THE OXFORD

MOVEMENT

Classics of British Historical Literature

JOHN CLIVE, EDITOR

R. W. Church

—

The Oxford
Movement

TWELVE YEARS, 1833-1845

EDITED AND WITH AN INTRODUCTION BY

GEOFFREY BEST

The University of Chicago Press
CHICAGO AND LONDON

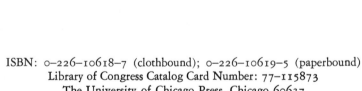

ISBN: 0–226–10618–7 (clothbound); 0–226–10619–5 (paperbound)
Library of Congress Catalog Card Number: 77–115873
The University of Chicago Press, Chicago 60637
The University of Chicago Press, Ltd., London
© 1970 by The University of Chicago
Published 1970
Printed in the United States of America

Contents

CONTENTS

Series Editor's Preface

This series of reprints has one major purpose: to put into the hands of students and other interested readers outstanding—and sometimes neglected—works dealing with British history which have either gone out of print or are obtainable only at a forbiddingly high price.

The phrase Classics of British Historical Literature requires some explanation, in view of the fact that the two companion series published by the University of Chicago Press are entitled Classic European Historians and Classic American Historians. Why, then, introduce the word *literature* into the title of this series?

One reason is obvious. History, if it is to live beyond its own generation, must be memorably written. The greatest British historians—Clarendon, Gibbon, Hume, Carlyle, Macaulay—survive today, not merely because they contributed to the cumulative historical knowledge about their subjects, but because they were masters of style and literary artists as well. And even historians of the second rank, if they deserve to survive, are able to do so only because they can still be read with pleasure. To emphasize this truth at the present time, when much eminently solid and worthy academic history suffers from being almost totally unreadable seems worth doing.

The other reason for including the word *literature* in the title of the series has to do with its scope. To read history is to learn about the past. But if, in trying to learn about the British past, one were to restrict oneself to the reading of formal works of history, one would miss a great deal. Often a historical novel, a sociological inquiry, or an account of events and institutions couched in semifictional form teaches us just as much about the past as does the "history" that calls itself by that name. And, not infrequently, these "informal" historical works turn out to be less well known than their merit deserves. By calling this series Classics of British Historical Literature it will be possible to include such books without doing violence to the usual nomenclature.

The continuing fascination and interest of Church's *Oxford Movement* is a good illustration of the fact that the history of British historiography can never be purely "progressive," in the sense that earlier works can safely be discarded as scholarship gradually and inevitably advances toward some absolute "truth" about men and events. Some works of very high quality have recently been written about the Oxford movement. And there is no doubt that the library shelves marked "John Henry Newman" will go on expanding. Still, in order to gain a real understanding of that remarkable group of men who tried, with some success, to infuse a new spirituality into the nineteenth-century Church of England, readers will have to keep turning to Church's pages. Why is this so?

Professor Best has answered that question in his introduction. The power of the work lies to a great extent in its author's having himself been a greatly concerned participant in the events to the depiction of which he applied his historical intelligence and judgment many years later on. It is this combination which helps to make the book both source and commentary, and lends it that sense of immediacy which later secondary works can no longer achieve.

The Oxford movement was part of a European reaction against what its founders believed to be the inimical aspects of that progress so confidently welcomed by early nineteenth-century liberals. It has often been condemned as over-donnish and academic. And, as Professor Best points out, there is still room for debate about its ultimate effects upon English thought and institutions. But the personalities of the men who made it what it was and what it became—above all, Newman's—continue to exert their spell. And Church's account will continue to stand as an example of one of the most delicate and difficult ways of writing history—the mingling of autobiographical reminiscence with retrospective historical analysis.

JOHN CLIVE

Editor's Introduction

R. W. Church and the Oxford Movement

Church, for all his European culture a man of profoundly English character, wrote this, his best historical book, chiefly for readers whom he assumed to understand the elements of such singular structures as the English established church and the most ancient English university. He seems further to have assumed, in respect of himself and his own involvement in the events of his story (an involvement sedulously concealed), that readers would either already know all they wanted to know about him or not particularly want to know anything about him. Neither assumption can now prudently be made even of English, Oxford-educated readers of this book. It is therefore necessary to begin with a few introductory notes about Church himself, about Oxford itself, and about the movement of which his remains the best history.

Richard William Church was born to mercantile parents in Lisbon on 25 April 1815, and lived abroad—mainly in Italy—until the death of his father in 1828. His mother, née Metzener, then settled in Bath and, unable to afford the fees of Winchester, sent him to a humdrum school of Evangelical character in Bristol. He went up to Oxford (Wadham College) in 1833, graduated in 1836, and continued study on his own until be became a fellow of Oriel College in 1838. There he remained, active equally in the academic, the religious, and the political life of the university until 1852, when, as the necessary and usual preliminary to marriage, he left Oxford and became a parson—as rector of Whatley, three miles west of Frome in Somerset. In 1871 he moved from the depths of the country to the hub of the metropolis, where he remained dean of Saint Paul's until his death on 9 December 1890.

Especially during his Whatley years, he was a copious writer for periodicals: long articles for the high church *Christian Remembrancer* between 1844 and 1855; weekly contributions of book reviews and political articles for the *Guardian* (which he had helped to found) between 1846 and 1871 and intermittently thereafter; regular contributions to the *Saturday Review* 1861–71 and frequent ones to the *Times* throughout his later years. He published several collections of these writings, many volumes of sermons and lectures, editions of St. Cyril's *Catechetical Lectures* and the first book of Hooker's *Ecclesiastical Polity*, as well as books on *Saint Anselm, The Beginning of the Middle Ages, Spenser, Bacon, Pascal,* and (what was not published until just after his death) *The Oxford Movement.* Although he never weakened in his adherence to that movement's side, the Catholic and high church side, of Anglicanism, as against both the low church Calvinist and the broad church Modernist sides, the charitable moderation of his manner and the scientific power of his mind made him seem less of a party man than perhaps he really was. These qualities also helped him acquire an unusual position in the Anglican establishment as at once scholarly and sensible, learned and likable, interested in politics without decisive political involvement, active and efficient in the things of this world but decidedly not of them. Not the sort of clergyman (and the Church of England had more than enough of them) who "moved in society" or much valued it, he nevertheless had a large circle of distinguished friends and acquaintances, extending far beyond his fellow travelers in the Oxford movement (notably Pusey's disciple and biographer H. P. Liddon, J. B. Mozley, George Moberly, E. S. Talbot, and his special friend from Oxford years onwards, Frederic Rogers Lord Blachford) to include Gladstone, Lord Acton, and the American scientist Asa Gray. Gladstone when prime minister relied upon him particularly for advice on church affairs, and he repeatedly declined offers of advancement, including, it was said (though the story seems to be apocryphal), Canterbury. His daughter published a tantalizingly brief selective biography of him in 1894,[1] and there is an admirably succinct sympathetic modern study of his life and ideas by B. A. Smith called *Dean Church: The Anglican Response to Newman*.[2]

The Oxford of Church's book was smaller, simpler, and more sequestered—by twenty preindustrial years—than that "beautiful city! So venerable, so lovely," of Matthew Arnold; "so unravaged by the fierce intellectual life of our century, so serene . . . whispering from her towers the last enchantments of the Middle Age." Church gives a good impression of its countrified quietness and civic singularity at the start of chapter 9, and a glance at the map reproduced here shows how small a city it was, and how little there was to it besides the colleges and university buildings. The 1831 census reported it as containing 20,649 persons, of whom not many more than a thousand or so can have been undergraduates and about seven hundred "dons" of one kind or another (not many of them engaged in teaching).[3] Apart from the profitable business of servicing the colleges and their sometimes wealthy members, Oxford's economic activities were no more than those naturally pertaining to a market town, agricultural center, and junction of roads and waterways, just over fifty miles from London via Maidenhead, Henley, and Dorchester or via High Wycombe and Wheatley. Both roads converged on the approach across Magdalen Bridge, and from the hill above it visitors first got that unforgettable impression of the "sweet city with its dreaming spires" (Matthew Arnold again) which lies at the heart of the romantic idea of the place.

Oxford University was in 1830 one of England's only two universities (London University, which effectively began with its "godless institution in Gower Street" in the late 1820s, was not statutorily recognized until 1836) and was the more conspicuously churchy of the two. No student could matriculate (that is, receive formal acceptance for a course of study leading to a degree) without subscribing to the Thirty-nine Articles of the Church of England; nearly all the dons were clergymen, and all

---

1. Mary C. Church (ed.), *Life and Letters of Dean Church* (London, 1894).
2. London, 1958.
3. The 1831 census showed 727 in the category "Capitalists, Bankers, Professional and other Educated Men" resident within colleges.

but the heads of houses (masters of colleges and "halls") and some professors were celibate; and the majority of the under-graduates who were there to work rather than to play intended to become clergymen themselves. The colleges were fiercely par-ticularistic and virtually autonomous corporations of varying size, wealth, and character, coming together as the University of Ox-ford only in respect of academic standards, examinations, and degrees (but not tuition, a college prerogative), the general discipline of students and to some small extent townsfolk, and participation in national politics. Most of the university's big public business, including the election of its two members of Parliament, was settled in Convocation, the assembly of all M.A.s whether resident or not. All matters relating to degrees were settled by Congregation, the assembly of virtually all resi-dent M.A.s. The effective executive body of the university was the Hebdomadal Board of the vice-chancellor, the heads of houses, and the two annually elected proctors.

Little about the Oxford movement itself need be said in the introduction to a book entirely about it. It was of immense impor-tance in the religious history of Britain and the English-speaking world on account both of its infusion (dramatic and sudden at first) of "Catholic consciousness" into the church and the dis-tinctive note of quiet, gentlemanly, humane piety which continues to mark the products of the theological colleges founded under its banner. It had significant political implications, both in its causes and consequences, as a religious and ecclesiastical wing of the Conservative counterattack against political Liberalism and Radicalism in the age of Whig-Liberal reforms (Roman Cath-olic emancipation, the Reform Bill, and the attempt to modernize the major national institutions of Great Britain and Ireland, including their established churches) and the radical and demo-cratic movements culminating at the end of the 1830s in Chartism. Its internal history, as Church well shows, was marked by dramatic events, tense confrontations, brilliant polemics, and soul-searching arguments over fundamental points of Christian principle.

It was in essence the bold proclamation by certain Oxford dons of ideas (some old, some new) about Christianity and the Church, directly and deliberately opposed to many dominant tendencies and fashionable isms of the age. Prominent among the older ideas (which though historic were in fact unfamiliar to the mass of British Christians and therefore tended to astound them) were the idea of an undivided but nonpopish Catholic Church, faithful in doctrine and ethos to the church of the fathers, in origins and authority absolutely independent of the kingdoms of this world; and the related principle of an apostolic succession of bishops and the validity of that priesthood alone upon which the hands of true bishops had been laid. Prominent among the newer ideas (which were more or less related to Romanticism) were readiness to respect and to learn from the "primitive," the unsophisticated, and the unfamiliar; reverence for the sublime, the mysterious, and the awe-ful; conviction that truth could as well be veiled and numinous as clear and sparkling, and that (to put it summarily) poetry, refinement, and goodness mattered at least as much as prose, calculation, and cleverness. The isms it set out to combat included materialism, utilitarianism, rationalism, scientism, latitudinarianism, and erastianism—most of them (with some reason) comprised by the men of the Oxford movement under the head of Liberalism; and, in English religious life, the vulgarities of Evangelicalism, Methodism, and aggressive antipopish Protestantism.

The interest of the movement was, and still is, enhanced by the intrinsic importance of many of the men involved in it. Several of its leading lights were already well known and distinguished in the pre-Victorian Church of England: John Keble's *Christian Year* had given him celebrity as a poet far beyond the university circles which revered him as a scholar and a saint; Hugh James Rose, Cambridge's only serious contributor to the movement, though not as great a man as Church (who knew him only by repute) makes out, stood forth at the beginning of the thirties as the high churchmen's chief intellectual hatchet man; while Edward Bouverie Pusey carried all the weight of a wealthy professor and canon of Christ Church who came from a county family. Others who, so to speak, grew up with the movement became distinguished and influential Anglicans of the next generation: Church himself and his Oxford friends, and other less wholly committed churchmen like Samuel Wilberforce who were nevertheless profoundly affected by the movement. And towering in interest and importance above them all was the figure of John Henry Newman, a man virtually unknown and of no importance outside Oxford in 1830, but whose star of reputation rose suddenly and brilliantly with and through the movement, and who penned in its service a sizable share of that remarkable corpus of writings about religion and the Christian Church which will continue to be studied so long as Christian scholarship survives. Church apparently came to know Newman better and to enjoy more of his confidences than any other of his Oxford friends after about 1838, and he early acquired for him a disciple's respect as well as a friend's affection. It is therefore not surprising that, when at last he decided to sum up and commit to print the reflections of half a century on the hectic twelve years which had provided the great formative experience of his life, he wound his narrative round what had by then to be called the Anglican career of Cardinal Newman: a biographical twist which adds to the interest his book possesses as an intelligent and sensitive insider's inside story.

Church's *Oxford Movement* is well worth a place in any collection of British historical classics, but not because Church was a great historian. There is some evidence that he could have been such if he had wished. Some of his earlier historical writings show much "professional" talent, as well as a style too reminiscent of Gibbon and Macaulay to be so entirely by accident. He cared greatly about history and approached its study with philosophical as well as religious seriousness. He knew about "scientific history" and he did not fail through ignorance or conceit to follow the bright German and French lights of his generation, as did so many of his historically minded contemporaries. But his interests were too wide and various and his sense of academic ambition insufficiently strong to make possible for him that concentration of time and energy which the rising scholarly standards of his age demanded. For one thing he was too conscientious in the exercise of his religious vocation, giving the prime of his energies to the pastoral, educational, and administrative duties of his appointments successively as Oxford don, country parson, and cathedral dignitary. For another thing, he was in his scholarly character too literary, and in his intellectual curiosity too psychological. Most of his historical writing was literary, biographical, or both: he valued nothing mortal more highly than the great works of prose and poetry through which gifted men had (in his understanding of history) reflected equally upon God and their fellows their sense of the magnificence and wonder of God's creation and the virtues of the civilization they had developed within it. He is after all best thought of as one of the great Victorian men of letters, one with stronger historical talents than most, who in his old age and as his last labor wrote a history of unusual qualities and, for students of religion in the English-speaking world, unique value.

Those literary, psychological, and biographical interests of Church's set their unmistakable stamp upon this book, and from them stem its strengths as well as its weaknesses. In this introductory essay I must try to point out such of them as will not be patent to any intelligent reader; and if I harp more on the limitations, it is only because they are the less apparent. The strengths (which greatly preponderate) are evident enough and call for little comment. The book is shapely, stylish, readable, cultivated, serious-minded, wise; it is reliable, accurate, and fair on almost all matters of fact and most of opinion; without being declamatory or melodramatic, it gives compelling impressions of great spiritual crises and exciting events; quiet and unpretentious, it nevertheless emanates hidden power and meaning, and invites the sensitive reader to read between the lines as well as along them. Above all it has the peculiar interest and importance of being a history of events written by that unusual historiographical character, a devoted insider who felt an obligation to look at them also as an outsider. Because of this inside experience, and because it mattered so much to him, there runs through Church's book a persistent autobiographical strain, although even a careful and critical reader might not notice it even if he were to ponder over the Preface, where it is most nearly explicit; and, although concealed and subdued, it is autobiography of a peculiarly intense kind, for what happened at Oxford between 1833 and 1845 was, to Church, a matter of spiritual life or death. He was not during those years entirely a cool, unemotional inside observer of the movement. He was immensely, intensely, involved in it both as a disciple of Newman's and as an activist on his and the movement's behalf in university affairs. The way he announces his purpose in the Preface (and in the letter to Lord Acton, cited in the Advertisement), admits the involvement and appears to promise little detachment. Yet it seems clear to me from the main body of the book (what would in any case be strongly suggested by one's knowledge of the rest of his writings) that his mind in writing it was largely governed by "scientific" considerations, inasmuch as he conscientiously felt an obligation to present a dispassionate view of the movement; an undertaking which required the specific rebuttal of certain, as he believed, unfair interpretations of parts of the story, as well as a judicial presentation of the whole. Despite what he says in the Preface, then, I am driven to regard the book as at once the distillation of an insider's personal experience of a movement and an outsider's professional history of it—an attempt, in effect, to run in harness potential incompatibilities, and therefore an exercise of a peculiarly difficult kind.

Its uniqueness lies in the qualities given it by the boldness of this attempt; its limitations and peculiarities, such as they inconspicuously are, spring from the insider's failure to detach himself sufficiently and the outsider's failure to take a broad enough view. Such failures (if such they indeed are) are not surprising. Plenty of scientifically minded historians who have not had Church's excuses have failed in detachment or in breadth of view. Plenty of historically minded men who have been personally involved in events have not, in setting them down for posterity, detached themselves nearly as much. One may doubt whether an attempt at historical detachment has ever, considering the effort needed to make it, been better made. For the effort was, in Church's case, very great. It meant an appraisal of the whole system of religious beliefs on which his life was founded; a self-examination, in the relative tranquillity of old age, about the pretexts and conduct of battles in which he had engaged fifty years before, and about the merits of the controversial cause to which he had since remained true; above all, it meant a last, long scrutiny of his relations, both personal and intellectual, with John Henry Newman, a scrutiny so serious and sustained, however muted by tactful self-effacement, that *The Oxford Movement* may fairly be read as Richard William Church's Apologia pro Vita Sua.

No reader of Church's narrative can fail to mark the pride of place given to Newman. A dominant note is struck in the first paragraph of the Preface, where Newman is characterized as "a man of genius, whose name is among the illustrious names of his age, a name which will always be connected with modern Oxford, and is likely to be long remembered wherever the English language is studied." Church perhaps chose 1833 as his official starting date for the movement because for Newman it had always been that; he certainly chose to end it in 1845 because the heart of that year's "catastrophe" (chap. 19) was Newman's quitting the Church of England for that of Rome. There is much more about Newman in the book than about any other individual, and the two individuals who by my rough calculations receive the next most attention are those whom one might, with not too much exaggeration, call respectively the good fairy who presided over Newman's introduction to the movement and the evil genius who engineered his abstraction from it, Hurrell Froude and W. G. Ward. To Newman the limelight keeps returning.

I am not sure whether that elementary observation constitutes mere comment or mild criticism. Church was obviously right to regard Newman as by far and away the most interesting mind of the movement, the only one of undisputed international caliber and permanent concern in the history of thought. (Who was the next most interesting? J. B. Mozley, implied Church; but most scholars would say Church himself.) Perhaps Newman's paramountcy needed emphasizing in 1890. It had always been asserted by Roman Catholic writers, but he himself had not made much of it in his *Apologia* (1864), and the fashion of calling the movement Puseyism through the same midcentury years that witnessed the growth of the cult of Keble no doubt suggested to many who had no better means of information that Keble and Pusey had been equally prominent earlier on. The 1883 expanded edition of William Palmer's *Narrative*[4] was almost outrageously hostile to Newman and may well have helped stimulate Church to put the record straight. But whatever might have been the case in 1890 for insisting on Newman's vital presence in the Oxford hub, it seems at least possible that his role was not appre-

4. *Narrative of Events Connected with the Publication of the Tracts for the Times.*

ciated (in either sense) along the spokes and towards the rim of
the wheel of influences that spread from Oxford up and down
the land. This is an aspect of the history of the Oxford movement
upon which Church had little to say, and by saying as little about
it but so much about Newman in a book so persuasive and affecting, he may have given a bias to subsequent study of the movement. To the Anglican throng which followed the movement at
more or less of a distance, many of them with misgivings, Newman was not for long—and perhaps never was—the only inspiration. His charisma was felt mainly by young men on the spot;
some of his writings always seemed to plain men of average intelligence too clever by half; and even during the years 1833–41,
when Newman really was (as Church so successfully insisted) the
man who mattered, there must have been many Anglicans who
set more store on the much less interesting and flighty things
Keble and Pusey and Williams were saying. Perhaps, who knows,
they were more influenced by what an active, articulate, and
respected non-don Tractarian like W. F. Hook was saying and
doing than they normally were by the academics.[5] But Church as
a young man knew the ecclesiastical world outside Oxford only
at second hand. Unlike so many of his university colleagues, he
was not born into a clerical clan; he knew (so far as I can make
out) nothing of the church before he went to Oxford; and he was
not slow in becoming one of Newman's circle of young followers,
though it is difficult to imagine that he ever fell into the sort of
extravagant adulation of Newman affected by his less stable or
sensible admirers. He was, however, an avowed disciple of Newman's, never then or in later life afraid or ashamed to admit it.
Of course he knew Keble and Pusey and the rest from the middle
thirties onwards, and he offers convincing assessments of their
respective contributions during the years before the catastrophe;
but it seems to me that he is not convincingly enthusiastic over
Keble and Pusey as he is over Newman.[6] There is some repetitive-
ness in his paragraphs on Keble, suggesting that he was guided

5. There is a light hint on page 16 that Church was aware of this possibility, though his chronology seems for once to be at fault: Hook moved to
Coventry in 1829 and did not reach Leeds until 1837.
6. And as he is also over Isaac Williams, Charles Marriott, and Richard
Hurrell Froude.

therein by loyalty and piety rather than by conviction; unless his views as a young man about *The Gifts of Civilization*[7] were very different from what they became later on, he cannot even in the thirties have found passages of Keble's assize sermon acceptable; and there are light ironic touches in what he writes about Pusey.[8] His comments on their intelligence and scholarship are non-committal. He duly acknowledges their enormous contemporary reputation as scholars, but he refrains (as well he might) from endorsing the criteria by which they were thus rightly rated.

But there is nothing noncommittal or evasive in his judgments on Newman or the other sharp mind of the movement, Ward. There, he wrote from knowledge and from the heart; and there we sense his autobiographical strain, as in his analysis of the changing mind of Newman he balances with tightrope delicacy the historian's objective judgment against the awed disciple's loyalty. Not that he was blind to Newman's failings. (Exactly when he became aware of which of them, however, he does not say.) He carefully notes Newman's defects as a party leader, and at several places he makes perfectly clear (as he had done before, most notably in his review of Newman's *Apologia* in the *Guardian*, 22 June 1864)[9] his opinion that Newman's mind had some strong bias at work in it which excited him and made him draw conclusions that Church and the "nonromanizing" Anglicans could only consider precipitate and unreasonable. Newman, he was bound to conclude, had been wrong so to abandon hope for Anglicanism and to submit his judgment to that of Rome. Yet how tenderly Church handles Newman's long agony! Again and again,[10] he dwells on this detail of his story, defending Newman (without perfect success, one may think) against the charge of dishonesty in not having come to a decision sooner; subtly depicting the state of a soul torn between conflicting fields of religious forces; and doing his charitable best to persuade the reader not to be irritated with Newman either for embarrassing his friends by hovering so long, or for ultimately deciding in favor of the wrong side.

7. The title of a notable group of lectures, first published in 1880.
8. See p. 69; pp. 97–98.
9. Reprinted in his *Occasional Papers* (London, 1897), 2: 379.
10. E.g., on pp. 156–57, 160–61, 183 ff; 205–6.

These passages are perhaps more interesting as exercises in religious psychology than as contributions to the history of the Oxford movement, and by some scholars' standards they must appear disproportionate; but to Church they were evidently of immense importance as the bridge of understanding between himself, who had made a different decision, and the leader and friend to whom he owed so much. A skeptical reader familiar with the Newman story and normally critical of the *Apologia* will at first think Church oversusceptible and extravagant in this matter; yet he may be led in the end to an admiring recognition that what drives Church through this painful exercise is nothing other than loyalty to a friend once so close and beloved that regard was undiminished even by a misjudgment so gross and a religious commitment so unacceptable. How much pain it gave Church to part company with Newman we cannot tell. Church characteristically kept the details of the great spiritual crisis of his life to himself; but it seems safe to assume that the grounds of his decision (whether conscious at the time or rationalized afterward) to stick to the Church of England were those he lists in chapter 19.[11] To the reviewer in the Roman Catholic journal *The Month*[12] they seemed somewhat unintelligible and slightly comic; so far as they meant anything, he wrote, they meant "that Anglicanism, though illogical in theory and incapable of an ideal," nevertheless worked quite well in practice. "It is the historical argument, and one which has great force with historical minds such as Dean Church's undoubtedly was." With that last comment at any rate most readers might agree. Church's Anglican attitude was in the last analysis national (rather than insular), patriotic, and pragmatic, perhaps in nonsectarian senses somewhat utilitarian and humanistic, and from Newman's point of view, indeed, illogical (though no more "illogical" from that point of view than his was "unreasonable" from Church's). It is an attitude which has remained close to the center of the Anglican tradition ever since, and which probably constitutes the Oxford movement's most enduring bequest to it.

The pride of place and special consideration given to Newman is justifiable in terms of Church's intention as a serious historian

11. Pp. 268–69.
12. Vol. 72 (May 1891), pp. 24–34.

to write an intellectual and, in a sense, social history, rather than an institutional or political one. That place and consideration are also explicable, if not so obviously justifiable, on account of Church's special relationship with Newman as disciple, friend, and sympathetic fellow Christian. Whether that special relationship caused Church to lose his historian's balance must be judged by each properly informed reader for himself, such judgment probably taking color from the reader's own religious beliefs. My own judgment of the matter is that Church's anxiety to redress the balance and ensure posthumous justice to the religious heroes of his youth betrays him into some exaggerations on his own side. His pleading of Newman's spiritual case (in itself well worth scrupulous analysis, since it was, so to speak, the supreme and signal test case by which so many of his friends' cases had to be judged) is eloquent and affecting, but it may leave one with a feeling that the critics who from early on alleged over-subtlety, excess of dialectical dexterity, and a "romanizing" tendency in Newman had more to be said for them than Church likes to admit. It is the romanizing charge by which he seems most embarrassed and upset, and he may be thought not satisfactorily to dismiss it by his repeated insistence that Newman was not conscious of the romanizing intentions attributed to him (not in the early stages, at all events), and that the man was incapable of deliberately playing a double game. That was no doubt true as far as it went, but it did not go far along the psychological road which Church in other contexts showed himself capable of exploring. The fact remains that some Oxford or ex-Oxford colleagues who by the later thirties were more detached from Newman than was Church may have understood one side of Newman better than Church did. Church's defensive action is skillfully conducted but imperfectly successful; and readers who consider it disproportionately lengthy may dare to suspect that Church himself was not wholly happy about it. Those who feel that way about it may be fortified by discerning a clearer instance of the same crippling honesty in another intimately Newmanite part of the story—that concerning Richard Hurrell Froude.

Here, surely, Church is on the defensive; loyally doing his best to defend the doubtfully defensible. Hurrell Froude (as he is generally called), member of a powerful clerical clan and elder brother of the historian James Anthony Froude, had a twofold interest for Church. He had played a major part in starting the movement; and he had been one of the young Newman's two dearest friends. Church never met Hurrell Froude and had to take on trust from his friends and masters their high estimation of his intellectual abilities, his stimulating influence upon them in the movement's formative years, and his delightful and loveable Christian character. Intellectual abilities of some high order were clear enough, and his personal influence was an unchallengeable fact. It was the proclamation of the loveliness of his character as a Christian that made difficulties for all students of the movement after the publication of his self-revealing *Remains* in 1838; and, in the train of doubts about the loveliness of *his* character, of course, came even more disturbing doubts about the loveliness of the characters of those who thought his so lovable. The coarse jibes of the ribald and prurient could be meekly borne and righteously dismissed; more disturbing by far were expressions of shock, amazement, nausea, and contempt by intelligent and pious men, from James Stephen in 1838[13] to Principal John Tulloch in 1885.[14] In chapter 3 Church does his conscientious best to report what he had been told and to make it all credible. My judgment of his Hurrell Froude passages is that the legend was not quite credible to Church himself.

On two other controversial parts of the story Church's defensive anxieties lead him into bold gestures of defiance and counter-attack; and these passages are among the most powerful and enjoyable bits of writing in the book. They may be so because in them the partisan element is more unabashed, more buoyant. The first of them is the Hampden affair, to which Church devotes many pages.[15] Renn Dickson Hampden, a theologian of Liberal or Modernist tendencies, was already a Tractarian bête noire on account of his supporting Whig-Liberal reform of church and state before Lord Melbourne, the Whig prime minister, appointed him to the regius chair of divinity early in 1836. This affair was

13. In the *Edinburgh Review* 67 (July 1838):500–535, reprinted in his *Essays in Ecclesiastical Biography* as "The Evangelical Succession."
14. In his *Movements of Religious Thought in Britain during the Nineteenth Century.*
15. Pp. 106, 108–12; chap. 9 from p. 115, 140–41, 216–20.

from the start one of the Tractarians' tenderest topics. By their apparently intolerant and unfair treatment of Hampden they gave their first hostage to fortune and drew from Thomas Arnold the first serious counterblast, his article titled (by the editor) "The Oxford Malignants," in the April 1836 *Edinburgh Review*.[16] Ever since, the issue between Hampden and the Tractarians has been in dispute, and (so much must one's judgment of it depend on theological and ecclesiastical preferences) it seems likely to remain so forever. Church obviously tried hard to be objective about it, but the passion of fifty years back had burnt too deep for him to come to any other conclusion than that the Tractarians were right to handle Hampden as toughly as they did; that Hampden, besides putting forward ideas which the Tractarians from their point of view rightly rejected, was culpably unclear and muddle-headed about them; and that his character had mealy-mouthed and vindictive sides to it which went far to justify the Tractarians' impatience and rancor. To non-Tractarians Hampden has never seemed as bad as they painted him, and to noncommitted historians he has not seemed to deserve even Church's strictures, which are mild compared with those contained in the bouncy *Reminiscences* of Tom Mozley.[17]

Interlocked at two junctures with the Tractarians' feud against Hampden is the other controversial matter on which Church really lets himself go: their battle against the Hebdomadal Board, the governing body through which the (as they maintained) stuffy, prejudiced, and obtuse older generation of dons enforced a cautious, conservative, and worldly-wise control of the university and prevented the change-minded younger generation from achieving much. Church's fierceness is the more impressive for his having had unrivaled opportunity to see the old gang at close quarters; he had been—though no reader could learn it from

16. Vol. 63, pp. 225–39.
17. *Reminiscences Chiefly of Oriel College and the Oxford Movement*, 2 vols. (London, 1882). Anglican scholars as dissimilar as V. F. Storr (*Development of English Theology in the Nineteenth Century* [London, 1913], pp. 99–106) and Charles Smyth (his article on Hampden in *Theology*, vol. 18) have found Hampden's ideas worthy of serious consideration, while one's judgment of the Macmullen business (chap. 16) may turn on how one reacts to the glimpses of the character of the man given in (for instance) W. R. W. Stephens's *Life and Letters of W. F. Hook* (London, 1878), 2: 195–200.

this book—a member of the Hebdomadal Board during his year as proctor, 1844–45, and ex officio bound to attend its weekly meetings! He recalls clearly and copiously, and evidently still sympathizes with, the righteous rage felt by the Tractarians at the heads' moral lethargy or worse. What he does not make nearly so clear is the extent to which this campaign, fought with all the variety of tactical maneuver, vendetta, backbiting, and bitterness of which a close community of dons and ecclesiastics is capable, was also a political one—not so much in the sense of national politics (though there were links with them) as of ordinary university politics, the same wherever twenty or thirty academic persons are gathered together and subjected to pressures to improve their institution.

Oxford University in the thirties and forties was under many pressures, and the Oxford movement was not the only important movement discernible within it. There was also a movement, firmly imbedded by 1830 though with still a long way to go, to improve the teaching, raise the academic standards, and make the university of greater national value. This movement had attractions not only for dons of Liberal persuasion, the Noetics[18] and their followers of the next generation, that of Stanley and Jowett. Ideals of higher standards, improved tutoring, and more evident public usefulness fired the minds also of earnest high Anglican dons, whose interpretation of goals and proposals for approaching them, however, would often take them into the opposite division lobby from the Liberals. Of this movement for university reform Church was very well aware but he hardly mentions it. It is, however, a part of the story about which the thoroughgoing investigator of the Oxford movement will wish to know more, since a fundamental aspect of the Tractarians' success, such as it was, was that for several years they gave leadership to the younger Oxford dons' campaign against the heads, and kept their flag flying as high as it did by means of a wind not wholly of their own creation. The reader may find it enthrallingly unraveled, in its sometimes sordid detail, by W. R. Ward.[19] To university men of

18. Church drily mentions these mildly adventurous scholars, with whom he seems to have had little sympathy, on page 19. Usually grouped with them are Hampden, Thomas Arnold, and Cambridge's Connop Thirlwall.

19. *Victorian Oxford* (London, 1965).

the 1970s it will seem engaging in the history of the Tractarians that even a friend could call Hurrell Froude an "agitator," that one who had been a zealous Newmanite recalled later how he had thrown himself into the "demonstrations" got up by Froude's successors,[20] and that its events included a threatened tutors' strike, an egregious mishandling of a discipline case, an unprecedented opposition to the conventional succession of vice-chancellors, and a party contest for the part-time poetry professorship.

The movement's role in the university politics of the time is thus not one of the aspects of its "total history" on which Church is informative. He is not indeed wholly silent about it—one must admiringly admit that hardly any aspects of that imagined total history are not hinted at or alluded to—but he was not particularly interested in it. About other aspects of the Oxford movement also Church was reticent or unconcerned. Conspicuous among them is the movement's relations with the immediately preceding religious movement of comparable importance, Evangelicalism. Some of the best recent histories have emphasized how close those relations were: they are painstakingly considered from all sides in Y. Brilioth, *The Anglican Revival*;[21] crisply accepted by Owen Chadwick, *The Mind of the Oxford Movement*,[22] which for all its brevity is the best introduction to the Tractarians' characteristic thoughts and feelings; rashly overpitched toward the end of Ford K. Brown's exciting *Fathers of the Victorians*,[23] which, however, retains much interest even after David Newsome's long review of it;[24] and carefully elucidated by Newsome himself in his *Parting of Friends*,[25] of which more in a moment. Newman never concealed his spiritual debt to the Evangelical teachers of his youth, and many Tractarians and semi-Tractarians, those who were not dons even more than those who were, came from Evangelical families. Church notices the intellectual and spiritual inadequacies of Evangelicalism in his few pages on that movement, but he makes no attempt to explore the extent to which it fortified the movement of his choice. It is difficult not to get the

20. Mark Pattison, *Memoirs* (London, 1885), p. 185.
21. London, 1925.
22. London, 1960.
23. Cambridge, 1961.
24. "Fathers and Sons," in the *Historical Journal* 6 (1963): 295–310.
25. London, 1966.

impression that Church disliked and deplored Evangelicalism, at
least in its Victorian forms. He writes coldly about it, more coldly
(as it seems to me) than he does about the Coleridgean[26] and
Noetic tendencies which the Tractarians set themselves also to
combat. W. Sanday noticed this in his excellent review of Church's
book in the *Critical Review*.[27] "The wealth of tender and affectionate remembrance which the book discloses is reserved," he
remarked, "for a limited circle. There are not, as it happens, many
kind words for those without." This is the more remarkable
if one considers the reputation for relatively nonpartisan churchmanship and humane breadth of understanding which Church
later in life justifiably enjoyed. Whatever his mature views may
have been about the Evangelical movement, it seems certain that
the cold shoulder he gives it in this book accurately reflects
what he felt about it during the years of his discipleship to Newman; and the historian must beware of drawing therefrom two
false conclusions: first, as already mentioned, that Evangelicalism
had no significant share in preparing the ground for Tractarianism; and second, that evangelicals in the 1830s were all wholly
hostile to it. Church gives that impression, but he should not
have done so. The wilder men of Evangelicalism, the ignorant
bibliolaters and obsessive proclaimers of "justification by faith
alone" and self-confident illuminists, were indeed hostile, and
so were some of the more sensible men too. But others were not.
Gladstone (who grew from evangelical origins to become a leading lay supporter of the Oxford movement), when in 1847 he
became second member of parliament for Oxford University,
found as his senior the moderate and cultivated Evangelical Sir
Robert Inglis, a Claphamite who had represented Oxford since
1829. Many intelligent Tory Evangelicals like Inglis went cor-
dially along for several years (though in most instances not
beyond the publication of Froude's *Remains!*) with the Tractarians in their campaigns to thwart Whiggism, to restore the self-
confidence of the established churches of England and Ireland

26. The essential Tractarian attitude to Coleridge is expressed in Keble's
and Froude's agreement to stigmatize the opinion that there were good men
in all parties as "the Coleridgian heresy." See J. T. Coleridge, *Memoir of
Keble,* 3d ed. (Oxford and London, 1870), p. 250.
27. Vol. 1 (1891), pp. 235–41.

and their authority over alarmingly licentious populaces, to clean up Oxford, and to stress the solemnity with which sacraments should be regarded. Some intelligent Anglicans of Evangelical origins or sympathies were much attracted by the high moral tone, the gentlemanly culture, the religious refinement and the ecclesiastical seriousness of the Oxford movement, and achieved a synthesis of what they thought were the best parts of each. Chief among these was Samuel Wilberforce, whom Newsome persuasively presents as *the essential Anglican*.[28] To that claim Church would presumably have been unwilling to assent. He appears to have believed, rightly or wrongly, that the Church of England's Catholic inheritance from the early fathers, the Caroline divines, and the spiritual heroes of later medieval and early modern Christendom, was substantial and authoritative enough to need no bolstering by post-Butlerian Wesleys and Wilberforces.

Newsome's recent book is, all things considered, the most important venture in Tractarian historiography since Brilioth's heavyweight contribution of over forty years ago, and Geoffrey Faber's original *Oxford Apostles*,[29] which remains the best readable book for a beginner to start with, as well as a refreshing one for a scholar to go back to. Like Church in the high importance he places on personalities and friendships, Newsome fills in some of Church's gaps by his reverent attention to Evangelical origins and connections, and by his concentration on the movement as it was experienced outside Oxford. From Newsome's narrative may also be obtained in palatable form a fuller account than Church allowed himself to give of the antecedents of the movement before 1833 and the consequences after 1845 (though Newsome is not the only historian to have written helpfully about the preparatory phase). The intellectual origins of the movement and the literature about them are still best approached through the classics of Storr and Brilioth and C. C. J. Webb;[30] to which, among more recent books, need only be added Chadwick's *Mind of the Oxford Movement*, for all its lack of bibliography. The movement's political origins on the counterrevolutionary side of

28. *Parting of Friends*, pp. 178–79; see also pp. 241, 248, 266, 329–37.
29. Second edition (London, 1936).
30. *Religious Thought in the Oxford Movement* (London, 1928).

the quasi revolution of 1828–32 have to be sought elsewhere. Church understood these well enough but chose to pass lightly over them. To historians who must measure the social and political dimensions of ostensibly religious movements, Church's inattention to such critical events as Roman Catholic emancipation and the Reform Bills will seem almost misleadingly inadequate. Newsome has many useful pages on this essential background, and so have Chadwick in part 1 of his *Victorian Church*,[31] Olive J. Brose in her *Church and Parliament: The Reshaping of the Church of England, 1828–1860*,[32] and also myself in *Temporal Pillars*.[33] Thus has the approach to 1833 become well lighted within the last decade. The aftermath of 1845 remains, however, in a darkness pierced so far only by Chadwick and Newsome. The implications of Newsome's chapter 7 are that wrong impressions may be gained from Church's elegiac tone and by his calling his closing chapter "Catastrophe," that the stouter hearts among the Tractarians were undismayed and undelayed, and that even in the later forties the movement, purged of its most embarrassing leaders and hangers-on, continued to make friends and influence people, outside Oxford if no longer within it (as he indeed admits). Church, concerned above all with the Oxford story and devoted above all to explaining and justifying Newman's part in it, could not regard Newman (though he could so regard Ward) as an embarrassment! And 1845 was so much of a catastrophe for him personally, that perhaps he could not grasp its being less of a shock for anyone else who cared about Catholicity.

Church must then be judged to have exaggerated the effects of the "catastrophe" outside Oxford. About its effects in Oxford he is nearer the mark. Oxford could certainly never be the same again for Newman's disciples, but not only because "the man who for fifteen years had to all Europe personated Oxford"[34] had left it. In a striking passage[35] (a passage which would come as less of a surprise had he said more earlier about the university

31. London, 1966.
32. Stanford, Calif., 1959.
33. Cambridge, 1964.
34. William Tuckwell, *Reminiscences of Oxford* (London, 1900), p. 187.
35. Pp. 261–63.

reform movement and the Tractarians' engagement in university politics), Church remarks that the "discomfiture" of the Tractarians made way for an ambitious rejuvenated movement of Liberalism, which was soon to be powerful enough to achieve reforms of the species fruitlessly advocated by Edinburgh Reviewers, Philosophic Radicals and the first wave (Coplestone's and Hampden's) of Oxbridge Liberals, and of a spirit perhaps more humane and (though in an utterly new nondogmatic style) religious for having been refined in the fire for twenty years between the ascetic piety and Latin sympathies of Newman and Pusey on the one side and the Germanic speculative boldness of Coleridge and Arnold on the other. Church's appeal from the old Liberals to the new was not wholly in vain, nor was his impression of their difference and the speed of their rise to ascendancy overdrawn. Another of Newman's former disciples, giving a pungent de-Newmanized don's version of these whirligig years, says: "If any Oxford man had gone to sleep in 1846 and had woke up again in 1850 he would have found himself in a totally new world."[36] Church was not bound to offer a complete explanation of the causes of this revolution, and readers who admire his *Oxford Movement* for what it is and for what the author put of himself into it will have no difficulty in excusing Church's failure to mention such profane matters as, for instance, the publication of J. S. Mill's *Logic* in 1843 and the arrival on 12 June 1844 of the first train from London at "that antique station which . . . does yet whisper to the tourist the last enchantments of the Middle Age."[37]

GEOFFREY BEST

---

36. Mark Pattison's *Memoirs*, p. 244.
37. Max Beerbohm, *Zuleika Dobson* (London, 1911), p. 1.

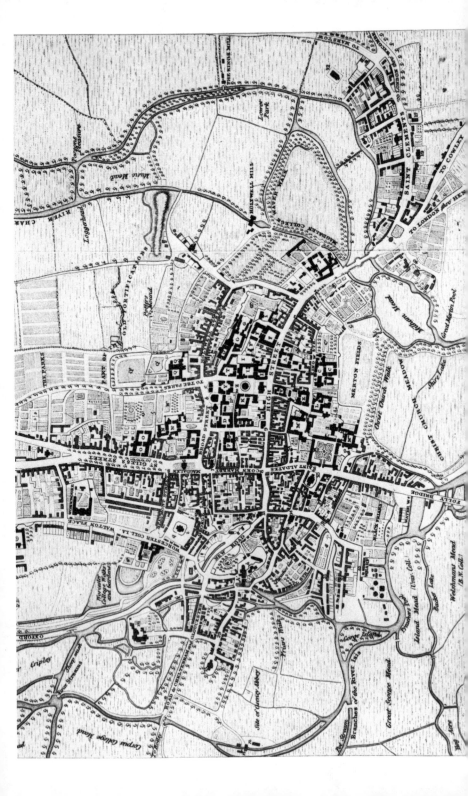

Plan of the City and University of Oxford
From James Ingram, *Memorials of Oxford* (1837), vol. 3.

THE OXFORD

MOVEMENT

Advertisement

The revision of these papers was a task to which the late Dean of St. Paul's gave all the work he could during the last months of his life. At the time of his death, fourteen of the papers had, so far as can be judged, received the form in which he wished them to be published; and these, of course, are printed here exactly as he left them. One more he had all but prepared for publication; the last four were mainly in the condition in which, six years ago, he had them privately put into type, for the convenience of his own further work upon them, and for the reading of two or three intimate friends. Those into whose care his work has now come have tried, with the help of his pencilled notes, to bring these four papers as nearly as they can into the form which they believe he would have had them take. But it has seemed better to leave unaltered a sentence here and there to which he might have given a more perfect shape, rather than to run the risk of swerving from the thought which was in his mind.

It is possible that the Dean would have made considerable changes in the preface which is here printed; for only that which seems the first draft of it has been found. But even thus it serves to show his wish and purpose for the work he had in hand; and it has therefore been thought best to publish it. Leave has been obtained to add here some fragments from a letter which, three years ago, he wrote to Lord Acton about these papers:

> If I ever publish them, I must say distinctly what I want to do, which is, not to pretend to write a history of the movement, or

to account for it or adequately to judge it and put it in its due place in relation to the religious and philosophical history of the time, but simply to preserve a contemporary memorial of what seems to me to have been a true and noble effort which passed before my eyes, a short scene of religious earnestness and aspiration, with all that was in it of self-devotion, affectionateness, and high and refined and varied character, displayed under circumstances which are scarcely intelligible to men of the present time; so enormous have been the changes in what was assumed and acted upon, and thought practicable and reasonable, "fifty years since." For their time and opportunities, the men of the movement, with all their imperfect equipment and their mistakes, still seem to me the salt of their generation. . . . I wish to leave behind me a record that one who lived with them, and lived long beyond most of them, believed in the reality of their goodness and height of character, and still looks back with deepest reverence to those forgotten men as the companions to whose teaching and example he owes an infinite debt, and not he only, but religious society in England of all kinds.

January 31st, 1891

Preface

The following pages relate to that stage in the Church revival of this century which is familiarly known as the Oxford Movement, or, to use its nickname, the Tractarian Movement. Various side influences and conditions affected it at its beginning and in its course; but the impelling and governing force was, throughout the years with which these pages are concerned, at Oxford. It was naturally and justly associated with Oxford, from which it received some of its most marked characteristics. Oxford men started it and guided it. At Oxford were raised its first hopes, and Oxford was the scene of its first successes. At Oxford were its deep disappointments, and its apparently fatal defeat. And it won and lost, as a champion of English theology and religion, a man of genius, whose name is among the illustrious names of his age, a name which will always be connected with modern Oxford, and is likely to be long remembered wherever the English language is studied.

We are sometimes told that enough has been written about the Oxford Movement, and that the world is rather tired of the subject. A good deal has certainly been both said and written about it, and more is probably still to come; and it is true that other interests, more immediate or more attractive, have thrown into the background what is severed from us by the interval of half a century. Still that movement had a good deal to do with what is going on in everyday life among us now; and feelings both of hostility to it, and of sympathy with it, are still lively and keen among those to whom religion is a serious subject, and even among some who are neutral in the questions which it raised, but who find in it a study of thought and character. I myself doubt whether the interest of it is so exhausted as is sometimes assumed. If it is, these pages will soon find their appropriate resting-place. But I venture to present them, because, though a good many judgments upon the movement have been put forth, they have come mostly from those who have been more or less avowedly opposed to it.[1] The men of most account among those who were attracted by it and represented it have, with one illustrious exception, passed away. A survivor of the generation which it stirred so deeply may not have much that is new to tell about it. He may not be able to affect much the judgment which will finally be accepted about it. But the fact is not unimportant, that a number of able and earnest men, men who both intellectually and morally would have been counted at the moment as part of the promise of the coming time, were fascinated and absorbed by it. It turned and governed their lives, lifting them out of custom and convention to efforts after something higher, something worthier of what they were. It seemed worth while to exhibit the course of the movement as it looked to these men—as it seemed to them viewed from the inside. My excuse for adding to so much that has been already written is, that I was familiar with many of the chief actors in the movement. And I do not like that the remembrance of friends and associates, men of singular purity of life and purpose, who raised the tone of living round them, and by their example, if not by their ideas, recalled both Oxford and the Church to a truer sense of their responsibilities, should, because no one would take the trouble to put things on record, "pass away like a dream."

The following pages were, for the most part, written, and put into printed shape, in 1884 and 1885. Since they were written, books have appeared, some of them important ones, going over most of the same ground; while yet more volumes may be expected. We have had ingenious theories of the genesis of the movement, and the filiation of its ideas. Attempts have been made to alter the proportions of the scene and of the several parts played

---

1. It is hardly necessary to say that these and the following words were written before Dr. Newman's death, and the publication of his letters.

upon it, and to reduce the common estimate of the weight and influence of some of the most prominent personages. The point of view of those who have thus written is not mine, and they tell their story (with a full right so to do) as I tell mine. But I do not propose to compare and adjust our respective accounts—to attack theirs, or to defend my own. I have not gone through their books to find statements to except to, or to qualify. The task would be a tiresome and unprofitable one. I understand their point of view, though I do not accept it. I do not doubt their good faith, and I hope that they will allow mine.

I

The Church
in the Reform Days

What is called the Oxford or Tractarian movement began, without doubt, in a vigorous effort for the immediate defence of the
Church against serious dangers, arising from the violent threatening temper of the days of the Reform Bill. It was one of several
and widely differing efforts. Viewed superficially it had its origin
in the accident of an urgent necessity.[1] The Church was really at
the moment imperilled amid the crude revolutionary projects of
the Reform epoch;[2] and something bolder and more effective than
the ordinary apologies for the Church was the call of the hour.
The official leaders of the Church were almost stunned and bewildered by the fierce outbreak of popular hostility. The answers

1. The suppression of the Irish bishoprics. Palmer, *Narrative* (1883), pp.
44, 101. Maurice, *Life,* 1:180.
2. "The Church, as it now stands, no human power can save" (Arnold to
Tyler, June 1832. *Life,* 1:326). "Nothing, as it seems to me, can save the
Church but an union with the Dissenters; now they are leagued with the antichristian party, and no merely internal reform will satisfy them" (Arnold to
Whately, January 1833, 1:348). He afterwards thought this exaggerated (*Life,*
1:336). "The Church has been for one hundred years without any government, and in such a stormy season it will not go on much longer without a
rudder" (Whately to Bp. Copleston, July 1832. *Life,* 1:167). "If such an
arrangement of the Executive Government is completed, it will be a difficult,
but great and glorious feat for your Lordship's ministry to preserve the establishment from utter overthrow" (Whately to Lord Grey, May 1832. *Life,*
1:156). It is remarkable that Dean Stanley should have been satisfied with
ascribing to the movement an "origin *entirely political,*" and should have seen
a proof of this "thoroughly political origin" in Newman's observing the date of
Mr. Keble's sermon "National Apostasy" as the birthday of the movement.
Edin. Rev. April 1880, pp. 309, 310.

put forth on its behalf to the clamour for extensive and even destructive change were the work of men surprised in a moment of security. They scarcely recognised the difference between what was indefensible and what must be fought for to the death; they mistook subordinate or unimportant points for the key of their position: in their compromises or in their resistance they wanted the guidance of clear and adequate principles, and they were vacillating and ineffective. But stronger and far-seeing minds perceived the need of a broad and intelligible basis on which to maintain the cause of the Church. For the air was full of new ideas; the temper of the time was bold and enterprising. It was felt by men who looked forward, that to hold their own they must have something more to show than custom or alleged expediency—they must sound the depths of their own convictions, and not be afraid to assert the claims of these convictions on men's reason and imagination as well as on their associations and feelings. The same dangers and necessities acted differently on different minds; but among those who were awakened by them to the presence of a great crisis were the first movers in what came to be known as the Tractarian movement. The stir around them, the perils which seemed to threaten, were a call to them to examine afresh the meaning of their familiar words and professions.

For the Church, as it had been in the quiet days of the eighteenth century, was scarcely adapted to the needs of more stirring times. The idea of clerical life had certainly sunk, both in fact and in the popular estimate of it. The disproportion between the purposes for which the Church with its ministry was founded and the actual tone of feeling among those responsible for its service had become too great. Men were afraid of principles; the one thing they most shrank from was the suspicion of enthusiasm. Bishop Lavington wrote a book to hold up to scorn the enthusiasm of Methodists and Papists; and what would have seemed reasonable and natural in matters of religion and worship in the age of Cranmer, in the age of Hooker, in the age of Andrewes, or in the age of Ken, seemed extravagant in the age which reflected the spirit of Tillotson and Secker, and even Porteus. The typical clergyman in English pictures of the manners of the day, in the *Vicar of Wakefield*, in Miss Austen's novels, in Crabbe's *Parish Register*, is represented, often quite unsuspiciously, as a kindly and respectable person, but certainly not alive to the greatness of his calling. He was often much, very much, to the society round him. When communication was so difficult and infrequent, he filled a place in the country life of England which no one else could fill. He was often the patriarch of his parish, its ruler, its doctor, its lawyer, its magistrate, as well as its teacher, before whom vice trembled and rebellion dared not show itself. The idea of the priest was not quite forgotten; but there was much— much even of what was good and useful—to obscure it. The beauty of the English Church in this time was its family life of purity and simplicity; its blot was quiet worldliness. It has some- times been the fashion in later days of strife and disquiet to re- gret that unpretending estimate of clerical duty and those easy- going days; as it has sometimes been the fashion to regret the pomp and dignity with which well-born or scholarly bishops, furnished with ample leisure and splendid revenues, presided in unapproachable state over their clergy and held their own among the great country families. Most things have a side for which something can be said; and we may truthfully and thankfully re- call that among the clergy of those days there were not a few but many instances, not only of gentle manners, and warm benevo- lence, and cultivated intelligence, but of simple piety and holy life.[3] But the fortunes of the Church are not safe in the hands of a clergy, of which a great part take their obligations easily. It was slumbering and sleeping when the visitation of days of change and trouble came upon it.

Against this state of things the Oxford movement was a de- termined revolt; but, as has been said, it was not the only one, nor the first. A profound discontent at the state of religion in England had taken possession of many powerful and serious minds in the generation which was rising into manhood at the close of the first quarter of the century; and others besides the leaders of the move- ment were feeling their way to firmer ground. Other writers of very different principles, and with different objects, had become alive, among other things, to the importance of true ideas about the Church, impatient at the ignorance and shallowness of the current views of it, and alarmed at the dangers which menaced it.

3. Readers of Wordsworth will remember the account of Mr. R. Walker (Notes to the "River Duddon").

Two Oxford teachers who commanded much attention by their force and boldness—Dr. Whately and Dr. Arnold—had developed their theories about the nature, constitution, and functions of the Church. They were dissatisfied with the general stagnation of religious opinion, on this as on other subjects. They agreed in resenting the unintelligent shortsightedness which relegated such a matter to a third or fourth rank in the scale of religious teaching. They agreed also in seizing the spiritual aspect of the Church, and in raising the idea of it above the level of the poor and worldly conceptions on the assumption of which questions relating to it were popularly discussed. But in their fundamental principles they were far apart. I assume, on the authority of Cardinal Newman, what was widely believed in Oxford, and never apparently denied, that the volume entitled *Letters of an Episcopalian*,[4] 1826, was, in some sense at least, the work of Dr. Whately. In it is sketched forth the conception of an organised body, introduced into the world by Christ Himself, endowed with definite spiritual powers and with no other, and, whether connected with the State or not, having an independent existence and inalienable claims, with its own objects and laws, with its own moral standard and spirit and character. From this book Cardinal Newman tells us that he learnt his theory of the Church, though it was, after all, but the theory received from the first appearance of Christian history; and he records also the deep impression which it made on others. Dr. Arnold's view was a much simpler one. He divided the world into Christians and non-Christians: Christians were all who professed to believe in Christ as a Divine Person and to worship Him,[5] and the brotherhood, the "Societas" of Christians, was all that was meant by "the Church" in the New Testament. It mattered, of course, to the conscience of each Christian what he had made up his mind to believe, but to no one else. Church organisation was, according to circumstances, partly inevitable or expedient, partly mischievous, but in no case of divine authority. Teaching, ministering the word, was a thing of divine appointment, but not so the mode of exercising it, either as to persons, forms, or methods. Sacraments there were, signs and pledges of divine love and help, in every action of life, in every sight of na-

4. Compare *Life of Whately* (ed. 1866), 1: 52, 68.
5. Arnold to W. Smith, *Life*, 1: 356–58; 2: 32.

ture, and eminently two most touching ones, recommended to Christians by the Redeemer Himself; but except as a matter of mere order, one man might deal with these as lawfully as another. Church history there was, fruitful in interest, instruction, and warning; for it was the record of the long struggle of the true idea of the Church against the false, and of the fatal disappearance of the true before the forces of blindness and wickedness.[6] Dr. Arnold's was a passionate attempt to place the true idea in the light. Of the difficulties of his theory he made light account. There was the vivid central truth which glowed through his soul and quickened all his thoughts. He became its champion and militant apostle. These doctrines, combined with his strong political liberalism, made the Midlands hot for Dr. Arnold. But he liked the fighting, as he thought, against the narrow and frightened orthodoxy round him. And he was in the thick of this fighting when another set of ideas about the Church—the ideas on which alone it seemed to a number of earnest and anxious minds that the cause of the Church could be maintained—the ideas which were the beginning of the Oxford movement, crossed his path. It was the old orthodox tradition of the Church, with fresh life put into it, which he flattered himself that he had so triumphantly demolished. This intrusion of a despised rival to his own teaching about the Church—teaching in which he believed with deep and fervent conviction—profoundly irritated him; all the more that it came from men who had been among his friends, and who, he thought, should have known better.[7]

But neither Dr. Whately's nor Dr. Arnold's attempts to put the old subject of the Church in a new light gained much hold on the public mind. One was too abstract; the other too unhistorical and revolutionary. Both in Oxford and in the country were men whose hearts burned within them for something less speculative and vague, something more reverent and less individual, more in sympathy with the inherited spirit of the Church. It did not need much searching to find in the facts and history of the Church ample evidence of principles distinct and inspiring, which, however long latent, or overlaid by superficial accretions, were as well

---

6. *Life,* 1:255 ff.
7. "I am vexed to find how much hopeless bigotry lingers in minds, οἷς ἥκιστα ἔχρη" (Arnold to Whately, Sept. 1832. *Life,* 1:331; 2: 3-7).

fitted as they ever were to animate its defenders in the struggle with the unfriendly opinion of the day. They could not open their Prayer Books, and think of what they read there, without seeing that on the face of it the Church claimed to be something very different from what it was assumed to be in the current controversies of the time, very different from a mere institution of the State, from a vague collection of Christian professions, from one form or denomination of religion among many, distinguished by larger privileges and larger revenues. They could not help seeing that it claimed an origin not short of the Apostles of Christ, and took for granted that it was to speak and teach with their authority and that of their Master. These were theological commonplaces; but now, the pressure of events and of competing ideas made them to be felt as real and momentous truths. Amid the confusions and inconsistencies of the semi-political controversy on Church reform, and on the defects and rights of the Church, which was going on in Parliament, in the press, and in pamphlets, the deeper thoughts of those who were interested in its fortunes were turned to what was intrinsic and characteristic in its constitution: and while these thoughts in some instances only issued in theory and argument, in others they led to practical resolves to act upon them and enforce them.

At the end of the first quarter of the century, say about 1825–30, two characteristic forms of Church of England Christianity were popularly recognised. One inherited the traditions of a learned and sober Anglicanism, claiming as the authorities for its theology the great line of English divines from Hooker to Waterland, finding its patterns of devotion in Bishop Wilson, Bishop Horne, and the "Whole Duty of Man," but not forgetful of Andrewes, Jeremy Taylor, and Ken,—preaching without passion or excitement, scholarlike, careful, wise, often vigorously reasoned discourses on the capital points of faith and morals and exhibiting in its adherents, who were many and important, all the varieties of a great and far-descended school, which claimed for itself rightful possession of the ground which it held. There was nothing effeminate about it, as there was nothing fanatical; there was nothing extreme or foolish about it; it was a manly school, distrustful of high-wrought feelings and professions, cultivating

14

self-command and shy of display, and setting up as its mark, in contrast to what seemed to it sentimental weakness, a reasonable and serious idea of duty. The divinity which it propounded, though it rested on learning, was rather that of strong common sense than of the schools of erudition. Its better members were highly cultivated, benevolent men, intolerant of irregularities both of doctrine and life, whose lives were governed by an unostentatious but solid and unfaltering piety, ready to burst forth on occasion into fervid devotion. Its worse members were jobbers and hunters after preferment, pluralists who built fortunes and endowed families out of the Church, or country gentlemen in orders, who rode to hounds and shot and danced and farmed, and often did worse things. Its average was what naturally in England would be the average, in a state of things in which great religious institutions have been for a long time settled and unmolested—kindly, helpful, respectable, sociable persons of good sense and character, workers rather in a fashion of routine which no one thought of breaking, sometimes keeping up their University learning, and apt to employ it in odd and not very profitable inquiries; apt, too, to value themselves on their cheerfulness and quick wit; but often dull and dogmatic and quarrelsome, often insufferably pompous. The custom of daily service and even of fasting was kept up more widely than is commonly supposed. The Eucharist, though sparingly administered, and though it had been profaned by the operation of the Test Acts, was approached by religious people with deep reverence. But besides the better, and the worse, and the average members of this, which called itself the Church party, there stood out a number of men of active and original minds, who, starting from the traditions of the party, were in advance of it in thought and knowledge, or in the desire to carry principles into action. At the Universities learning was still represented by distinguished names. At Oxford, Dr. Routh was still living and at work, and Van Mildert was not forgotten. Bishop Lloyd, if he had lived, would have played a considerable part; and a young man of vast industry and great Oriental learning, Mr. Pusey, was coming on the scene. Davison, in an age which had gone mad about the study of prophecy, had taught a more intelligent and sober way of regarding it; and Mr. John

Miller's Bampton Lectures, now probably only remembered by a striking sentence, quoted in a note to the *Christian Year*,[8] had impressed his readers with a deeper sense of the uses of Scripture. Cambridge, besides scholars like Bishop Kaye, and accomplished writers like Mr. Le Bas and Mr. Lyall, could boast of Mr. Hugh James Rose, the most eminent person of his generation as a divine. But the influence of this learned theology was at the time not equal to its value. Sound requires atmosphere; and there was as yet no atmosphere in the public mind in which the voice of this theology could be heard. The person who first gave body and force to Church theology, not to be mistaken or ignored, was Dr. Hook. His massive and thorough Churchmanship was the independent growth of his own thoughts and reading. Resolute, through good report and evil report, rough but very generous, stern both against Popery and Puritanism, he had become a power in the Midlands and the North, and first Coventry, then Leeds, were the centres of a new influence. He was the apostle of the Church to the great middle class.

These were the orthodox Churchmen, whom their rivals, and not their rivals only,[9] denounced as dry, unspiritual, formal, unevangelical, self-righteous; teachers of mere morality at their best, allies and servants of the world at their worst. In the party which at this time had come to be looked upon popularly as best entitled to be the *religious* party, whether they were admired as Evangelicals, or abused as Calvinists, or laughed at as the Saints, were inheritors not of Anglican traditions, but of those which had grown up among the zealous clergymen and laymen who had sympathised with the great Methodist revival, and whose theology and life had been profoundly affected by it. It was the second or third generation of those whose religious ideas had been formed and governed by the influence of teachers like Hervey, Romaine, Cecil, Venn, Fletcher, Newton, and Thomas Scott. The fathers of the Evangelical school were men of naturally strong and vigorous understandings, robust and rugged, and sometimes eccen-

8. St. Bartholomew's Day.
9. "The mere barren orthodoxy which, from all that I can hear, is characteristic of Oxford." Maurice in 1829 (*Life,* 1:103). In 1832 he speaks of his "high endeavours to rouse Oxford from its lethargy having so signally failed" (1:143).

tric, but quite able to cope with the controversialists, like Bishop Tomline, who attacked them. These High Church controversialists were too half-hearted and too shallow, and understood their own principles too imperfectly, to be a match for antagonists who were in deadly earnest, and put them to shame by their zeal and courage. But Newton and Romaine and the Milners were too limited and narrow in their compass of ideas to found a powerful theology. They undoubtedly often quickened conscience. But their system was a one-sided and unnatural one, indeed in the hands of some of its expounders threatening morality and soundness of character.[10] It had none of the sweep which carried the justification doctrines of Luther, or the systematic predestinarianism of Calvin, or the "platform of discipline" of John Knox and the Puritans. It had to deal with a society which laid stress on what was "reasonable," or "polite," or "ingenious," or "genteel," and unconsciously it had come to have respect to these requirements. The one thing by which its preachers carried disciples with them was their undoubted and serious piety, and their brave, though often fantastic and inconsistent, protest against the world. They won consideration and belief by the mild persecution which this protest brought on them—by being proscribed as enthusiasts by comfortable dignitaries, and mocked as "Methodists" and "Saints" by wits and worldlings. But the austere spirit of Newton and Thomas Scott had, between 1820 and 1830, given way a good deal to the influence of increasing popularity. The profession of Evangelical religion had been made more than respectable by the adhesion of men of position and weight. Preached in the pulpits of fashionable chapels, this religion proved to be no more exacting than its "High and Dry" rival. It gave a gentle stimulus to tempers which required to be excited by novelty. It recommended itself by gifts of flowing words or high-pitched rhetoric to those who expected *some* demands to be made on them, so that these demands were not too strict. Yet Evangelical religion had not been unfruitful, especially in public results. It had led Howard and Elizabeth Fry to assail the brutalities of the prisons. It had led Clarkson and Wilberforce to overthrow the slave trade, and ultimately slavery itself. It had created great Mis-

10. Abbey and Overton, *English Church in the Eighteenth Century*, 2:180, 204.

sionary Societies. It had given motive and impetus to countless philanthropic schemes. What it failed in was the education and development of character; and this was the result of the increasing meagreness of its writing and preaching. There were still Evangelical preachers of force and eloquence—Robert Hall, Edward Irving, Chalmers, Jay of Bath—but they were not Churchmen. The circle of themes dwelt on by this school in the Church was a contracted one, and no one had found the way of enlarging it. It shrank, in its fear of mere moralising, in its horror of the idea of merit or of the value of good works, from coming into contact with the manifold realities of the spirit of man: it never seemed to get beyond the "first beginnings" of Christian teaching, the call to repent, the assurance of forgiveness: it had nothing to say to the long and varied process of building up the new life of truth and goodness: it was nervously afraid of departing from the consecrated phrases of its school, and in the perpetual iteration of them it lost hold of the meaning they may once have had. It too often found its guarantee for faithfulness in jealous suspicions, and in fierce bigotries, and at length it presented all the characteristics of an exhausted teaching and a spent enthusiasm. Claiming to be exclusively spiritual, fervent, unworldly, the sole announcer of the free grace of God amid self-righteousness and sin, it had come, in fact, to be on very easy terms with the world. Yet it kept its hold on numbers of spiritually-minded persons, for in truth there seemed to be nothing better for those who saw in the affections the main field of religion. But even of these good men, the monotonous language sounded to all but themselves inconceivably hollow and wearisome; and in the hands of the average teachers of the school, the idea of religion was becoming poor and thin and unreal.

But besides these two great parties, each of them claiming to represent the authentic and unchanging mind of the Church, there were independent thinkers who took their place with neither and criticised both. Paley had still his disciples at Cambridge, or if not disciples, yet representatives of his masculine but not very profound and reverent way of thinking; and a critical school, represented by names afterwards famous, Connop Thirlwall and Julius Hare, strongly influenced by German speculation, both in theology and history, began to attract attention. And at Cambridge was growing, slowly and out of sight, a mind and an influence which were to be at once the counterpart and the rival of the Oxford movement, its ally for a short moment, and then its earnest and often bitter enemy. In spite of the dominant teaching identified with the name of Mr. Simeon, Frederic Maurice, with John Sterling and other members of the Apostles' Club, was feeling for something truer and nobler than the conventionalities of the religious world.[11] In Oxford, mostly in a different way, more dry, more dialectical, and, perhaps it may be said, more sober, definite, and ambitious of clearness, the same spirit was at work. There was a certain drift towards Dissent among the warmer spirits. Under the leading of Whately, questions were asked about what was supposed to be beyond dispute with both Churchmen and Evangelicals. Current phrases, the keynotes of many a sermon, were fearlessly taken to pieces. Men were challenged to examine the meaning of their words. They were cautioned or ridiculed as the case might be, on the score of "confusion of thought" and "inaccuracy of mind"; they were convicted of great logical sins, *ignoratio elenchi*, or *undistributed middle terms*; and bold theories began to make their appearance about religious principles and teaching, which did not easily accommodate themselves to popular conceptions. In very different ways and degrees, Davison, Copleston, Whately, Hawkins, Milman, and not least, a brilliant naturalised Spaniard who sowed the seeds of doubt around him, Blanco White, had broken through a number of accepted opinions, and had presented some startling ideas to men who had thought that all religious questions lay between the orthodoxy of Lambeth and the orthodoxy of Clapham and Islington. And thus the foundation was laid, at least, at Oxford of what was then called the Liberal School of Theology. Its theories and paradoxes, then commonly associated with the *"Noetic"* character of one college, Oriel, were thought startling and venturesome when discussed in steady-going common-rooms and country parsonages; but they were still cautious and old-fashioned compared with what was to come after them. The distance is indeed great between those early disturbers of lecture-rooms and University pulpits, and their successors.

11. *V*. Maurice, *Life,* 1:108–111; Trench's *Letters;* Carlyle's *Sterling.*

While this was going on within the Church, there was a great movement of thought going on in the country. It was the time when Bentham's utilitarianism had at length made its way into prominence and importance. It had gained a hold on a number of powerful minds in society and political life. It was threatening to become the dominant and popular philosophy. It began, in some ways beneficially, to affect and even control legislation. It made desperate attempts to take possession of the whole province of morals. It forced those who saw through its mischief, who hated and feared it, to seek a reason, and a solid and strong one, for the faith which was in them as to the reality of conscience and the mysterious distinction between right and wrong. And it entered into a close alliance with science, which was beginning to assert its claims, since then risen so high, to a new and undefined supremacy, not only in the general concerns of the world, but specially in education. It was the day of Holland House. It was the time when a Society of which Lord Brougham was the soul, and which comprised a great number of important political and important scientific names, was definitely formed for the *Diffusion of Useful Knowledge.* Their labours are hardly remembered now in the great changes for which they paved the way; but the Society was the means of getting written and of publishing at a cheap rate a number of original and excellent books on science, biography, and history. It was the time of the *Library of Useful Knowledge,* and its companion, the *Library of Entertaining Knowledge*; of the *Penny Magazine,* and its Church rival, the *Saturday Magazine,* of the *Penny Cyclopædia,* and *Lardner's Cabinet Cyclopædia,* and *Murray's Family Library*: popular series, which contained much of the work of the ablest men of the day, and which, though for the most part superseded now, were full of interest then. Another creation of this epoch, and an unmistakable indication of its tendencies, was the British Association for the Advancement of Science, which met for the first time at Oxford in June 1832, not without a good deal of jealousy and misgiving, partly unreasonable, partly not unfounded, among men in whose hearts the cause and fortunes of religion were supreme.

Thus the time was ripe for great collisions of principles and aims; for the decomposition of elements which had been hitherto united; for sifting them out of their old combinations, and regrouping them according to their more natural affinities. It was a time for the formation and development of unexpected novelties in teaching and practical effort. There was a great historic Church party, imperfectly conscious of its position and responsibilities;[12] there was an active but declining pietistic school, resting on a feeble intellectual basis and narrow and meagre interpretations of Scripture, and strong only in its circle of philanthropic work; there was, confronting both, a rising body of inquisitive and, in some ways, menacing thought. To men deeply interested in religion, the ground seemed confused and treacherous. There was room, and there was a call, for new effort; but to find the resources for it, it seemed necessary to cut down deep below the level of what even good men accepted as the adequate expression of Christianity, and its fit application to the conditions of the nineteenth century. It came to pass that there were men who had the heart to make this atempt. As was said at starting, the actual movement began in the conviction that a great and sudden danger to the Church was at hand, and that an unusual effort must be made to meet it. But if the occasion was in a measure accidental, there was nothing haphazard or tentative in the line chosen to encounter the danger. From the first it was deliberately and distinctively taken. The choice of it was of the result of convictions which had been forming before the occasion came which called on them. The religious ideas which governed the minds of those who led the movement had been traced, in outline at least, firmly and without faltering.

The movement had its spring in the consciences and character of its leaders. To these men religion really meant the most awful and most seriously personal thing on earth. It had not only a theological basis; it had still more deeply a moral one. What that basis was is shown in a variety of indications of ethical temper and habits, before the movement, in those who afterwards directed it. The *Christian Year* was published in 1827, and tells us distinctly by what kind of standard Mr. Keble moulded his judgment and aims. What Mr. Keble's influence and teaching did, in training an apt pupil to deep and severe views of truth and duty, is to be

12. "In what concerns the Established Church, the House of Commons seems to feel no other principle than that of vulgar policy. The old High Church race is worn out." Alex. Knox (June 1816), 1:54.

seen in the records of purpose and self-discipline, often so pain-ful, but always so lofty and sincere, of Mr. Hurrell Froude's journal. But these indications are most forcibly given in Mr. New-man's earliest preaching. As tutor at Oriel, Mr. Newman had made what efforts he could, sometimes disturbing to the authori-ties, to raise the standard of conduct and feeling among his pupils. When he became a parish priest, his preaching took a singularly practical and plain-spoken character. The first sermon of the series, a typical sermon, "Holiness necessary for future Blessed-ness," a sermon which has made many readers grave when they laid it down, was written in 1826, before he came to St. Mary's; and as he began he continued. No sermons, except those which his great opposite, Dr. Arnold, was preaching at Rugby, had appealed to conscience with such directness and force. A passionate and sus-tained earnestness after a high moral rule, seriously realised in conduct, is the dominant character of these sermons. They showed the strong reaction against slackness of fibre in the religious life; against the poverty, softness, restlessness, worldliness, the blunted and impaired sense of truth, which reigned with little check in the recognised fashions of professing Christianity; the want of depth both of thought and feeling; the strange blindness to the real sternness, nay the austerity, of the New Testament. Out of this ground the movement grew. Even more than a theological reform, it was a protest against the loose unreality of ordinary religious morality. In the first stage of the movement, moral earnestness and enthusiasm gave its impulse to theological interest and zeal.

II

The Beginning
of the Movement—
John Keble

Long before the Oxford movement was thought of, or had any definite shape, a number of its characteristic principles and ideas had taken strong hold of the mind of a man of great ability and great seriousness, who, after a brilliant career at Oxford as student and tutor, had exchanged the University for a humble country cure. John Keble, by some years the senior, but the college friend and intimate of Arnold, was the son of a Gloucestershire country clergyman of strong character and considerable scholarship. He taught and educated his two sons at home, and then sent them to Oxford, where both of them made their mark, and the elder, John, a mere boy when he first appeared at his college, Corpus, carried off almost everything that the University could give in the way of distinction. He won a double first; he won the Latin and English Essays in the same year; and he won what was the still greater honour of an Oriel Fellowship. His honours were borne with meekness and simplicity; to his attainments he joined a temper of singular sweetness and modesty, capable at the same time, when necessary, of austere strength and strictness of principle. He had become one of the most distinguished men in Oxford, when about the year 1823 he felt himself bound to give himself more exclusively to the work of a clergyman, and left Oxford to be his father's curate. There was nothing very unusual in his way of life, or singular and showy in his work as a clergyman; he went in and out among the poor, he was not averse to society, he preached plain, unpretending, earnest sermons; he kept up his

literary interests. But he was a deeply convinced Churchman, finding his standard and pattern of doctrine and devotion in the sober
earnestness and dignity of the Prayer Book, and looking with
great and intelligent dislike at the teaching and practical working
of the more popular system which, under the name of Evangelical Christianity, was aspiring to dominate religious opinion, and
which, often combining some of the most questionable features
of Methodism and Calvinism, denounced with fierce intolerance
everything that deviated from its formulas and watchwords. And
as his loyalty to the Church of England was profound and intense,
all who had shared her fortunes, good or bad, or who professed
to serve her, had a place in his affections; and any policy which
threatened to injure or oppress her, and any principles which were
hostile to her influence and teaching, roused his indignation and
resistance. He was a strong Tory, and by conviction and religious
temper a thorough High Churchman.

But there was nothing in him to foreshadow the leader in a
bold and wide-reaching movement. He was absolutely without
ambition. He hated show and mistrusted excitement. The thought
of preferment was steadily put aside both from temper and definite principle. He had no popular aptitudes, and was very suspicious of them. He had no care for the possession of influence; he
had deliberately chosen the *fallentis semita vitae*, and to be what
his father had been, a faithful and contented country parson, was
all that he desired. But idleness was not in his nature. Born a poet,
steeped in all that is noblest and tenderest and most beautiful in
Greek and Roman literature, with the keenest sympathy with that
new school of poetry which, with Wordsworth as its representative, was searching out the deeper relations between nature and
the human soul, he found in poetical composition a vent and relief for feelings stirred by the marvels of glory and of awfulness,
and by the sorrows and blessings, amid which human life is
passed. But his poetry was for a long time only for himself and
his intimate friends; his indulgence in poetical composition was
partly playful, and it was not till after much hesitation on his own
part and also on theirs, and with a contemptuous undervaluing of
his work, which continued to the end of his life, that the anony-
mous little book of poems was published which has since become
familiar wherever English is read, as the *Christian Year*. His serious interests were public ones. Though living in the shade, he

followed with anxiety and increasing disquiet the changes which went on so rapidly and so formidably, during the end of the first quarter of this century, in opinion and in the possession of political power. It became more and more plain that great changes were at hand, though not so plain what they would be. It seemed likely that power would come into the hands of men and parties hostile to the Church in their principles, and ready to use to its prejudice the advantages which its position as an establishment gave them; and the anticipation grew in Keble's mind, that in the struggles which seemed likely, not only for the legal rights but for the faith of the Church, the Church might have both to claim more, and to suffer more, at the hands of Government. Yet though these thoughts filled his mind, and strong things were said in the intercourse with friends about what was going on about them, no definite course of action had been even contemplated when Keble went into the country in 1823. There was nothing to distinguish him from numbers of able clergymen all over England, who were looking on with interest, with anxiety, often with indignation, at what was going on. Mr. Keble had not many friends and was no party chief. He was a brilliant university scholar overlaying the plain, unworldly country parson; an old-fashioned English Churchman, with great veneration for the Church and its bishops, and a great dislike of Rome, Dissent, and Methodism, but with a quick heart; with a frank, gay humility of soul, with great contempt of appearances, great enjoyment of nature, great unselfishness, strict and severe principles of morals and duty.

What was it that turned him by degrees into so prominent and so influential a person? It was the result of the action of his convictions and ideas, and still more of his character, on the energetic and fearless mind of a pupil and disciple, Richard Hurrell Froude. Froude was Keble's pupil at Oriel, and when Keble left Oriel for his curacy at the beginning of the Long Vacation of 1823, he took Froude with him to read for his degree. He took with him ultimately two other pupils, Robert Wilberforce and Isaac Williams of Trinity. One of them, Isaac Williams, has left some reminiscences of the time, and of the terms on which the young men were with their tutor, then one of the most famous men at Oxford. They were on terms of the utmost freedom. "Master is the greatest boy of them all," was the judgment of the rustic who was gardener, groom, and parish clerk to Mr. Keble. Froude's was a keen logical mind, not easily satisfied, contemptuous of compromises and evasions, and disposed on occasion to be mischievous and aggressive; and with Keble, as with anybody else, he was ready to dispute and try every form of dialectical experiment. But he was open to higher influences than those of logic, and in Keble he saw what subdued and won him to boundless veneration and affection. Keble won the love of the whole little society; but in Froude he had gained a disciple who was to be the mouthpiece and champion of his ideas, and who was to react on himself and carry him forward to larger enterprises and bolder resolutions than by himself he would have thought of. Froude took in from Keble all he had to communicate—principles, convictions, moral rules and standards of life, hopes, fears, antipathies. And his keenly-tempered intellect, and his determination and high courage, gave a point and an impulse of their own to Keble's views and purposes. As things came to look darker, and dangers seemed more serious to the Church, its faith or its rights, the interchange of thought between master and disciple, in talk and in letter, pointed more and more to the coming necessity of action; and Froude at least had no objections to the business of an agitator. But all this was very gradual; things did not yet go beyond discussion; ideas, views, arguments were examined and compared; and Froude, with all his dash, felt as Keble felt, that he had much to learn about himself, as well as about books and things. In his respect for antiquity, in his dislike of the novelties which were invading Church rules and sentiments, as well as its creeds, in his jealousy of the State, as well as in his seriousness of self-discipline, he accepted Keble's guidance and influence more and more; and from Keble he had more than one lesson of self-distrust, more than one warning against the temptations of intellect. "Froude told me many years after," writes one of his friends, "that Keble once, before parting with him, seemed to have something on his mind which he wished to say, but shrank from saying, while waiting, I think, for a coach. At last he said, just before parting, 'Froude, you thought Law's *Serious Call* was a clever book; it seemed to me as if you had said the Day of Judgment will be a pretty sight.' This speech, Froude told me, had a great effect on his after life."[1]

1. Isaac Williams's MS. Memoir.

At Easter 1826 Froude was elected Fellow of Oriel. He came back to Oxford, charged with Keble's thoughts and feelings, and from his more eager and impatient temper, more on the look-out for ways of giving them effect. The next year he became tutor, and he held the tutorship till 1830. But he found at Oriel a colleague, a little his senior in age and standing, of whom Froude and his friends as yet knew little except that he was a man of great ability, that he had been a favourite of Whately's, and that in a loose and rough way he was counted among the few Liberals and Evangel-icals in Oxford. This was Mr. Newman. Keble had been shy of him, and Froude would at first judge him by Keble's standard. But Newman was just at this time "moving," as he expresses it, "out of the shadow of Liberalism." Living not apart like Keble, but in the same college, and meeting every day, Froude and New-man could not but be either strongly and permanently repelled, or strongly attracted. They were attracted; attracted with a force which at last united them in the deepest and most unreserved friendship. Of the steps of this great change in the mind and for-tunes of each of them we have no record: intimacies of this kind grow in college out of unnoticed and unremembered talks, agree-ing or differing, out of unconscious disclosures of temper and purpose, out of walks and rides and quiet breakfasts and common-room arguments, out of admirations and dislikes, out of letters and criticisms and questions; and nobody can tell afterwards how they have come about. The change was gradual and deliberate. Froude's friends in Gloucestershire, the Keble family, had their misgivings about Newman's supposed liberalism; they did not much want to have to do with him. His subtle and speculative temper did not always square with Froude's theology. "N. is a fellow that I like more, the more I think of him," Froude wrote in 1828; "only I would give a few odd pence if he were not a heretic."[2] But Froude, who saw him every day, and was soon associated with him in the tutorship, found a spirit more akin to his own in depth and freedom and daring, than he had yet en-countered. And Froude found Newman just in that maturing state of religious opinion in which a powerful mind like Froude's would be likely to act decisively. Each acted on the other. Froude represented Keble's ideas, Keble's enthusiasm. Newman gave

2. *Rem.* 1:232, 233. In 1828, Newman had preferred Hawkins to Keble, for Provost.

shape, foundation, consistency, elevation to the Anglican theology, when he accepted it, which Froude had learned from Keble. "I knew him first," we read in the *Apologia*, "in 1826, and was in the closest and most affectionate friendship with him from about 1829 till his death in 1836."[3] But this was not all. Through Froude, Newman came to know and to be intimate with Keble; and a sort of *camaraderie* arose, of very independent and outspoken people, who acknowledged Keble as their master and counsellor.

"The true and primary author of it" (the Tractarian movement), we read in the *Apologia*, "as is usual with great motive powers, was out of sight. . . . Need I say that I am speaking of John Keble?" The statement is strictly true. Froude never would have been the man he was but for his daily and hourly intercourse with Keble; and Froude brought to bear upon Newman's mind, at a critical period of its development, Keble's ideas and feelings about religion and the Church, Keble's reality of thought and purpose, Keble's transparent and saintly simplicity. And Froude, as we know from a well-known saying of his,[4] brought Keble and Newman to understand one another, when the elder man was shy and suspicious of the younger, and the younger, though full of veneration for the elder, was hardly yet in full sympathy with what was most characteristic and most cherished in the elder's religious convictions. Keble attracted and moulded Froude: he impressed Froude with his strong Churchmanship, his severity and reality of life, his poetry and high standard of scholarly excellence. Froude learned from him to be anti-Erastian, anti-methodistical, anti-sentimental, and as strong in his hatred of the world, as contemptuous of popular approval, as any Methodist. Yet all this might merely have made a strong impression, or formed one more marked school of doctrine, without the fierce energy which received it and which it inspired. But Froude, in accepting Keble's ideas, resolved to make them active, public, aggressive; and he found in Newman a colleague whose bold origi-

3. *Apol.* p. 84.
4. *Remains*, 1:438; *Apol.* p. 77. "Do you know the story of the murderer who had done one good thing in his life? Well, if I was asked what good deed I have ever done, I should say I had brought Keble and Newman to understand each other."

nality responded to his own. Together they worked as tutors; together they worked when their tutorships came to an end; together they worked when thrown into companionship in their Mediterranean voyage in the winter of 1832 and the spring of 1833. They came back, full of aspirations and anxieties which spurred them on; their thoughts had broken out in papers sent home from time to time to Rose's *British Magazine*—"Home Thoughts Abroad," and the "Lyra Apostolica." Then came the meeting at Hadleigh, and the beginning of the Tracts. Keble had given the inspiration, Froude had given the impulse; then Newman took up the work, and the impulse henceforward, and the direction, were his.

Doubtless, many thought and felt like them about the perils which beset the Church and religion. Loyalty to the Church, belief in her divine mission, allegiance to her authority, readiness to do battle for her claims, were anything but extinct in her ministers and laity. The elements were all about of sound and devoted Churchmanship. Higher ideas of the Church than the popular and political notion of it, higher conceptions of Christian doctrine than those of the ordinary evangelical theology—echoes of the meditations of a remarkable Irishman, Mr. Alexander Knox —had in many quarters attracted attention in the works and sermons of his disciple, Bishop Jebb, though it was not till the movement had taken shape that their full significance was realised. Others besides Keble and Froude and Newman were seriously considering what could best be done to arrest the current which was running strong against the Church, and discussing schemes of resistance and defence. Others were stirring up themselves and their brethren to meet the new emergencies, to respond to the new call. Some of these were in communication with the Oriel men, and ultimately took part with them in organising vigorous measures. But it was not till Mr. Newman made up his mind to force on the public mind, in a way which could not be evaded, the great article of the Creed—"I believe one Catholic and Apostolic Church"—that the movement began. And for the first part of its course, it was concentrated at Oxford. It was the direct result of the searchings of heart and the communings for seven years, from 1826 to 1833, of the three men who have been the subject of this chapter.

III

Richard Hurrell Froude

The names of those who took the lead in this movement are familiar—Keble, Newman, Pusey, Hugh James Rose, William Palmer. Much has been written about them by friends and enemies, and also by one of themselves, and any special notice of them is not to the purpose of the present narrative. But besides these, there were men who are now almost forgotten, but who at the time interested their contemporaries, because they were supposed to represent in a marked way the spirit and character of the movement, or to have exercised influence upon it. They ought not to be overlooked in an account of it. One of them has been already mentioned, Mr. Hurrell Froude.[1] Two others were Mr. Isaac Williams and Mr. Charles Marriott. They were all three of them men whom those who knew them could never forget—could never cease to admire and love.

Hurrell Froude soon passed away before the brunt of the fighting came. His name is associated with Mr. Newman and Mr. Keble, but it is little more than a name to those who now talk of the origin of the movement. Yet all who remember him agree in assigning to him an importance as great as that of any, in that little knot of men whose thoughts and whose courage gave birth to it.

Richard Hurrell Froude was born in 1803, and was thus two

1. I ought to say that I was not personally acquainted with Mr. Froude. I have subjoined to this chapter some recollections of him by Lord Blachford, who was his pupil and an intimate friend.

years younger than Mr. Newman, who was born in 1801. He went to Eton, and in 1821 to Oriel, where he was a pupil of Mr. Keble, and where he was elected Fellow, along with Robert Wilberforce, at Easter 1826. He was College Tutor from 1827 to 1830, having Mr. Newman and R. Wilberforce for colleagues. His health failed in 1831 and led to much absence in warm climates. He went with Mr. Newman to the south of Europe in 1832–33, and was with him at Rome. The next two winters, with the intervening year, he spent in the West Indies. Early in 1836 he died at Dartington—his birthplace. He was at the Hadleigh meeting, in July 1833, when the foundations of the movement were laid; he went abroad that winter, and was not much in England afterwards. It was through correspondence that he kept up his intercourse with his friends.

Thus he was early cut off from direct and personal action on the course which things took. But it would be a great mistake to suppose that his influence on the line taken and on the minds of others was inconsiderable. It would be more true to say that with one exception no one was more responsible for the impulse which led to the movement; no one had more to do with shaping its distinct aims and its moral spirit and character in its first stage; no one was more daring and more clear, as far as he saw, in what he was prepared for. There was no one to whom his friends so much looked up with admiration and enthusiasm. There was no "wasted shade"[2] in Hurrell Froude's disabled, prematurely shortened life.

Like Henry Martyn he was made by strong and even merciless self-discipline over a strong and for a long time refractory nature. He was a man of great gifts, with much that was most attractive and noble; but joined with this there was originally in his character a vein of perversity and mischief, always in danger of breaking out, and with which he kept up a long and painful struggle. His inmost thought and knowledge of himself have been laid bare in the papers which his friends published after his death. He was in the habit of probing his motives to the bottom, and of recording without mercy what he thought his self-deceits

2. "In this mortal journeying wasted shade
Is worse than wasted sunshine."
Henry Taylor, *Sicilian Summer*, v. 3.

31

and affectations. The religious world of the day made merry over his methods of self-discipline; but whatever may be said of them, and such things are not easy to judge of, one thing is manifest, that they were true and sincere efforts to conquer what he thought evil in himself, to keep himself in order, to bring his inmost self into subjection to the law and will of God. The self-chastening, which his private papers show, is no passion or value for asceticism, but a purely moral effort after self-command and honesty of character; and what makes the struggle so touching is its perfect reality and truth. He "turned his thoughts on that desolate wilderness, his own conscience, and said what he saw there."[3] A man who has had a good deal to conquer in himself, and has gone a good way to conquer it, is not apt to be indulgent to self-deceit or indolence, or even weakness. The basis of Froude's character was a demand which would not be put off for what was real and thorough; an implacable scorn and hatred for what he counted shams and pretences. "His highest ambition," he used to say, "was to be a humdrum."[4] The intellectual and the moral parts of his character were of a piece. The tricks and flimsinesses of a bad argument provoked him as much as the imposture and "flash" of insincere sentiment and fine talking; he might be conscious of "flash" in himself and his friends, and he would admit it unequivocally; but it was as unbearable to him to pretend not to see a fallacy as soon as it was detected, as it would have been to him to arrive at the right answer of a sum or a problem by tampering with the processes. Such a man, with strong affections and keen perception of all forms of beauty, and with the deepest desire to be reverent towards all that had a right to reverence, would find himself in the most irritating state of opposition and impatience with much that passed as religion round him. Principles not attempted to be understood and carried into practice, smooth self-complacency among those who looked down on a blind and unspiritual world, the continual provocation of worthless reasoning and ignorant platitudes, the dull unconscious stupidity of people who could not see that the times were critical—that truth had to be defended, and that it was no easy or lighthearted business to defend

3. *Remains*, Second Part, 1:47.
4. *Remains*, 1:82.

it—threw him into an habitual attitude of defiance, and half-amused, half-earnest contradiction, which made him feared by loose reasoners and pretentious talkers, and even by quiet easy-going friends, who unexpectedly found themselves led on blindfold, with the utmost gravity, into traps and absurdities by the wiles of his mischievous dialectic. This was the outside look of his relentless earnestness. People who did not like him, or his views, and who, perhaps, had winced under his irony, naturally put down his strong language, which on occasion could certainly be unceremonious, to flippancy and arrogance. But within the circle of those whom he trusted, or of those who needed at any time his help, another side disclosed itself—a side of the most genuine warmth of affection, an awful reality of devoutness, which it was his great and habitual effort to keep hidden, a high simplicity of unworldliness and generosity, and in spite of his daring mockeries of what was commonplace or showy, the most sincere and deeply felt humility with himself. Dangerous as he was often thought to be in conversation, one of the features of his character which has impressed itself on the memory of one who knew him well, was his "patient, winning considerateness in discussion, which, with other qualities, endeared him to those to whom he opened his heart."[5] "It is impossible," writes James Mozley in 1833, with a mixture of amusement, speaking of the views about celibacy which were beginning to be current, "to talk with Froude without committing one's self on such subjects as these, so that by and by I expect the tergiversants will be a considerable party." His letters, with their affectionately playful addresses, δαιμόνιε, αἰνότατε, πέπον, Carissime, "Sir, my dear friend," or "'Aργείων ὄχ' ἄριστε, have you not been a spoon?" are full of the most delightful ease and verve and sympathy.

With a keen sense of English faults he was, as Cardinal Newman has said, "an Englishman to the backbone"; and he was, further, a fastidious, high-tempered English gentleman, in spite of his declaiming about "pampered aristocrats" and the "gentleman heresy." His friends thought of him as of the "young Achilles," with his high courage, and noble form, and "eagle eye," made for such great things, but appointed so soon to die.

5. *Apologia,* p. 84.

"Who can refrain from tears at the thought of that bright and beautiful Froude?" is the expression of one of them shortly before his death, and when it was quite certain that the doom which had so long hung over him was at hand.[6] He had the love of doing, for the mere sake of doing, what was difficult or even dangerous to do, which is the mainspring of characteristic English sports and games. He loved the sea; he liked to sail his own boat, and enjoyed rough weather, and took interest in the niceties of seamanship and shipcraft. He was a bold rider across country. With a powerful grasp on mathematical truths and principles, he entered with whole-hearted zest into inviting problems, or into practical details of mechanical or hydrostatic or astronomical science. His letters are full of such observations, put in a way which he thought would interest his friends, and marked by his strong habit of getting into touch with what was real and of the substance of questions. He applied his thoughts to architecture with a power and originality which at the time were not common. No one who only cared for this world could be more attracted and interested than he was by the wonder and beauty of its facts and

6. The following shows the feeling about him in friends apt to be severe critics:—"The contents of the present collection are rather fragments and sketches than complete compositions. This might be expected in the works of a man whose days were few and interrupted by illness, if indeed that may be called an interruption, which was every day sensibly drawing him to his grave. In Mr. Froude's case, however, we cannot set down much of this incompleteness to the score of illness. The strength of his religious impressions, the boldness and clearness of his views, his long habits of self-denial, and his unconquerable energy of mind, triumphed over weakness and decay, till men with all their health and strength about them might gaze upon his attenuated form, struck with a certain awe of wonderment at the brightness of his wit, the intenseness of his mental vision, and the iron strength of his argument. . . . We will venture a remark as to that ironical turn, which certainly does appear in various shapes in the first part of these *Remains*. Unpleasant as irony may sometimes be, there need not go with it, and in this instance there did not go with it, the smallest real asperity of temper. Who that remembers the inexpressible sweetness of his smile, and the deep and melancholy pity with which he would speak of those whom he felt to be the victims of modern delusions, would not be forward to contradict such a suspicion? Such expressions, we will venture to say, and not harshness, anger, or gloom, animate the features of that countenance which will never cease to haunt the memory of those who knew him. His irony arose from that peculiar mode in which he viewed all earthly things, himself and all that was dear to him not excepted. It was his poetry." From an article in the *British Critic*, April 1840, p. 396, by Mr. Thomas Mozley, quoted in *Letters of J. B. Mozley*, p. 102.

appearances. With the deepest allegiance to his home and reverence for its ties and authority, a home of the old-fashioned ecclesiastical sort, manly, religious, orderly, he carried into his wider life the feelings with which he had been brought up; bold as he was, his reason and his character craved for authority, but authority which morally and reasonably he could respect. Mr. Keble's goodness and purity subdued him, and disposed him to accept without reserve his master's teaching: and towards Mr. Keble, along with an outside show of playful criticism and privileged impertinence, there was a reverence which governed Froude's whole nature. In the wild and rough heyday of reform, he was a Tory of the Tories. But when authority failed him, from cowardice or stupidity or self-interest, he could not easily pardon it; and he was ready to startle his friends by proclaiming himself a Radical, prepared for the sake of the highest and greatest interests to sacrifice all second-rate and subordinate ones.

When his friends, after his death, published selections from his journals and letters, the world was shocked by what seemed his amazing audacity both of thought and expression about a number of things and persons which it was customary to regard as almost beyond the reach of criticism. The *Remains* lent themselves admirably to the controversial process of culling choice phrases and sentences and epithets surprisingly at variance with conventional and popular estimates. Friends were pained and disturbed; foes naturally enough could not hold in their overflowing exultation at such a disclosure of the spirit of the movement. Sermons and newspapers drew attention to Froude's extravagances with horror and disgust. The truth is that if the off-hand sayings in conversation or letters of any man of force and wit and strong convictions about the things and persons that he condemns, were made known to the world, they would by themselves have much the same look of flippancy, injustice, impertinence to those who disagreed in opinion with the speaker or writer; they are allowed for, or they are not allowed for by others, according to what is known of his general character. The friends who published Froude's *Remains* knew what he was; they knew the place and proportion of the fierce and scornful passages; they knew that they really did not go beyond the liberty and the frank speaking which most people give themselves in the *abandon* and understood exaggeration of intimate correspondence and talk. But they miscalculated the effect on those who did not know him, or whose interest it was to make the most of the advantage given them. They seem to have expected that the picture which they presented of their friend's transparent sincerity and singleness of aim, manifested amid so much pain and self-abasement, would have touched readers more. They miscalculated in supposing that the proofs of so much reality of religious earnestness would carry off the offence of vehement language, which without these proofs might naturally be thought to show mere random violence. At any rate the result was much natural and genuine irritation, which they were hardly prepared for. Whether on general grounds they were wise in startling and vexing friends, and putting fresh weapons into the hands of opponents by their frank disclosure of so unconventional a character, is a question which may have more than one answer; but one thing is certain, they were not wise, if they only desired to forward the immediate interests of their party or cause. It was not the act of cunning conspirators; it was the act of men who were ready to show their hands, and take the consequences. Undoubtedly, they warned off many who had so far gone along with the movement, and who now drew back. But if the publication was a mistake, it was the mistake of men confident in their own straightforwardness.

There is a natural Nemesis to all over-strong and exaggerated language. The weight of Froude's judgments was lessened by the disclosure of his strong words, and his dashing fashion of condemnation and dislike gave a precedent for the violence of shallower men. But to those who look back on them now, though there can be no wonder that at the time they excited such an outcry, their outspoken boldness hardly excites surprise. Much of it might naturally be put down to the force of first impressions; much of it is the vehemence of an Englishman who claims the liberty of criticising and finding fault at home; much of it was the inevitable vehemence of a reformer. Much of it seems clear foresight of what has since come to be recognised. His judgments on the Reformers, startling as they were at the time, are not so very different, as to the facts of the case, from what most people on all sides now agree in; and as to their temper and theology, from what most churchmen would now agree in. Whatever allowances may be made for the difficulties of their time, and these allowances ought to be very great, and however well they may have done parts of their work, such as the translations and adaptations of the Prayer Book, it is safe to say that the divines of the Reformation never can be again, with their confessed Calvinism, with their shifting opinions, their extravagant deference to the foreign oracles of Geneva and Zurich, their subservience to bad men in power, the heroes and saints of churchmen. But when all this is said, it still remains true that Froude was often intemperate and unjust. In the hands of the most self-restrained and considerate of its leaders, the movement must anyhow have provoked strong opposition, and given great offence. The surprise and the general ignorance were too great; the assault was too rude and unexpected. But Froude's strong language gave it a needless exasperation.

Froude was a man strong in abstract thought and imagination, who wanted adequate knowledge. His canons of judgment were not enlarged, corrected, and strengthened by any reading or experience commensurate with his original powers of reasoning or invention. He was quite conscious of it, and did his best to fill up the gap in his intellectual equipment. He showed what he might have done under more favouring circumstances in a very interesting volume on Becket's history and letters. But circumstances were hopelessly against him; he had not time, he had not health and strength, for the learning which he so needed, which he so longed for. But wherever he could, he learned. He was quite ready to submit his prepossessions to the test and limitation of facts. Eager and quick-sighted, he was often apt to be hasty in conclusions from imperfect or insufficient premises; but even about what he saw most clearly he was willing to hold himself in suspense, when he found that there was something more to know. Cardinal Newman has noted two deficiencies which, in his opinion, were noticeable in Froude. "He had no turn for theology as such"; and, further, he goes on: "I should say that his power of entering into the minds of others was not equal to his other gifts"—a remark which he illustrates by saying that Froude could not believe that "I really held the Roman Church to be antichristian." The want of this power—in which he stood in such sharp contrast to his friend—might be either a strength or a weakness; a strength, if his business was only to fight; a weakness, if it was to attract and persuade. But Froude was made for conflict, not to win disciples. Some wild solemn poetry, marked by deep feeling and direct expression, is scattered through his letters,[7] kindled always by things and thoughts of the highest significance, and breaking forth with force and fire. But probably the judgment passed on him by a clever friend, from the examination of his handwriting, was a true one: "This fellow has a great deal of imagination, but not the imagination of a poet." He felt that even beyond poetry there are higher things than anything that imagination can work upon. It was a feeling which made him blind to the grandeur of Milton's poetry. He saw in it only an intrusion into the most sacred of sanctities.

It was this fearless and powerful spirit, keen and quick to see inferences and intolerant of compromises, that the disturbances of Roman Catholic Emancipation and of the Reform time roused from the common round of pursuits, natural to a serious and thoughtful clergyman of scholarlike mind and as yet no definite objects, and brought him with all his enthusiasm and thoroughness into a companionship with men who had devoted their lives, and given up every worldly object, to save the Church by raising it to its original idea and spirit. Keble had lifted his pupil's thoughts above mere dry and unintelligent orthodoxy, and Froude had entered with earnest purpose into Church ways of practical self-discipline and self-correction. Bishop Lloyd's lectures had taught him and others, to the surprise of many, that the familiar and venerated Prayer Book was but the reflexion of mediaeval and primitive devotion, still embodied in its Latin forms in the Roman Service books; and so indirectly had planted in their minds the idea of the historical connexion, and in a very profound way the spiritual sympathy, of the modern with the pre-Reformation Church. But it is not till 1829 or 1830 that we begin in his *Remains* to see in him the sense of a pressing and anxious crisis in religious matters. In the summer of 1829 he came more closely than hitherto across Mr. Newman's path. They had been Fellows together since 1826, and Tutors since 1827. Mr. Froude, with his Toryism and old-fashioned churchmanship, would not

7. Such as the "Daniel" in the *Lyra Apostolica,* the "Dialogue between Old Self and New Self," and the lines in the *Remains* (1:208, 209).

unnaturally be shy of a friend of Whately's with his reputation for theological liberalism. Froude's first letter to Mr. Newman is in August 1828. It is the letter of a friendly and sympathising colleague in college work, glad to be free from the "images of impudent undergraduates"; he inserts some lines of verse, talks about Dollond and telescopes, and relates how he and a friend got up at half-past two in the morning, and walked half a mile to see Mercury rise; he writes about his mathematical studies and reading for orders, and how a friend had "read half through Prideaux and yet accuses himself of idleness"; but there is no interchange of intimate thought. Mr. Newman was at this time, as he has told us, drifting away from under the shadow of liberalism; and in Froude he found a man who, without being a liberal, was as quick-sighted, as courageous, and as alive to great thoughts and new hopes as himself. Very different in many ways, they were in this alike, that the commonplace notions of religion and the Church were utterly unsatisfactory to them, and that each had the capacity for affectionate and whole-hearted friendship. The friendship began and lasted on, growing stronger and deeper to the end. And this was not all. Froude's friendship with Mr. Newman overcame Mr. Keble's hesitations about Mr. Newman's supposed liberalism. Mr. Newman has put on record what he thought and felt about Froude; no one, probably, of the many whom Cardinal Newman's long life has brought round him, ever occupied Froude's place in his heart. The correspondence shows in part the way in which Froude's spirit rose, under the sense of having such a friend to work with in the cause which day by day grew greater and more sacred in the eyes of both. Towards Mr. Keble Froude felt like a son to a father; towards Mr. Newman like a soldier to his comrade, and him the most splendid and boldest of warriors. Each mind caught fire from the other, till the high enthusiasm of the one was quenched in an early death.

Shortly after this friendship began, the course of events also began which finally gave birth to the Oxford movement. The break-up of parties caused by the Roman Catholic emancipation was followed by the French and Belgian revolutions of 1830, and these changes gave a fresh stimulus to all the reforming parties in England—Whigs, Radicals, and liberal religionists. Froude's letters mark the influence of these changes on his mind. They stirred in him the fiercest disgust and indignation, and as soon as the necessity of battle became evident to save the Church—and such a necessity was evident—he threw himself into it with all his heart, and his attitude was henceforth that of a determined and uncompromising combatant. "Froude is growing stronger and stronger in his sentiments every day," writes James Mozley, in 1832, "and cuts about him on all sides. It is extremely fine to hear him talk. The aristocracy of the country at present are the chief objects of his vituperation, and he decidedly sets himself against the modern character of the gentleman, and thinks that the Church will eventually depend for its support, as it always did in its most influential times, on the very poorest classes." "I would not set down anything that Froude says for his deliberate opinion," writes James Mozley a year later, "for he really hates the present state of things so excessively that any change would be a relief to him." . . . "Froude is staying up, and I see a great deal of him." . . . "Froude is most enthusiastic in his plans, and says, 'What fun it is living in such times as these! how could one now go back to the times of old Tory humbug?'" From hence-forth his position among his friends was that of the most impatient and aggressive of reformers, the one who most urged on his fellows to outspoken language and a bold line of action. They were not men to hang back and be afraid, but they were cautious and considerate of popular alarms and prejudices, compared with Froude's fearlessness. Other minds were indeed moving—minds as strong as his, indeed, it may be, deeper, more complex, more amply furnished, with a wider range of vision and a greater command of the field. But while he lived, he appears as the one who spurs on and incites, where others hesitate. He is the one by whom are visibly most felt the *gaudia certaminis,* and the confidence of victory, and the most profound contempt for the men and ideas of the boastful and short-sighted present.

In this unsparing and absorbing warfare, what did Froude aim at—what was the object he sought to bring about, what were the obstacles he sought to overthrow?

He was accused, as was most natural, of Romanising; of wishing to bring back Popery. It is perfectly certain that this was not what he meant, though he did not care for the imputation of it.

He was, perhaps, the first Englishman who attempted to do justice to Rome, and to use friendly language of it, without the intention of joining it. But what he fought for was not Rome, not even a restoration of unity, but a Church of England such as it was conceived of by the Caroline divines and the Non-jurors. The great break-up of 1830 had forced on men the anxious question, "What is the Church as spoken of in England? Is it the Church of Christ?" and the answers were various. Hooker had said it was "the nation"; and in entirely altered circumstances, with some qualifications, Dr. Arnold said the same. It was "the Establishment" according to the lawyers and politicians, both Whig and Tory. It was an invisible and mystical body, said the Evangelicals. It was the aggregate of separate congregations, said the Non-conformists. It was the parliamentary creation of the Reformation, said the Erastians. The true Church was the communion of the Pope, the pretended Church was a legalised schism, said the Roman Catholics. All these ideas were floating about, loose and vague, among people who talked much about the Church. Whately, with his clear sense, had laid down that it was a divine religious society, distinct in its origin and existence, distinct in its attributes from any other. But this idea had fallen dead, till Froude and his friends put new life into it. Froude accepted Whately's idea that the Church of England was the one historic uninterrupted Church, than which there could be no other, locally in England; but into this Froude read a great deal that never was and never could be in Whately's thoughts. Whately had gone very far in viewing the Church from without as a great and sacred corporate body. Casting aside the Erastian theory, he had claimed its right to exist, and if necessary, govern itself, separate from the state. He had recognised excommunication as its natural and indefeasible instrument of government. But what the internal life of the Church was, what should be its teaching and organic system, and what was the standard and proof of these, Whately had left unsaid. And this outline Froude filled up. For this he went the way to which the Prayer Book, with its Offices, its Liturgy, its Ordination services, pointed him. With the divines who had specially valued the Prayer Book, and taught in its spirit, Bishop Wilson, William Law, Hammond, Ken, Laud, Andrewes, he went back to the times and the sources from which the Prayer

Book came to us, the early Church, the reforming Church—
for such with all its faults it was—of the eleventh, twelfth, and
thirteenth centuries, before the hopelessly corrupt and fatal times
of the fourteenth and fifteenth centuries, which led to the break-
up of the sixteenth. Thus to the great question, What is the
Church? he gave without hesitation, and gave to the end, the same
answer that Anglicans gave and are giving still. But he added two
points which were then very new to the ears of English Churchmen: (1) that there were great and to most people unsuspected
faults and shortcomings in the English Church, for some of which
the Reformation was gravely responsible; (2) that the Roman
Church was more right than we had been taught to think in many
parts both of principle and practice, and that our quarrel with it
on these points arose from our own ignorance and prejudices. To
people who had taken for granted all their lives that the Church
was thoroughly "Protestant" and thoroughly right in its Protestantism, and that Rome was Antichrist, these confident statements
came with a shock. He did not enter much into dogmatic questions. As far as can be judged from his *Remains,* the one point
of doctrine on which he laid stress, as being inadequately recognised and taught in the then condition of the English Church,
was the primitive doctrine of the Eucharist. His other criticisms
pointed to practical and moral matters; the spirit of Erastianism,
the low standard of life and purpose and self-discipline in the
clergy, the low tone of the current religious teaching. The Evangelical teaching seem to him a system of unreal works. The opposite school was too self-complacent, too comfortable, too
secure in its social and political alliances; and he was bent on
shaming people into severer notions. "We will have a *vocab-
ularium apostolicum,* and I will start with four words: 'pampered aristocrats,' 'resident gentlemen,' 'smug parsons,' and
'*pauperes Christi.*' I shall use the first on all occasions; it seems
to me just to hit the thing." "I think of putting the view forward
(about new monasteries), under the title of a 'Project for Reviving Religion in Great Towns.' Certainly colleges of unmarried
priests (who might, of course, retire to a living, when they
could and liked) would be the cheapest possible way of providing
effectively for the spiritual wants of a large population." And his
great quarrel with the existing state of things was that the spiritual

objects of the Church were overlaid and lost sight of in the anxiety not to lose its political position. In this direction he was, as he proclaims himself, an out-and-out Radical, and he was prepared at once to go very far. "If a national Church means a Church without discipline, my argument for discipline is an argument against a national Church; and the best thing we can do is to unnationalise ours as soon as possible"; "let us tell the truth and shame the devil; let us give up a *national* Church and have a *real* one." His criticism did not diminish in severity, or his proposals become less daring, as he felt that his time was growing short and the hand of death was upon him. But to the end, the elevation and improvement of the English Church remained his great purpose. To his friend as we know, the Roman Church was *either* the Truth or Antichrist. To Froude it was neither the whole truth nor Antichrist; but like the English Church itself, a great and defective Church, whose defects were the opposite to ours, and which we should do wisely to learn from rather than abuse. But to the last his allegiance never wavered to the English Church.

It is very striking to come from Froude's boisterous freedom in his letters to his sermons and the papers he prepared for publication. In his sermons his manner of writing is severe and restrained even to dryness. If they startle it is by the force and searching point of an idea, not by any strength of words. The style is chastened, simple, calm, with the most careful avoidance of over-statement or anything rhetorical. And so in his papers, his mode of argument, forcible and cogent as it is, avoids all appearance of exaggeration or even illustrative expansion; it is all muscle and sinew; it is modelled on the argumentative style of Bishop Butler, and still more, of William Law. No one could suppose from these papers Froude's fiery impetuosity, or the frank daring of his disrespectful vocabulary. Those who can read between the lines can trace the grave irony which clung everywhere to his deep earnestness.

There was yet another side of Froude's character which was little thought of by his critics, or recognised by all his friends. With all his keenness of judgment and all his readiness for conflict, some who knew him best were impressed by the melancholy which hung over his life, and which, though he ignored it, they could detect. It is remembered still by Cardinal Newman. "I thought," wrote Mr. Isaac Williams, "that knowing him, I better understood Hamlet, a person most natural, but so original as to be unlike any one else, hiding depth of delicate thought in apparent extravagances. *Hamlet,* and the *Georgics* of Virgil, he used to say, he should have bound together." "Isaac Williams," wrote Mr. Copeland, "mentioned to me a remark made on Froude by S. Wilberforce in his early days: 'They talk of Froude's fun, but somehow I cannot be in a room with him alone for ten minutes without feeling so intensely melancholy, that I do not know what to do with myself. At Brightstone, in my Eden days, he was with me, and I was overwhelmed with the deep sense which possessed him of yearning which nothing could satisfy and of the unsatisfying nature of all things.' "[8]

Froude often reminds us of Pascal. Both had that peculiarly bright, brilliant, sharp-cutting intellect which passes with ease through the coverings and disguises which veil realities from men. Both had mathematical powers of unusual originality and clearness; both had the same imaginative faculty; both had the same keen interest in practical problems of science; both felt and followed the attraction of deeper and more awful interests. Both had the same love of beauty; both suppressed it. Both had the same want of wide or deep learning; they made skilful use of what books came to their hand, and used their reading as few readers are able to use it; but their real instrument of work was their own quick and strong insight, and power of close and vigorous reasoning. Both had the greatest contempt for fashionable and hollow "shadows of religion." Both had the same definite, unflinching judgment. Both used the same clear and direct language. Both had a certain grim delight in the irony with which they pursued their opponents. In both it is probable that their unmeasured and unsparing criticism recoiled on the cause which they had at heart. But in the case of both of them it was not the temper of the satirist, it was no mere love of attacking what was vulnerable, and indulgence in the cruel pleasure of stinging and putting to shame, which inspired them. Their souls were moved by the dis-

8. A few references to the *Remains* illustrating this are subjoined if any one cares to compare them with these recollections, 1:7, 13, 18, 26, 106, 184, 199, 200–204.

honour done to religion, by public evils and public dangers. Both of them died young, before their work was done. They placed before themselves the loftiest and most unselfish objects, the restoration of truth and goodness in the Church, and to that they gave their life and all that they had. And what they called on others to be they were themselves. They were alike in the sternness, the reality, the perseverance, almost unintelligible in its methods to ordinary men, of their moral and spiritual self-discipline.

Supplementary to Chapter 3

Hurrell Froude[9] was, when I, as an undergraduate, first knew him in 1828, tall and very thin, with something of a stoop, with a large skull and forehead, but not a large face, delicate features, and penetrating gray eyes, not exactly piercing, but bright with internal conceptions, and ready to assume an expression of amusement, careful attention, inquiry or stern disgust, but with a basis of softness. His manner was cordial and familiar, and assured you, as you knew him well, of his affectionate feeling, which encouraged you to speak your mind (with certain limits), subject to the consideration that if you said anything absurd it would not be allowed to fall to the ground. He had more of the undergraduate in him than any "don" whom I ever knew; absolutely unlike Newman in being always ready to skate, sail, or ride with his friends—and, if in a scrape, not pharisaical as to his means of getting out of it. I remember, *e.g.*, climbing Merton gate with him in my undergraduate days, when we had been out too late boating or skating. And unless authority or substantial decorum was really threatened he was very lenient—or rather had an amused sympathy with the irregularities that are mere matters of mischief or high spirits. In lecture it was, *mutatis mutandis,* the same man. Seeing, from his *Remains,* the "high view of his own capacities of which he could not divest himself," and his determination not to exhibit or be puffed up by it, and looking back on his tutorial man-

9. I am indebted for these recollections to the late Lord Blachford. They were written in Oct. 1884.

ner (I was in his lectures both in classics and mathematics), it was strange how he disguised, not only his *sense* of superiority, but the appearance of it, so that his pupils felt him more as a fellow-student than as the refined scholar or mathematician which he was. This was partly owing to his carelessness of those formulae, the familiarity with which gives even second-rate lecturers a position of superiority which is less visible in those who, like their pupils, are themselves always struggling with principles—and partly to an effort, perhaps sometimes overdone, not to put himself above the level of others. In a lecture on the *Supplices* of Aeschylus, I have heard him say *tout bonnement,* "I can't construe that—what do you make of it, A. B.?" turning to the supposed best scholar in the lecture; or, when an objection was started to his mode of getting through a difficulty, "Ah! I had not thought of that—perhaps your way is the best." And this mode of dealing with himself and the undergraduates whom he liked, made them like him, but also made them really undervalue his talent, which, as we now see, was what he meant they should do. At the same time, though watchful over his own vanity, he was keen and prompt in snubs—playful and challenging retort—to those he liked, but in the nature of scornful exposure, when he had to do with coarseness or coxcombry, or shallow display of sentiment. It was a paradoxical consequence of his suppression of egotism that he was more solicitous to show that you were wrong than that he was right.

He also wanted, like Socrates or Bishop Butler, to make others, if possible, think for themselves.

However, it is not to be inferred that his conversation was made of controversy. To a certain extent it turned that way, because he was fond of paradox. (His brother William used to say that he, William, never felt he had really mastered a principle till he had thrown it into a paradox.) And paradox, of course, invites contradiction, and so controversy. On subjects upon which he considered himself more or less an apostle, he liked to stir people's minds by what startled them, waking them up, or giving them "nuts to crack." An almost solemn gravity with amusement twinkling behind it—not invisible—and ready to burst forth into a bright low laugh when gravity had been played out, was a very frequent posture with him.

46

But he was thoroughly ready to amuse and instruct, or to be amused and instructed, as an eager and earnest speaker or listener on most matters of interest. I do not remember that he had any great turn for beauty of colour; he had none, I think, or next to none, for music—nor do I remember in him any great love of humour—but for beauty of physical form, for mechanics, for mathematics, for poetry which had a root in true feeling, for wit (including that perception of a quasi-logical absurdity of position), for history, for domestic incidents, his sympathy was always lively, and he would throw himself naturally and warmly into them. From his general demeanour (I need scarcely say) the "odour of sanctity" was wholly absent. I am not sure that his height and depth of aim and lively versatility of talent did not leave his *compassionate* sympathies rather undeveloped; certainly to himself, and, I suspect, largely in the case of others, he would view suffering not as a thing to be cockered up or made much of, though of course to be alleviated if possible, but to be viewed calmly as a Providential discipline for those who can mitigate, or have to endure it.

J. H. N. was once reading me a letter just received from him in which (in answer to J. H. N.'s account of his work and the possibility of his breaking down) he said in substance: "I daresay you have more to do than your health will bear, but I would not have you give up anything except perhaps the deanery" (of Oriel). And then J. H. N. paused, with a kind of inner exultant chuckle, and said, "Ah! there's a Basil for you"; as if the friendship which sacrificed its friend, as it would sacrifice itself to a cause, was the friendship which was really worth having.

As I came to know him in a more manly way, as a brother Fellow, friend, and collaborateur, the character of "ecclesiastical agitator" was of course added to this.

In this capacity his great pleasure was taking bulls by their horns. Like the "gueux" of the Low Countries, he would have met half-way any opprobrious nickname, and I believe coined the epithet "apostolical" for his party because it was connected with everything in Spain which was obnoxious to the British public. I remember one day his grievously shocking Palmer of Worcester, a man of an opposite texture, when a council in J. H. N.'s rooms had been called to consider some memorial or other to which Palmer wanted to collect the signatures of many, and particularly of dignified persons, but in which Froude wished to express the determined opinions of a few. Froude stretched out his long length on Newman's sofa, and broke in upon one of Palmer's judicious harangues about Bishops and Archdeacons and such like, with the ejaculation, "I don't see why we should disguise from ourselves that our object is to dictate to the clergy of this country, and I, for one, do not want any one else to get on the box." He thought that true Churchmen must be few before they were many—that the sin of the clergy in all ages was that they tried to make out that Christians were many when they were only few, and sacrificed to this object the force derivable from down-right and unmistakable enforcement of truth in speech or action.

As simplicity in thought, word, and deed formed no small part of his ideal, his tastes in architecture, painting, sculpture, rhetoric, or poetry were severe. He had no patience with what was artistically dissolute, luscious, or decorated more than in proportion to its animating idea—wishy-washy or sentimental. The ornamental parts of his own rooms (in which I lived in his absence) were a slab of marble to wash upon, a print of Rubens's "Deposition," and a head (life-size) of the Apollo Belvidere. And I remember still the tall scorn, with something of surprise, with which, on entering my undergraduate room, he looked down on some Venuses, Cupids, and Hebes, which, freshman-like, I had bought from an Italian.

He was not very easy even under conventional vulgarity, still less under the vulgarity of egotism; but, being essentially a partisan, he could put up with both in a man who was really in earnest and on the right side. Nothing, however, I think, would have induced him to tolerate false sentiment, and he would, I think, if he had lived, have exerted himself very trenchantly to prevent his cause being adulterated by it.

He was, I should say, sometimes misled by a theory that genius cut through a subject by logic or intuition, without looking to the right or left, while common sense was always testing every step by consideration of surroundings (I have not got his terse mode of statement), and that genius was right, or at least had only to be corrected here and there by common sense. This, I take it, would hardly have answered if his trenchancy had not been in practice corrected by J. H. N.'s wider political circumspection.

He submitted, I suppose, to J. H. N.'s axiom, that if the movement was to do anything it must become "respectable"; but it was against his nature.

He would (as we see in the *Remains*) have wished Ken to have the "courage of his convictions" by excommunicating the Jurors in William III.'s time, and setting up a little Catholic Church, like the Jansenists in Holland. He was not (as has been observed) a theologian, but he was as jealous for orthodoxy as if he were. He spoke slightingly of Heber as having ignorantly or carelessly communicated with (?) Monophysites. But he probably knew no more about that and other heresies than a man of active and penetrating mind would derive from textbooks. And I think it likely enough—not that his reverence for the Eucharist, but—that his special attention to the details of Eucharistic doctrine was due to the consideration that it was the foundation of ecclesiastical discipline and authority—matters on which his mind fastened itself with enthusiasm.

IV

Mr. Newman's
Early Friends—
Isaac Williams

In the early days of the movement, among Mr. Newman's greatest friends, and much in his confidence, were two Fellows of
Trinity—a college which never forgot that Newman had once
belonged to it,—Isaac Williams and William John Copeland. In
mind and character very different, they were close friends, with
the affection characteristic of those days; and for both of them
Mr. Newman "had the love which passes that of common relation."[1] Isaac Williams was born among the mountains of Wales,
and had the true poetic gift, though his power of expression was
often not equal to what he wanted to say: Copeland was a Lon-
doner, bred up in the strict school of Churchmanship represented
by Mr. Norris of Hackney, tempered by sympathies with the Non-
jurors. At Oxford he lived, along with Isaac Williams, in the
very heart of the movement, which was the interest of his life;
but he lived, self-forgetting or self-effacing, a wonderful mixture
of tender and inexhaustible sympathy, and of quick and keen wit,
which yet, somehow or other, in that time of exasperation and
bitterness, made him few enemies. He knew more than most men
of the goings on of the movement, and he ought to have been its
chronicler. But he was fastidious and hard to satisfy, and he left
his task till it was too late.

Isaac Williams was born in Wales in 1802, a year after Newman, ten years after John Keble. His early life was spent in Lon-

---

1. Mozley, *Reminiscences*, 1:18.

don, but his affection for Wales and its mountain scenery was great and undiminished to the end of his life. At Harrow, where Henry Drury was his tutor, he made his mark by his mastery of Latin composition and his devotion to Latin language and literature. "I was so used to think in Latin that when I had to write an English theme, which was but seldom, I had to translate my ideas, which ran in Latin, into English";[2] and later in life he complained of the Latin current which disturbed him when he had to write English. He was also a great cricketer; and he describes himself as coming up to Trinity, were he soon got a scholarship, an ambitious and careless youth, who had never heard a word about Christianity, and to whom religion, its aims and its restraints, were a mere name.

This was changed by what, in the language of devotional schools, would have been called his conversion. It came about, as men speak, as the result of accidents; but the whole course of his thoughts and life was turned into a channel from which it nevermore diverged. An old Welsh clergyman gave the undergraduate an introduction to John Keble, who then held a place in Oxford almost unique. But the Trinity undergraduate and the Oriel don saw little of one another till Isaac Williams won the Latin prize poem, *Ars Geologica*. Keble then called on Isaac Williams and offered his help in criticising the poem and polishing it for printing. The two men plainly took to one another at first sight; and that service was followed by a most unexpected invitation on Keble's part. He had chanced to come to Williams's room, and on Williams saying that he had no plan of reading for the approaching vacation, Keble said, "I am going to leave Oxford for good. Suppose you come and read with me. The Provost has asked me to take Wilberforce, and I declined; but if you would come, you would be companions." Keble was going down to Southrop, a little curacy near his father's; there Williams joined him with two more—Robert Wilberforce and R. H. Froude; and there the Long Vacation of 1823 was spent, and Isaac Williams's character and course determined. "It was this very trivial accident, this short walk of a few yards, and a few words spoken, which was the turning-point of my life. If a merciful God had miraculously

2. I. Williams, MS. Memoir.

interposed to arrest my course, I could not have had a stronger assurance of His presence than I always had in looking back to that day." It determined Isaac Williams's character, and it determined for good and all his theological position. He had before him all day long in John Keble a spectacle which was absolutely new to him. Ambitious as a rising and successful scholar at college, he saw a man, looked up to and wondered at by every one, absolutely without pride and without ambition. He saw the most distinguished academic of his day, to whom every prospect was open, retiring from Oxford in the height of his fame to bury himself with a few hundred of Gloucestershire peasants in a miserable curacy. He saw this man caring for and respecting the ignorant and poor as much as others respected the great and the learned. He saw this man, who had made what the world would call so great a sacrifice, apparently unconscious that he had made any sacrifice at all, gay, unceremonious, bright, full of play as a boy, ready with his pupils for any exercise, mental or muscular— for a hard ride, or a crabbed bit of Aeschylus, or a logic fence with disputations and paradoxical undergraduates, giving and taking on even ground. These pupils saw one, the depth of whose religion none could doubt, "always endeavouring to do them good as it were unknown to themselves and in secret, and ever avoiding that his kindness should be felt and acknowledged"; showing in the whole course of daily life the purity of Christian love, and taking the utmost pains to make no profession or show of it. This unostentatious and undemonstrative religion—so frank, so generous in all its ways—was to Isaac Williams "quite a new world." It turned his mind in upon itself in the deepest reverence, but also with something of morbid despair of ever reaching such a standard. It drove all dreams of ambition out of his mind. It made humility, self-restraint, self-abasement, objects of unceasing, possibly not always wise and healthy, effort. But the result was certainly a character of great sweetness, tenderness, and lowly unselfishness, pure, free from all worldliness, and deeply resigned to the will of God. He caught from Mr. Keble, like Froude, two characteristic habits of mind—a strong depreciation of mere intellect compared with the less showy excellences of faithfulness to conscience and duty; and a horror and hatred of everything that seemed like display or the desire of applause or of immediate effect. Intellectual depreciators of intellect may deceive themselves, and do not always escape the snare which they fear; but in Isaac Williams there was a very genuine carrying out of the Psalmist's words: "Surely I have behaved and quieted myself; I refrain my soul and keep it low, as a child that is weaned from his mother." This fear of display in a man of singularly delicate and fastidious taste came to have something forced and morbid on it. It seemed sometimes as if in preaching or talking he aimed at being dull and clumsy. But in all that he did and wrote he aimed at being true at all costs and in the very depths of his heart; and though, in his words, we may wish sometimes for what we should feel to be more natural and healthy in tone, we never can doubt that we are in the presence of one who shrank from all conscious unreality like poison.

From Keble, or, it may be said, from the Kebles, he received his theology. The Kebles were all of them men of the old-fashioned High Church orthodoxy, of the Prayer Book and the Catechism—the orthodoxy which was professed at Oxford, which was represented in London by Norris of Hackney and Joshua Watson; which valued in religion sobriety, reverence, and deference to authority, and in teaching, sound learning and the wisdom of the great English divines; which vehemently disliked the Evangelicals and Methodists for their poor and loose theology, their love of excitement and display, their hunting after popularity. This Church of England divinity was the theology of the old Vicar of Coln St. Aldwyn's, a good scholar and a good parish priest, who had brought up his two sons at home to be scholars; and had impressed his solid and manly theology on them so strongly that amid all changes they remained at bottom true to their paternal training. John Keble added to it great attainments and brilliant gifts of imagination and poetry; but he never lost the plain, downright, almost awkward ways of conversation and manner of his simple home—ways which might have seemed abrupt and rough but for the singular sweetness and charm of his nature. To those who looked on the outside he was always the homely, rigidly orthodox country clergyman. On Isaac Williams, with his ethical standard, John Keble also impressed his ideas of religious truth; he made him an old-fashioned High Churchman, suspicious of excitement and "effect," suspicious of the loud-talking religious world, suspicious of its novelties and shallowness, and clinging with his whole soul to ancient ways and sound Church of England doctrine reflected in the Prayer Book. And from John Keble's influence he passed under the influence of Thomas Keble, the Vicar of Bisley, a man of sterner type than his brother, with strong and definite opinions on all subjects; curt and keen in speech; intolerant of all that seemed to threaten wholesome teaching and the interests of the Church; and equally straightforward, equally simple, in manners and life. Under him Isaac Williams began his career as a clergyman; he spent two years of solitary and monotonous life in a small cure, seeking comfort from solitude in poetical composition ("It was very calm and subduing," he writes); and then he was recalled to Oxford as Fellow and Tutor of his college, to meet a new and stronger influence, which it was part of the work and trial of the rest of his life both to assimilate and to resist.

For, with Newman, with whom he now came into contact, he did both. There opened to him from intercourse with Newman a new world of thought; and yet while feeling and answering to its charm, he never was quite at ease with him. But Williams and Froude had always been great friends since the reading party of 1823, in spite of Froude's audacities. Froude was now residing in Oxford, and had become Newman's most intimate friend, and he brought Newman and Williams together. "Living at that time," he says, "so much with Froude, I was now in consequence for the first time brought into intercourse with Newman. We almost daily walked and often dined together." Newman and Froude had ceased to be tutors; their thoughts were turned to theology and the condition of the Church. Newman had definitely broken with the Evangelicals, to whom he had been supposed to belong, and Whately's influence over him was waning, and with Froude he looked up to Keble as the pattern of religious wisdom. He had accepted the position of a Churchman as it was understood by Keble and Froude; and thus there was nothing to hinder Williams's full sympathy with him. But from the first there seems to have been an almost impalpable bar between them, which is the more remarkable because Williams appears to have seen with equanimity Froude's apparently more violent and dangerous outbreaks of paradox and antipathy. Possibly, after the catastrophe, he may, in looking back, have exaggerated his early alarms. But from the first he says he saw in Newman what he had learned to look upon as the gravest of dangers—the preponderance of intellect among the elements of character and as the guide of life. "I was greatly delighted and charmed with Newman, who was extremely kind to me, but did not altogether trust his opinions; and though Froude was in the habit of stating things in an extreme and paradoxical manner, yet one always felt conscious of a ground of entire confidence and agreement; but it was not so with Newman, even though one appeared more in unison with his more moderate views."

But, in spite of all this, Newman offered and Isaac Williams accepted the curacy of St. Mary's. "Things at Oxford [1830-32] at that time were very dull." "Froude and I seemed entirely alone, with Newman only secretly, as it were, beginning to sympathise. I became at once very much attached to Newman, won by his kindness and delighted by his good and wonderful qualities; and he proposed that I should be his curate at St. Mary's. . . . I can remember a strong feeling of difference I first felt on acting together with him from what I had been accustomed to: that he was in the habit of looking for effect, and for what was sensibly effective, which from the Bisley and Fairford School I had been long habituated to avoid; but to do one's duty in faith and leave it to God, and that all the more earnestly, because there were no sympathies from without to answer. There was a felt but unexpressed difference of this kind, but perhaps it became afterwards harmonised as we acted together."[3]

Thus early, among those most closely united, there appeared the beginnings of those different currents which became so divergent as time went on. Isaac Williams, dear as he was to Newman, and returning to the full Newman's affection, yet represented from the first the views of what Williams spoke of as the "Bisley and Fairford School," which, though sympathising and co-operating with the movement, was never quite easy about it, and was not sparing of its criticism on the stir and agitation of the Tracts.

Isaac Williams threw himself heartily into the early stages of

3. I. Williams, MS. Memoir.

the movement; in his poetry into its imaginative and poetical side, and also into its practical and self-denying side. But he would have been quite content with its silent working, and its apparent want of visible success. He would have been quite content with preaching simple homely sermons on the obvious but hard duties of daily life, and not seeing much come of them; with finding a slow abatement of the self-indulgent habits of university life, with keeping Fridays, with less wine in common room. The Bisley maxims bade men to be very stiff and uncompromising in their witness and in their duties, but to make no show and expect no recognition or immediate fruit, and to be silent under misconstruction. But his was not a mind which realised great possibilities of change in the inherited ways of the English Church. The spirit of change, so keenly discerned by Newman, as being both certain and capable of being turned to good account as well as bad, to him was unintelligible or bad. More reality, more severity and consistency, deeper habits of self-discipline on the accepted lines of English Church orthodoxy, would have satisfied him as the aim of the movement, as it undoubtedly was a large part of its aim; though with Froude and Newman it also aimed at a widening of ideas, of interests and sympathies, beyond what had been common in the English Church.

In the history of the movement Isaac Williams took a forward part in two of its events, with one of which his connexion was most natural, with the other grotesquely and ludicrously incongruous. The one was the plan and stating of the series of *Plain Sermons* in 1839, to which not only the Kebles, Williams, and Copeland contributed their volumes, but also Newman and Dr. Pusey. Isaac Williams has left the following account of his share in the work.

> It seemed at this time (about 1838–39) as if Oxford, from the strength of principle shown there (and an almost unanimous and concentrated energy), was becoming a rallying point for the whole kingdom: but I watched from the beginning and saw greater dangers among ourselves than those from without; which I endeavoured to obviate by publishing the *Plain Sermons*. [*Plain Sermons,* by contributors to the *Tracts for the Times,* 1st Series, January 1839.] I attempted in vain to get the Kebles to publish, in order to keep pace with Newman, and so maintain a more

practical turn in the movement. I remember C. Cornish (C. L. Cornish, Fellow and Tutor of Exeter) coming to me and saying as we walked in Trinity Gardens, "People are a little afraid of being carried away by Newman's brilliancy; they want more of the steady sobriety of the Kebles infused into the movement to keep us safe; we have so much sail and want ballast." And the effect of the publication of the *Plain Sermons* was at the time very quieting. In first undertaking the *Plain Sermons,* I had no encouragement from any one, not even from John Keble; ac-quiescence was all that I could gain. But I have heard J. K. mention a saying of Judge Coleridge, long before the *Tracts* were thought of: "If you want to propagate your opinions you should lend your sermons; the clergy would then preach them, and adopt your opinions." Now this has been the effect of the publi-cation of the *Plain Sermons.*

Isaac Williams, if any man, represented in the movement the moderate and unobtrusive way of religious teaching. But it was his curious fate to be dragged into the front ranks of the fray, and to be singled out as almost the most wicked and dangerous of the Tractarians. He had the strange fortune to produce the first of the Tracts[4] which was by itself held up to popular indignation as embodying all the mischief of the series and the secret aims of the movement. The Tract had another effect. It made Williams the object of the first great Tractarian battle in the University, the contest for the Poetry Professorship: the first decisive and open trial of strength, and the first Tractarian defeat. The contest, even more than the result, distressed him greatly; and the course of things in the movement itself aggravated his distress. His general distrust of intellectual restlessness had now passed into the special and too well grounded fear that the movement, in some of its most prominent representatives, was going definitely in the direc-tion of Rome. A new generation was rising into influence, to whom the old Church watchwords and maxims, the old Church habits of mind, the old Church convictions, had completely lost their force, and were become almost objects of dislike and scorn; and for this change Newman's approval and countenance were freely and not very scrupulously quoted. Williams's relation to

4. The history of this famous Tract, No. 80, on *Reserve in communicating Religious Knowledge,* belongs to a later stage of the movement.

him had long been a curious mixture of the most affectionate attachment and intimacy with growing distrust and sense of divergence. Newman was now giving more and more distinct warning that he was likely to go where Williams could not follow him, and the pain on both sides was growing. But things moved fast, and at length the strain broke.

The estrangement was inevitable; but both cherished the warmest feelings of affection, even though such a friendship had been broken. But Oxford became distasteful to Williams, and he soon afterwards left it for Bisley and Stinchcombe, the living of his brother-in-law, Sir G. Prevost. There he married (22d June 1842), and spent the remainder of his life devoting himself to the preparation of those devotional commentaries, which are still so well known. He suffered for the greatest part of his life from a distressing and disabling chronic asthma—from the time that he came back to Oxford as Fellow and Tutor—and he died in 1865. The old friends met once more shortly before Isaac Williams's death; Newman came to see him, and at his departure Williams accompanied him to the station.

Isaac Williams wrote a great deal of poetry, first during his solitary curacy at Windrush, and afterwards at Oxford. It was in a lower and sadder key than the *Christian Year*, which no doubt first inspired it; it wanted the elasticity and freshness and variety of Keble's verse, and it was often careless in structure and wanting in concentration. But it was the outpouring of a very beautiful mind, deeply impressed with the realities of failure in the Church and religion, as well as in human life, full of tenderness and pathetic sweetness, and seeking a vent for its feelings, and relief for its trouble, in calling up before itself the images of God's goodness and kingdom of which nature and the world are full. His poetry is a witness to the depth and earnestness and genuine delicacy of what seemed hard and narrow in the Bisley school; there are passages in it which are not easily forgotten; but it was not strong enough to arrest the excitement which soon set in, and with its continual obscurity and its want of finish it never had the recognition really due to its excellence. Newman thought it too soft. It certainly wanted the fire and boldness and directness which he threw into his own verse when he wrote; but serious earnestness and severity of tone it certainly did not want.

V

Charles Marriott

Charles Marriott was a man who was drawn into the movement, almost in spite of himself, by the attraction of the character of the leaders, the greatness of its object, and the purity and nobleness of the motives which prompted it. He was naturally a man of metaphysical mind, given almost from a child to abstract and indeed abstruse thought.[1] He had been a student of S. T. Coleridge, whom the Oriel men disliked as a misty thinker. He used to discuss Coleridge with a man little known then, but who gained a high reputation on the Continent as a first-rate Greek scholar, and became afterwards Professor of Greek in the University of Sydney, Charles Badham. Marriott also appreciated Hampden as a philosopher, whom the Oriel men thoroughly distrusted as a theologian. He might easily under different conditions have become a divine of the type of F. D. Maurice. He was by disposition averse to anything like party, and the rough and sharp proceedings which party action sometimes seems to make natural. His temper was eminently sober, cautious and conciliatory in his way of looking at important questions. He was a man with many friends of different sorts and ways, and of boundless though undemonstrative sympathy. His original tendencies would have made him an eclectic, recognising the strength of position in opposing schools or theories, and welcoming all that was good and

1. "He told me," writes a relative, "that questions about trade used to occupy him very early in life. He used to ponder how it could be right to sell things for more than they cost you."

59

high in them. He was profoundly and devotedly religious, without show, without extravagance. His father, who died when he was only fourteen, had been a distinguished man in his time. He was a Christ Church man, and one of two in the first of the Oxford Honour lists in 1802, with E. Copleston, H. Phillpotts, and S. P. Rigaud for his examiners. He was afterwards tutor to the Earl of Dalkeith, and he became the friend of Walter Scott, who dedicated to him the Second Canto of *Marmion*; and having ready and graceful poetical talent, he contributed several ballads to the *Minstrelsy of the Scottish Border, The Feast of Spurs,* and *Archie Armstrong's Aith.* He was a good preacher; his sympathies—of friendship, perhaps, rather than of definite opinion—were with men like Mr. John Bowdler and the Thorntons. While he lived he taught Charles Marriott himself. After his death, Charles, a studious boy, with ways of his own of learning, and though successful and sure in his work, very slow in the process of doing it, after a short and discouraging experiment at Rugby, went to read with a private tutor till he went to Oxford. He was first at Exeter, and then gained a scholarship at Balliol. He gained a Classical First Class and a Mathematical Second in the Michaelmas Term of 1832, and the following Easter he was elected Fellow at Oriel.

For a man of his power and attainments he was as a speaker, and in conversation, surprisingly awkward. He had a sturdy, penetrating, tenacious, but embarrassed intellect—embarrassed, at least, by the crowd and range of jostling thoughts, in its outward process and manifestations, for he thoroughly trusted its inner workings, and was confident of the accuracy of the results, even when helplessly unable to justify them at the moment.[2] In matters of business he seemed at first sight utterly unpractical. In discussing with keen, rapid, and experienced men like the Provost, the value of leases, or some question of the management of College property, Marriott, who always took great interest in such inquiries, frequently maintained some position which to the quicker wits round him seemed a paradox or a mare's nest. Yet it often happened that after a dispute, carried on with a brisk fire

2. "He had his own way of doing everything, and used most stoutly to protest that it was quite impossible that he should do it in any other."–MS. Memoir by his brother, John Marriott.

of not always respectful objections to Marriott's view, and in which his only advantage was the patience with which he clumsily, yet surely, brought out the real point of the matter, overlooked by others, the debate ended in the recognition that he had been right. It was often a strange and almost distressing sight to see the difficulty under which he sometimes laboured of communicating his thoughts, as a speaker at a meeting, or as a teacher to his hearers, or even in the easiness of familiar talk. The comfort was that he was not really discouraged. He was wrestling with his own refractory faculty of expression and speech; it may be, he was busy deeper down in the recesses and storehouses of his mind; but he was too much taken up with the effort to notice what people thought of it, or even if they smiled; and what he had to say was so genuine and veracious, as an expression of his meaning, so full of benevolence, charity, and generosity, and often so weighty and unexpected, that men felt it a shame to think much of the peculiarities of his long look of blank silence, and the odd, clumsy explanations which followed it. He was a man, under an uncouth exterior, of the noblest and most affectionate nature; most patient, indulgent, and hopeful to all in whom he took an interest, even when they sorely tried his kindness and his faith in them. Where he loved and trusted and admired, he was apt to rate very highly, sometimes too highly. His gratitude was boundless. He was one of those who deliberately gave up the prospect of domestic life, to which he was naturally drawn, for the sake of his cause. Capable of abstract thought beyond most men of his time, and never unwilling to share his thoughts with those at all disposed to venture with him into deep waters, he was always ready to converse or to discuss on much more ordinary ground. As an undergraduate and a young bachelor, he had attained, without seeking it, a position of almost unexampled authority in the junior University world that was hardly reached by any one for many years at least after him. He was hopeless as a speaker in the Union; but with all his halting and bungling speeches, that democratic and sometimes noisy assembly bore from him with kindly amusement and real respect what they would bear from no one else, and he had an influence in its sometimes turbulent debates which seems unaccountable. He was the *vir pietate gravis*. In a once popular squib, occasioned by one of the fiercest of these debates, this unique position is noticed and commemorated—

Οὐδ' ἔλαθεν Μαρίωτα, φιλαίτατον 'Ωρειήλων

· · · · · · · · · · ·

῏Ηλθε μέγα γρώνων, Μασιχοῖς καὶ πᾶσ' ἀλαπητός,
Καὶ σμείλων, προσέφη πάντας κείνδοις ἐπέεσιν.[3]

His ways and his talk were such as to call forth not unfrequent mirth among those who most revered him. He would meet you and look you in the face without speaking a word. He was not without humour; but his jokes, carried off by a little laugh of his own, were apt to be recondite in their meaning and allusions. With his great power of sympathy, he yet did not easily divine other men's lighter or subtler moods, and odd and sometimes even distressing mistakes were the consequence. His health was weak, and a chronic tenderness of throat and chest made him take precautions which sometimes seemed whimsical; and his well-known figure in a black cloak, with a black veil over his college cap, and a black comforter round his neck, which at one time in Oxford acquired his name, sometimes startled little boys and sleepy college porters when he came on them suddenly at night.

With more power than most men of standing alone, and of arranging his observations on life and the world in ways of his own, he had pre-eminently above all men round him, in the highest and noblest form, the spirit of a disciple. Like most human things, discipleship has its good and its evil, its strong and its poor and dangerous side; but it really has, what is much forgotten now, a good and a strong side. Both in philosophy and religion, the μαθητὴς is a distinct character, and Charles Marriott was an example of it at its best. He had its manly and reasonable humility, its generous trustfulness, its self-forgetfulness; he had, too, the enthusiasm of having and recognising a great master and teacher, and doing what he wanted done; and he learned from the love of his master to love what he believed truth still more. The character of the disciple does not save a man from difficulties, from trouble and perplexity; but it tends to save him from

3. *Uniomachia*, 1833.

idols of his own making. It is something, in the trials of life and faith, to have the consciousness of knowing or having known some one greater and better and wiser than oneself, of having felt the spell of his guidance and example. Marriott's mind, quick to see what was real and strong, and at once reverent to it as soon as he saw it, came very much, as an undergraduate at Balliol, under the influence of a very able and brilliant tutor, Moberly, afterwards Headmaster of Winchester and Bishop of Salisbury; and to the last his deference and affection to his old tutor remained unimpaired. But he came under a still more potent charm when he moved to Oriel, and became the friend of Mr. Newman. Master and disciple were as unlike as any two men could be; they were united by their sympathy in the great crisis round them, by their absorbing devotion to the cause of true religion. Marriott brought to the movement, and especially to its chief, a great University character, and an unswerving and touching fidelity. He placed himself, his life, and all that he could do, at the service of the great effort to elevate and animate the Church; to the last he would gladly have done so under him whom he first acknowledged as his master. This was not to be; and he transferred his allegiance, as unreservedly, with equal loyalty and self-sacrifice, to his successor. But to the end, while his powers lasted, with all his great gifts and attainments, with every temptation to an independent position and self-chosen employment, he continued a disciple. He believed in men wiser than himself; he occupied himself with what they thought best for him to do.

This work was, for the most part, in what was done to raise the standard of knowledge of early Christian literature, and to make that knowledge accurate and scholarlike. He was, for a time, the Principal of the Theological College at Chichester, under Bishop Otter. He was also for a time Tutor at Oriel, and later, Vicar of St. Mary's. He was long bent on setting on foot some kind of Hall for poor students; and he took over from Mr. Newman the buildings at Littlemore, which he turned into a place for printing religious works. But though he was connected more or less closely with numberless schemes of Christian work in Oxford and out of it, his special work was that of a theological student. Marriott had much to do with the Library of the Fathers, with correcting translations, collating manuscripts, editing texts.[4] Somehow, the most interesting portions hardly came to his share; and what he did in the way of original writing, little as it was, causes regret that so much of his time was spent on the drudgery of editing. Some sermons, a little volume of *Thoughts on Private Devotion*, and another on the *Epistle to the Romans*, are nearly all that he has left of his own. Novelty of manner or thought in them there is none, still less anything brilliant or sharp in observation or style; but there is an undefinable sense, in their calm, severe pages, of a deep and serious mind dwelling on deep and very serious things. It is impossible not to wish that a man who could so write and impress people might have had the leisure to write more.

But Marriott never had any leisure. It has been said above that he placed himself at the service of those whom he counted his teachers. But the truth is that he was at every one's service who wanted or who asked his help. He had a large, and what must have been often a burdensome, correspondence. With pupils or friends he was always ready for some extra bit of reading. To strangers he was always ready to show attention and hospitality, though Marriott's parties were as quaint as himself. His breakfast parties in his own room were things to have seen—a crowd of undergraduates, finding their way with difficulty amid lanes and piles of books, amid a scarcity of chairs and room, and the host, perfectly unconscious of anything grotesque, sitting silent during the whole of the meal, but perfectly happy, at the head of the table. But there was no claimant on his purse or his interest who was too strange for his sympathy—raw freshmen, bores of every kind, broken-down tradesmen, old women, distressed foreigners, converted Jews, all the odd and helpless wanderers from beaten ways, were to be heard of at Marriott's rooms; and all, more or less, had a share of his time and thoughts, and perhaps counsel.

---

4. "This became the main task of his life as long as health was continued to him. All who knew him well will remember how laboriously he worked at it, and how, in one shape or another, it was always on hand. Either he was translating, or correcting the translation of others; or he was collating MSS., or correcting the press. This last work was carried on at all times and wherever he was—on a journey, after dinner—even in a boat, he would pull out a sheet and go to write upon it in haste to get it finished for the next post. The number of volumes in the Library of the Fathers which bear the signature C. M. attest his diligence."—John Marriott's Memoir of him (MS.)

He was sensible of worry as he grew older; but he never relaxed his efforts to do what any one asked of him. There must be even now some still living who know what no one else knows, how much they owe, with no direct claim on him, to Charles Marriott's inexhaustible patience and charity. The pains which he would take with even the most uncongenial and unpromising men, who somehow had come in his way, and seemed thrown on his charge, the patience with which he would bear and condone their follies and even worse, were not to be told, for, indeed, few knew what they were.

> He was always ready to be the friend of any one whose conduct gave proofs of high principle, however inferior to himself in knowledge or acquirements, and his friendship once gained was not easily lost. I believe there was nothing in his power which he was not ready to do for a friend who wanted his help. It is not easy to state instances of such kindness without revealing what for many reasons had better be left untold. But many such have come to my knowledge, and I believe there are many more known only to himself and to those who derived benefit from his disinterested friendship.[5]

Marriott's great contribution to the movement was his solid, simple goodness, his immovable hope, his confidence that things would come right. With much imaginativeness open to poetical grandeur and charm, and not without some power of giving expression to feeling, he was destitute of all that made so many others of his friends interesting as men. He was nothing, as a person to know and observe, to the genius of the two Mozleys, to the brilliant social charm of Frederic Faber, to the keen, refined intelligence of Mark Pattison, to the originality and clever eccentricity of William Palmer of Magdalen. And he was nothing as a man of practical power for organising and carrying out successful schemes: such power was not much found at Oxford in those days. But his faith in his cause, as the cause of goodness and truth, was proof against mockery or suspicion or disaster. When ominous signs disturbed other people he saw none. He had an almost perverse subtlety of mind which put a favourable interpretation on what seemed most formidable. As his master drew more and more

5. J. M., MS. Memoir.

out of sympathy with the English Church, Marriott, resolutely loyal to it and to him, refused to understand hints and indications which to others were but too plain. He vexed and even provoked Newman, in the last agonies of the struggle, by the optimism with which he clung to useless theories and impossible hopes. For that unquenchable hoping against hope, and hope unabated still when the catastrophe had come, the English Church at least owes him deep gratitude. Throughout those anxious years he never despaired of her.

All through his life he was a beacon and an incitement to those who wished to make a good use of their lives. In him all men could see, whatever their opinions and however little they liked him, the simplicity and the truth of a self-denying life of suffering —for he was never well—of zealous hard work, unstinted, unrecompensed; of unabated lofty hopes for the great interests of the Church and the University; of deep unpretending matter-of-course godliness and goodness—without "form or comeliness" to attract any but those who cared for them, for themselves alone. It is almost a sacred duty to those who remember one who cared nothing for his own name or fame to recall what is the truth— that no one did more to persuade those round him of the solid underground religious reality of the movement. Mr. Thomas Mozley, among other generous notices of men whom the world and their contemporaries have forgotten, has said what is not more than justice.[6] Speaking of the enthusiasm of the movement, and the spirit of its members, "There had never been seen at Oxford, indeed seldom anywhere, so large and noble a sacrifice of the most precious gifts and powers to a sacred cause," he points out what each of the leaders gave to it:

> Charles Marriott threw in his scholarship and something more, for he might have been a philosopher, and he had poetry in his veins, being the son of the well-known author of the "Devonshire Lane." No one sacrificed himself so entirely to the cause, giving to it all that he had and all that he was, as Charles Marriott. He did not gather large congregations; he did not write works of genius to spread his name over the land, and to all time; he had few of the pleasures or even of the comforts that spontaneously offer themselves in any field of enterprise. He

6. *Rem.*, 1:447.

laboured day and night in the search and defence of Divine Truth. His admirers were not the thousands, but the scholars who could really appreciate. I confess to have been a little ashamed of myself when Bishop Burgess asked me about Charles Marriott, as one of the most eminent scholars of the day. Through sheer ignorance I had failed in adequate appreciation.

In his later years he became a member of the new Hebdomadal Council at Oxford, and took considerable part in working the new constitution of the University. In an epidemic of smallpox at Oxford in 1854, he took his full share in looking after the sick, and caught the disorder; but he recovered. At length, in the midst of troublesome work and many anxieties, his life of toil was arrested by a severe paralytic seizure, 29th June 1855. He partially rallied, and survived for some time longer; but his labours were ended. He died at Bradfield, 25th September 1858. He was worn out by variety and pressure of unintermitted labour, which he would scarcely allow any change or holiday to relieve. Exhaustion made illness, when it came, fatal.

VI

The Oxford Tracts

"On 14th July 1833," we read in Cardinal Newman's *Apologia*,
"Mr. Keble preached the assize sermon in the University Pulpit.
It was published under the title of *National Apostasy*. I have ever
considered and kept the day as the start of the religious movement
of 1833.[1]

This memorable sermon was a strong expression of the belief
common to a large body of Churchmen amid the triumphs of the
Reform Bill, that the new governors of the country were preparing to invade the rights, and to alter the constitution, and even the
public documents of the Church. The suppression of ten Irish
Bishoprics, in defiance of Church opinion, showed how ready the
Government was to take liberties in a high-handed way with the
old adjustments of the relations of Church and State. Churchmen
had hitherto taken for granted that England was "a nation which
had for centuries acknowledged, as an essential part of its theory
of government, that, *as* a Christian nation, she is also a part of
Christ's Church, and bound, in all her legislation and policy, by
the fundamental laws of that Church." When "a Government
and people, so constituted, threw off the restraint which in many
respects such a principle would impose upon them, nay, disavowed the principle itself," this, to those whose ideas Mr. Keble
represented, seemed nothing short of a "direct disavowal of the
sovereignty of God. If it be true anywhere that such enactments
are forced on the legislature by public opinion, is Apostasy too

1. *Apol.,* p. 100.

hard a word to describe the temper of such a nation?" The sermon was a call to face in earnest a changed state of things, full of immediate and pressing danger; to consider how it was to be met by Christians and Churchmen, and to watch motives and tempers.

> Surely it will be no unworthy principle if any man is more circumspect in his behaviour, more watchful and fearful of himself, more earnest in his petitions for spiritual aid, from a dread of disparaging the holy name of the English Church in her hour of peril by his own personal fault and negligence. As to those who, either by station or temper, feel themselves more deeply interested, they cannot be too careful in reminding themselves that one chief danger in times of change and excitement arises from their tendency to engross the whole mind. Public concerns, ecclesiastical or civil, will prove indeed ruinous to those who permit them to occupy all their care and thought, neglecting or undervaluing ordinary duties, more especially those of a devotional kind. These cautions being duly observed, I do not see how any person can devote himself too entirely to the cause of the Apostolic Church in these realms. There may be, as far as he knows, but a very few to sympathise with him. He may have to wait long, and very likely pass out of this world, before he see any abatement in the triumph of disorder and irreligion. But, *if he be consistent,* he possesses to the utmost the personal consolations of a good Christian; and as a true Churchman, he has the encouragement which no other cause in the world can impart in the same degree: he is calmly, soberly, demonstrably *sure* that, sooner or later, *his will be the winning side,* and that the victory will be complete, universal, eternal.

But if Mr. Keble's sermon was the first word of the movement, its first step was taken in a small meeting of friends, at Mr. Hugh James Rose's parsonage at Hadleigh, in Suffolk, between the 25th and the 29th of the same July. At this little gathering, the ideas and anxieties which for some time past had filled the thoughts of a number of earnest Churchmen, and had brought them into communication with one another, came to a head, and issued in the determination to move. Mr. Rose, a man of high character and distinction in his day, who had recently started the *British Magazine,* as an organ of Church teaching and opinion, was the natural person to bring about such a meeting.[2] It was arranged that a few

2. Palmer, *Narrative,* 1843 (republished 1883), pp. 5, 18.

representative men, or as many as were able, should meet towards the end of July at Hadleigh Rectory. They were men in full agreement on the main questions, but with great differences in temperament and habits of thought. Mr. Rose was the person of most authority, and next to him, Mr. Palmer; and these, with Mr. A. Perceval, formed as it were the right wing of the little council. Their Oxford allies were the three Oriel men, Mr. Keble, Mr. Froude, and Mr. Newman, now fresh from his escape from death in a foreign land, and from the long solitary musings in his Mediterranean orange-boat, full of joyful vigour and ready for enterprise and work.[3] In the result, Mr. Keble and Mr. Newman were not present, but they were in active correspondence with the others.[4] From this meeting resulted the *Tracts for the Times*, and the agitation connected with them.

These friends were all devoted Churchmen, but, as has been said, each had his marked character, not only as a man but as a Churchman. The most important among them was as yet the least prominent. Two of them were men of learning, acquainted with the great world of London, and who, with all their zeal, had some of the caution which comes of such experience. At the time, the most conspicuous was Mr. Hugh James Rose.

Mr. Rose was a man whose name and whose influence, as his friends thought, have been overshadowed and overlooked in the popular view of the Church revival. It owed to him, they held, not only its first impulse, but all that was best and most hopeful in it; and when it lost him, it lost its wisest and ablest guide and inspirer. It is certainly true that when that revival began he was a much more distinguished and important person than any of the other persons interested in it. As far as could be seen at the time, he was the most accomplished divine and teacher in the English Church. He was a really learned man. He had the intellect and energy and literary skill to use his learning. He was a man of singularly elevated and religious character; he had something of the eye and temper of a statesman, and he had already a high position. He was profoundly loyal to the Church, and keenly interested in whatever affected its condition and its fortunes. As early as 1825 he had in some lectures at Cambridge called the at-

3. Palmer (1883), pp. 40, 43, "June 1833, when he joined us at Oxford."
4. See Palmer's account (1883), pp. 45–47, and (1843), pp. 6, 7.

tention of English Churchmen to the state of religious thought and speculation in Germany, and to the mischiefs likely to react on English theology from the rationalising temper and methods which had supplanted the old Lutheran teaching; and this had led to a sharp controversy with Mr. Pusey, as he was then, who thought that Mr. Rose[5] had both exaggerated the fact itself and had not adequately given the historical account of it. He had the prudence, but not the backwardness, of a man of large knowledge, and considerable experience of the world. More alive to difficulties and dangers than his younger associates, he showed his courage and his unselfish earnestness in his frank sympathy with them, daring and outspoken as they were, and in his willingness to share with them the risks of an undertaking of which no one knew better than he what were likely to be the difficulties. He certainly was a person who might be expected to have a chief part in directing anything with which he was connected. His countenance and his indirect influence were very important elements, both in the stirring of thought which led to the Hadleigh resolutions, and in giving its form to what was then decided upon. But his action in the movement was impeded by his failure in health, and cut short by his early death, January 1839. How he would have influenced the course of things if he had lived, it is not now easy to say. He must have been reckoned with as one of the chiefs. He would have been opposed to anything that really tended towards Rome. But there is no reason to think that he would have shrunk from any step only because it was bold. He had sympathy for courage and genius, and he had knowledge and authority which would have commanded respect for his judgment and opinion. But it is too much to say either that the movement could not have been without him, or that it was specially his design and plan, or that he alone could have given the impulse which led to it; though

5. "Mr. Rose . . . was the one commanding figure and very lovable man, that the frightened and discomfited Church people were now rallying round. Few people have left so distinct an impression of themselves as this gentleman. For many years after, when he was no more, and Newman had left Rose's standpoint far behind, he could never speak of him or think of him without renewed tenderness" (Mr. T. Mozley, *Reminiscences,* 1:308).

In November 1838, shortly before Mr. Rose's death, Mr. Newman had dedicated a volume of sermons to him—"who, when hearts were failing, bade us stir up the gift that was in us, and betake ourselves to our true mother" (*Parochial Sermons,* vol. 4).

it seemed at one time as if he was to be its leader and chief. Certainly he was the most valuable and the most loyal of its early auxiliaries.

Another coadjutor, whose part at the time also seemed rather that of a chief, was Mr. William Palmer, of Worcester College. He had been educated at Trinity College, Dublin, but he had transferred his home to Oxford, both in the University and the city. He was a man of exact and scholastic mind, well equipped at all points in controversial theology, strong in clear theories and precise definitions, familiar with objections current in the schools and with the answers to them, and well versed in all the questions, arguments, and authorities belonging to the great debate with Rome. He had definite and well-arranged ideas about the nature and office of the Church; and, from his study of the Roman controversy, he had at command the distinctions necessary to discriminate between things which popular views confused, and to protect the doctrines characteristic of the Church from being identified with Romanism. Especially he had given great attention to the public devotional language and forms of the Church, and had produced by far the best book in the English language on the history and significance of the offices of the English Church—the *Origines Liturgicae,* published at the University Press in 1832. It was a book to give a man authority with divines and scholars; and among those with whom at this time he acted no one had so compact and defensible a theory, even if it was somewhat rigid and technical, of the peculiar constitution of the English Church as Mr. Palmer. With the deepest belief in this theory, he saw great dangers threatening, partly from general ignorance and looseness of thought, partly from antagonistic ideas and principles only too distinct and too popular; and he threw all his learning and zeal on the side of those who, like himself, were alive to those dangers, and were prepared for a great effort to counteract them.

The little company which met at Hadleigh Rectory, from 25th to 29th July 1833, met—as other knots of men have often met, to discuss a question or a policy, or to found an association, or a league, or a newspaper—to lay down the outlines of some practical scheme of work; but with little foresight of the venture they were making, or of the momentous issues which depended on their meeting. Later on, when controversy began, it became a favourite rhetorical device to call it by the ugly name of a "conspiracy." Certainly Froude called it so, and Mr. Palmer; and Mr. Perceval wrote a narrative to answer the charge. It was a "conspiracy," as any other meeting would be of men with an object which other men dislike.

Of the Oriel men, only Froude went to Hadleigh. Keble and Newman were both absent, but in close correspondence with the others. Their plans had not taken any definite shape; but they were ready for any sacrifice and service, and they were filled with wrath against the insolence of those who thought that the Church was given over into their hands, and against the apathy and cowardice of those who let her enemies have their way. Yet with much impatience and many stern determinations in their hearts, they were all of them men to be swayed by the judgment and experience of their friends.

The state of mind under which the four friends met at the Hadleigh conference has been very distinctly and deliberately recorded by all of them. Churchmen in our days hardly realise what the face of things then looked like to men who, if they felt deeply, were no mere fanatics or alarmists, but sober and sagacious observers, not affected by mere cries, but seeing clearly beneath the surface of things their certain and powerful tendencies.

> We felt ourselves [writes Mr. Palmer some years afterwards] assailed by enemies from without and foes within. Our Prelates insulted and threatened by Ministers of State. In Ireland ten bishoprics suppressed. We were advised to feel thankful that a more sweeping measure had not been adopted. What was to come next? . . . Was the same principle of concession to popular clamour . . . to be exemplified in the dismemberment of the English Church? . . . We were overwhelmed with pamphlets on Church reform. Lord Henley, brother-in-law of Sir Robert Peel, Dr. Burton, and others of name and influence led the way. Dr. Arnold of Rugby ventured to propose that all sects should be united by Act of Parliament with the Church of England. Reports, apparently well founded, were prevalent that some of the Prelates were favourable to alterations in the Liturgy. Pamphlets were in wide circulation recommending the abolition of the Creeds (at least in public worship), especially urging the expulsion of the Athanasian Creed; the removal of all mention of the Blessed Trinity; of the doctrine of baptismal regeneration; of

the practice of absolution. We knew not to what quarter to look for support. A Prelacy threatened and apparently intimidated; a Government making its power subservient to agitators, who avowedly sought the destruction of the Church. . . . And, worst of all, *no principle in the public mind to which we could appeal;* an utter ignorance of all rational grounds of attachment to the Church; an oblivion of its spiritual character, as an institution not of man but of God; the grossest Erastianism most widely prevalent, especially amongst all classes of politicians. There was in all this enough to appal the stoutest heart; and those who can recall the feeling of those days will at once remember the deep depression into which the Church had fallen, and the gloomy forebodings universally prevalent.[6]

"Before the spirit and temper of those who met at the conference is condemned as extravagant," writes Mr. Perceval in 1842,[7] "let the reader call to mind what was then actually the condition as well as the prospect of the Church and nation: an agrarian and civic insurrection against the bishops and clergy, and all who desired to adhere to the existing institutions of the country; the populace goaded on, openly by the speeches, covertly (as was fully believed at the time) by the paid emissaries of the ministers of the Crown; the chief of those ministers in his place in Parliament bidding the bishops 'set their house in order'; the mob taking him at his word, and burning to the ground the palace of the Bishop of Bristol, with the public buildings of the city, while they shouted the Premier's name in triumph on the ruins." The pressing imminence of the danger is taken for granted by the calmest and most cautious of the party, Mr. Rose, in a letter of February 1833. "That something is requisite, is certain. The only thing is, that whatever is done ought to be *quickly* done, for the danger is immediate, and *I should have little fear if I thought that we could stand for ten or fifteen years as we are.*"[8] In the *Apologia* Cardinal Newman recalls what was before him in those days.

6. *Narrative of Events Connected with the Publication of Tracts for the Times,* by W. Palmer (published 1843, republished 1883), pp. 96–100 (abridged).

7. *Collection of Papers Connected with the Theological Movement of 1833,* by A. P. Perceval (1842), p. 25.

8. Palmer's *Narrative* (1833), p. 101.

The Whigs had come into power; Lord Grey had told the bishops to "set their house in order," and some of the prelates had been insulted and threatened in the streets of London. The vital question was, How were we to keep the Church from being Liberalised? There was so much apathy on the subject in some quarters, such imbecile alarm in others; the true principles of Churchmanship seemed so radically decayed, and there was such distraction in the councils of the clergy. The Bishop of London of the day, an active and open-hearted man, had been for years engaged in diluting the high orthodoxy of the Church by the introduction of the Evangelical body into places of influence and trust. He had deeply offended men who agreed with myself by an off-hand saying (as it was reported) to the effect that belief in the apostolical succession had gone out with the Non-jurors. "*We can count you,*" he said to some of the gravest and most venerated persons of the old school. . . . I felt affection for my own Church, but not tenderness: I felt dismay at her prospects, anger and scorn at her do-nothing perplexity. I thought that if Liberalism once got a footing within her, it was sure of victory in the event. I saw that Reformation principles were powerless to rescue her. As to leaving her, the thought never crossed my imagination: still I ever kept before me that there was something greater than the Established Church, and that that was the Church Catholic and Apostolic, set up from the beginning, of which she was but the local presence and organ. She was nothing unless she was this. She must be dealt with strongly or she would be lost. There was need of a second Reformation.

"If *I thought that we could stand ten or fifteen years as we are,* I should have little fear," said Mr. Rose. He felt that, if only he could secure a respite, he had the means and the hope of opening the eyes of Churchmen. They were secure and idle from long prosperity, and now they were scared and perplexed by the suddenness of an attack for which they were wholly unprepared. But he had confidence in his own convictions. He had around him ability and zeal, in which he had the best reason to trust. He might hope, if he had time, to turn the tide. But this time to stand to arms was just what he had not. The danger, he felt, was upon him. He could not wait. So he acquiesced in an agitation which so cautious and steady a man would otherwise hardly have chosen. "That *something must be done* is certain. The only thing is, that whatever is done ought to be *quickly* done." Nothing can show more forcibly the imminence and pressure of the crisis than words like these, not merely from Froude and his friends, but from such a man as Mr. Hugh James Rose.

"Something must be done," but what? This was not easy to say. It was obvious that men must act in concert, and must write; but beyond these general points, questions and difficulties arose. The first idea that suggested itself at Hadleigh was a form of association, which would have been something like the *English Church Union* or the *Church Defence Association* of our days. It probably was Mr. Palmer's idea; and for some time the attempt to carry it into effect was followed up at Oxford. Plans of "Association" were drawn up and rejected. The endeavour brought out differences of opinion—differences as to the rightness or the policy of specific mention of doctrines; differences as to the union of Church and State, on the importance of maintaining which, as long as possible, Mr. Newman sided with Mr. Palmer against Mr. Keble's more uncompromising view. A *"third* formulary" was at length adopted. "Events," it said, "have occurred within the last few years calculated to inspire the true members and friends of the Church with the deepest uneasiness." It went on to notice that political changes had thrown power into the hands of the professed enemies of the Church as an establishment; but it was not merely as an establishment that it was in most serious danger.

> Every one [it says] who has become acquainted with the literature of the day, must have observed the sedulous attempts made in various quarters to reconcile members of the Church to alterations in its doctrines and discipline. Projects of change, which include the annihilation of our Creeds and the removal of doctrinal statements incidentally contained in our worship, have been boldly and assiduously put forth. Our services have been subjected to licentious criticism, with the view of superseding some of them and of entirely remodelling others. The very elementary principles of our ritual and discipline have been rudely questioned; our apostolical polity has been ridiculed and denied.

The condition of the times made these things more than ordinarily alarming, and the pressing danger was urged as a reason for the formation, by members of the Church in various parts of the kingdom, of an association on a few broad principles of union for the defence of the Church. "They feel strongly," said the authors of the paper, "that no fear of the appearance of forwardness should dissuade them from a design, which seems to be demanded of them by their affection towards that spiritual community to which they owe their hopes of the world to come, and by a sense of duty to that God and Saviour who is its Founder and Defender." But the plan of an Association, or of separate Associations, which was circulated in the autumn of 1833, came to nothing. "Jealousy was entertained of it in high quarters." Froude objected to any association less wide than the Church itself. Newman had a horror of committees and meetings and great people in London. And thus, in spite of Mr. Palmer's efforts, favoured by a certain number of influential and dignified friends, the Association would not work. But the stir about it was not without result. Mr. Palmer travelled about the country with the view of bringing the state of things before the clergy. In place of the Association, an Address to the Archbishop of Canterbury was resolved upon. It was drawn up by Mr. Palmer, who undertook the business of circulating it. In spite of great difficulties and trouble—of the alarm of friends like Mr. Rose, who was afraid that it would cause schism in the Church; of the general timidity of the dignified clergy; of the distrust and the crotchets of others; of the coldness of the bishops and the opposition of some of them—it was presented with the signatures of some 7000 clergy to the Archbishop in February 1834. It bore the names, among others, of Dr. Christopher Wordsworth, Master of Trinity; Dr. Gilbert, of Brasenose College; Dr. Faussett, and Mr. Keble. And this was not all. A Lay Address followed. There were difficulties about the first form proposed, which was thought to say too much about the doctrine and discipline of the Church; and it was laid aside for one with more vague expressions about the "consecration of the State," and the practical benefits of the Established Church. In this form it was signed by 230,000 heads of families, and presented to the Archbishop in the following May. "From these two events," writes Mr. Perceval in 1842, "we may date the commencement of the turn of the tide, which had threatened to overwhelm our Church and our religion."[9] There can, at any rate, be little doubt that as regards the external position of the Church in the country, this agitation was a success. It rallied the courage of Churchmen, and showed that they were stronger and more resolute than their enemies thought. The revolutionary temper of the times had thrown all Churchmen on the Conservative side; and these addresses were partly helped by political Conservatism, and also reacted in its favour.

Some of the Hadleigh friends would probably have been content to go on in this course, raising and keeping alive a strong feeling in favour of things as they were, creating a general sympathy with the Church, and confidence in the peculiar excellency of its wise and sober institutions, sedulously but cautiously endeavouring to correct popular mistakes about them, and to diffuse a sounder knowledge and a sounder tone of religious feeling. This is what Mr. H. J. Rose would have wished, only he felt that he could not insure the "ten or fifteen years" which he wanted to work this gradual change. Both he and Mr. Palmer would have made London, to use a military term, their base of operations. The Oriel men, on the other hand, thought that "Universities are the natural centres of intellectual movements"; they were for working more spontaneously in the freedom of independent study; they had little faith in organisation; "living movements," they said, "do not come of committees." But at Hadleigh it was settled that there was writing to be done, in some way or other; and on this, divergence of opinion soon showed itself, both as to the matter and the tone of what was to be written.

For the writers of real force, the men of genius, were the three Oriel men, with less experience, at that time, with less extensive learning, than Mr. Rose and Mr. Palmer. But they were bolder and keener spirits; they pierced more deeply into the real condition and prospects of the times; they were not disposed to smooth over and excuse what they thought hollow and untrue, to put up with decorous compromises and half-measures, to be patient towards apathy, negligence, or insolence. They certainly had more in them of the temper of warfare. We know from their

9. *Collection of Papers*, p. 12.

own avowals that a great anger possessed them, that they were indignant at the sacred idea of the Church being lost and smothered by selfishness and stupidity; they were animated by the spirit which makes men lose patience with abuses and their apologists, and gives them no peace till they speak out. Mr. Newman felt that, though associations and addresses might be very well, what the Church and the clergy and the country wanted was plain speaking; and that plain speaking could not be got by any papers put forth as joint manifestoes, or with the revision and sanction of "safe" and "judicious" advisers. It was necessary to write, and to write as each man felt: and he determined that each man should write and speak for himself, though working in concert and sympathy with others towards the supreme end— the cause and interests of the Church.

And thus were born the *Tracts for the Times*.[10] For a time Mr. Palmer's line and Mr. Newman's line ran on side by side; but Mr. Palmer's plan had soon done all that it could do, important as that was; it gradually faded out of sight, and the attention of all who cared for, or who feared or who hated the movement, was concentrated on the "Oxford Tracts." They were the watchword and the symbol of an enterprise which all soon felt to be a remarkable one—remarkable, if in nothing else, in the form in which it was started. Great changes and movements have been begun in various ways; in secret and underground communications, in daring acts of self-devotion or violence, in the organisation of an institution, in the persistent display of a particular temper and set of habits, especially in the form of a stirring and enthralling eloquence, in popular preaching, in fierce appeals to the passions. But though tracts had become in later times familiar instruments of religious action, they had, from the fashion of using them, become united in the minds of many with rather disparaging associations. The pertinacity of good ladies who pressed them on chance strangers, and who extolled their efficacy as if it was that of a quack medicine, had lowered the general respect for them. The last thing that could have been thought of was a great religious revolution in motion by tracts and leaflets, and taking its character and name from them.

10. "That portentous birth of time, the *Tracts for the Times*."—Mozley, *Remin.*, 1:311.

But the ring of these early Tracts was something very different from anything of the kind yet known in England. They were clear, brief, stern appeals to conscience and reason, sparing of words, utterly without rhetoric, intense in purpose. They were like the short, sharp, rapid utterances of men in pain and danger and pressing emergency. The first one gave the keynote of the series. Mr. Newman "had out of his own head begun the Tracts": he wrote the opening one in a mood which he has himself described. He was in the "exultation of health restored and home regained": he felt, he says, an "exuberant and joyous energy which he never had before or since"; "his health and strength had come back to him with such a rebound" that some of his friends did not know him.

> I had the consciousness that I was employed in that work which I had been dreaming about, and which I felt to be so momentous and inspiring. I had a supreme confidence in our cause; we were upholding that primitive Christianity which was delivered for all time by the early teachers of the Church, and which was registered and attested in the Anglican formularies and by the Anglican divines. That ancient religion had well-nigh faded out of the land through the political changes of the last 150 years, and it must be restored. It would be, in fact, a second Reformation—a better Reformation, for it would return, not to the sixteenth century, but to the seventeenth. No time was to be lost, for the Whigs had come to do their worst, and the rescue might come too late. Bishoprics were already in course of suppression; Church property was in course of confiscation; sees would be soon receiving unsuitable occupants. We knew enough to begin preaching, and there was no one else to preach. I felt [he goes on, with a characteristic recollection of his own experience when he started on his voyage with Froude in the *Hermes*] as on a vessel, which first gets under weigh, and then clears out the deck, and stores away luggage and live stock into their proper receptacles.[11]

The first three Tracts bear the date of 9th September 1833. They were the first public utterance of the movement. The opening words of this famous series deserve to be recalled. They are new to most of the present generation.

11. Froude, *Remains*, 1:265.

TO MY BRETHREN IN THE SACRED MINISTRY, THE PRESBYTERS
AND DEACONS OF THE CHURCH OF CHRIST IN ENGLAND,
ORDAINED THEREUNTO BY THE HOLY GHOST AND THE
IMPOSITION OF HANDS.

FELLOW-LABOURERS,—I am but one of yourselves—a Presbyter;
and therefore I conceal my name, lest I should take too much on
myself by speaking in my own person. Yet speak I must; for
the times are very evil, yet no one speaks against them.

Is not this so? Do not we "look one upon another," yet
perform nothing? Do we not all confess the peril into which the
Church is come, yet sit still each in his own retirement, as if
mountains and seas cut off brother from brother? Therefore
suffer me, while I try to draw you forth from those pleasant re-
treats, which it has been our blessedness hitherto to enjoy, to
contemplate the condition and prospects of our Holy Mother in
a practical way; so that one and all may unlearn that idle habit,
which has grown upon us, of owning the state of things to be
bad, yet doing nothing to remedy it.

Consider a moment. Is it fair, is it dutiful, to suffer our bishops
to stand the brunt of the battle without doing our part to support
them? Upon them comes "the care of all the Churches." This
cannot be helped; indeed it is their glory. Not one of us would
wish in the least to deprive them of the duties, the toils, the
responsibilities of their high office. And, black event as it would
be for the country, yet (as far as they are concerned) we could
not wish them a more blessed termination of their course than
the spoiling of their goods and martyrdom.

To them then we willingly and affectionately relinquish their
high privileges and honours; we encroach not upon the rights of
the SUCCESSORS OF THE APOSTLES; we touch not their sword and
crozier. Yet surely we may be their shield-bearers in the battle
without offence; and by our voice and deeds be to them what
Luke and Timothy were to St. Paul.

Now then let me come at once to the subject which leads me
to address you. Should the Government and the Country so far
forget their God as to cast off the Church, to deprive it of its
temporal honours and substance, *on what* will you rest the claim
of respect and attention which you make upon your flocks?
Hitherto you have been upheld by your birth, your education,
your wealth, your connexions; should these secular advantages
cease, on what must Christ's Ministers depend? Is not this a
serious practical question? We know how miserable is the state

of religious bodies not supported by the State. Look at the Dissenters on all sides of you, and you will see at once that their Ministers, depending simply upon the people, become the *creatures* of the people. Are you content that this should be your case? Alas! can a greater evil befall Christians, than for their teachers to be guided by them, instead of guiding? How can we "hold fast the form of sound words," and "keep that which is committed to our trust," if our influence is to depend simply on our popularity? Is it not our very office to *oppose* the world? Can we then allow ourselves to *court* it? to preach smooth things and prophesy deceits? to make the way of life easy to the rich and indolent, and to bribe the humbler classes by excitements and strong intoxicating doctrine? Surely it must not be so;—and the question recurs, *on what* are we to rest our authority when the State deserts us?

Christ has not left His Church without claim of its own upon the attention of men. Surely not. Hard Master He cannot be, to bid us oppose the world, yet give us no credentials for so doing. There are some who rest their divine mission on their own unsupported assertion; others, who rest it upon their popularity; others, on their success; and others, who rest it upon their temporal distinctions. This last case has, perhaps, been too much our own; I fear we have neglected the real ground on which our authority is built—OUR APOSTOLICAL DESCENT.

We have been born, not of blood, nor of the will of the flesh, nor of the will of man, but of God. The Lord Jesus Christ gave His Spirit to His Apostles; they in turn laid their hands on those who should succeed them; and these again on others; and so the sacred gift has been handed down to our present bishops, who have appointed us as their assistants, and in some sense representatives.

Now every one of us believes this. I know that some will at first deny they do; still they do believe it. Only, it is not sufficiently, practically impressed on their minds. They *do* believe it; for it is the doctrine of the Ordination Service, which they have recognised as truth in the most solemn season of their lives. In order, then, not to prove, but to remind and impress, I entreat your attention to the words used when you were made ministers of Christ's Church.

The office of Deacon was thus committed to you: "Take thou authority to execute the office of a Deacon in the Church of God committed unto thee: In the name, etc."

And the Priesthood thus:

"Receive the Holy Ghost, for the office and work of a Priest, in the Church of God, now committed unto thee by the imposition of our hands. Whose sins thou dost forgive, they are forgiven; and whose sins thou dost retain, they are retained. And be thou a faithful dispenser of the Word of God, and of His Holy Sacraments: In the name, etc."

These, I say, were words spoken to us, and received by us, when we were brought nearer to God than at any other time of our lives. I know the grace of ordination is contained in the laying on of hands, not in any form of words;—yet in our own case (as has ever been usual in the Church) words of blessing have accompanied the act. Thus we have confessed before God our belief that the bishop who ordained us gave us the Holy Ghost, gave us the power to bind and to loose, to administer the Sacraments, and to preach. Now *how* is he able to give these great gifts? *Whence* is his right? Are these words idle (which would be taking God's name in vain), or do they express merely a wish (which surely is very far below their meaning), or do they not rather indicate that the speaker is conveying a gift? Surely they can mean nothing short of this. But whence, I ask, his right to do so? Has he any right, except as having received the power from those who consecrated him to be a bishop? He could not give what he had never received. It is plain then that he but *transmits*; and that the Christian Ministry is a *succession*. And if we trace back the power of ordination from hand to hand, of course we shall come to the Apostles at last. We know we do, as a plain historical fact; and therefore all we, who have been ordained clergy, in the very form of our ordination acknowledged the doctrine of the APOSTOLIC SUCCESSION.

And for the same reason, we must necessarily consider none to be *really* ordained who have not *thus* been ordained. For if ordination is a divine ordinance, it must be necessary; and if it is not a divine ordinance, how dare we use it? Therefore all who use it, all of *us*, must consider it necessary. As well might we pretend the Sacraments are not necessary to salvation, while we make use of the offices in the Liturgy; for when God appoints means of grace, they are *the* means.

I do not see how any one can escape from this plain view of the subject, except (as I have already hinted) by declaring that the words do not mean all that they say. But only reflect what a most unseemly time for random words is that in which ministers are set apart for their office. Do we not adopt a Liturgy *in order* to hinder inconsiderate idle language, and shall we, in the most sacred of all services, write down, subscribe, and use again and again forms of speech which have not been weighed, and cannot be taken strictly?

Therefore, my dear brethren, act up to your professions. Let it not be said that you have neglected a gift; for if you have the Spirit of the Apostles on you, surely this *is* a great gift. "Stir up the gift of God which is in you." Make much of it. Show your value of it. Keep it before your minds as an honourable badge, far higher than that secular respectability, or cultivation, or polish, or learning, or rank, which gives you a hearing with the many. Tell *them* of your gift. The times will soon drive you to do this, if you mean to be still anything. But wait not for the times. Do not be compelled, by the world's forsaking you, to recur as if unwillingly to the high source of your authority. Speak out now, before you are forced, both as glorying in your privilege and to insure your rightful honour from your people. A notion has gone abroad that they can take away your power. They think they have given and can take it away. They think it lies in the Church property, and they know that they have politically the power to confiscate that property. They have been deluded into a notion that present palpable usefulness, producible results, acceptableness to your flocks, that these and such like are the tests of your divine commission. Enlighten them in this matter. Exalt our Holy Fathers the bishops, as representatives of the Apostles, and the Angels of the Churches; and magnify your office, as being ordained by them to take part in their Ministry.

But, if you will not adopt my view of the subject, which I offer to you, not doubtingly, yet (I hope) respectfully, at all events, CHOOSE YOUR SIDE. To remain neuter much longer will be itself to take a part. *Choose* your side; since side you shortly must, with one or other party, even though you do nothing. Fear to be of those whose line is decided for them by chance circumstances, and who may perchance find themselves with the enemies of Christ, while they think but to remove themselves from worldly politics. Such abstinence is impossible in troublous times. HE THAT IS NOT WITH ME IS AGAINST ME, AND HE THAT GATHERETH NOT WITH ME SCATTERETH ABROAD.

While Mr. Palmer was working at the Association and the Address, Mr. Newman with his friends was sending forth the Tracts, one after another, in rapid succession, through the autumn and winter of 1833. They were short papers, in many cases mere short notes, on the great questions which had suddenly sprung into such interest, and were felt to be full of momentous consequence—the true and essential nature of the Christian Church, its relation to the primitive ages, its authority and its polity and government, the current objections to its claims in England, to its doctrines and its services, the length of the prayers, the Burial Service, the proposed alterations in the Liturgy, the neglect of discipline, the sins and corruptions of each branch of Christendom. The same topics were enforced and illustrated again and again as the series went on; and then there came extracts from English divines, like Bishop Beveridge, Bishop Wilson, and Bishop Cosin, and under the title "Records of the Church," translations from the early Fathers, Ignatius, Justin, Irenaeus, and others. Mr. Palmer contributed to one of these papers, and later on Mr. Perceval wrote two or three; but for the most part these early Tracts were written by Mr. Newman, though Mr. Keble and one or two others also helped. Afterwards, other writers joined in the series. They were at first not only published with a notice that any one might republish them with any alterations he pleased, but they were distributed by zealous coadjutors, ready to take any trouble in the cause. Mr. Mozley has described how he rode about Northamptonshire, from parsonage to parsonage, with bundles of the Tracts. The *Apologia* records the same story. "I called upon clergy," says the writer, "in various parts of the country, whether I was acquainted with them or not, and I attended at the houses of friends where several of them were from time to time assembled. . . . I did not care whether my visits were made to High Church or Low Church: I wished to make a strong pull in union with all who were opposed to the principles of Liberalism, whoever they might be." He adds that he does not think that much came of these visits, or of letters written with the same purpose, "except that they advertised the fact that a rally in favour of the Church was commencing."

The early Tracts were intended to startle the world, and they succeeded in doing so. Their very form, as short earnest leaflets, was perplexing; for they came, not from the class of religionists who usually deal in such productions, but from distinguished University scholars, picked men of a picked college; and from men, too, who as a school were the representatives of soberness and self-control in religious feeling and language, and whose usual style of writing was specially marked by its severe avoidance of excitement and novelty; the school from which had lately come the *Christian Year,* with its memorable motto *"In quietness and confidence shall be your strength."* Their matter was equally unusual. Undoubtedly they "brought strange things to the ears" of their generation. To Churchmen now these "strange things" are such familiar commonplaces, that it is hard to realise how they should have made so much stir. But they were novelties, partly audacious, partly unintelligible, then. The strong and peremptory language of the Tracts, their absence of qualifications or explanations, frightened friends like Mr. Palmer, who, so far, had no ground to quarrel with their doctrine, and he wished them to be discontinued. The story went that one of the bishops, on reading one of the Tracts on the Apostolical Succession, could not make up his mind whether he held the doctrine or not. They fell on a time of profound and inexcusable ignorance on the subjects they discussed, and they did not spare it. The cry of Romanism was inevitable, and was soon raised, though there was absolutely nothing in them but had the indisputable sanction of the Prayer Book, and of the most authoritative Anglican divines. There was no Romanism in them, nor anything that showed a tendency to it. But custom, and the prevalence of other systems and ways, and the interest of later speculations, and the slackening of professional reading and scholarship in the Church, had made their readers forget some of the most obvious facts in Church history, and the most certain Church principles; and men were at sea as to what they knew or believed on the points on which the Tracts challenged them. The scare was not creditable; it was like the Italian scare about cholera with its quarantines and fumigations; but it was natural. The theological knowledge and learning were wanting which would have been familiar with the broad line of difference between what is Catholic and what is specially Roman. There were many whose teaching was impugned, for it was really Calvinist or Zwinglian, and not Anglican. There were hopeful and ambitious theological Liberals, who recognised in that appeal to Anglicanism the most effective counter-stroke to their own schemes and theories. There were many whom the movement forced to think, who did not want such addition to

their responsibilities. It cannot be thought surprising that the new
Tracts were received with surprise, dismay, ridicule, and indignation. But they also at once called forth a response of eager sympathy from numbers to whom they brought unhoped-for relief
and light in a day of gloom, of rebuke and blasphemy. Mr. Keble,
in the preface to his famous assize sermon, had hazarded the belief that there were "hundreds, nay, thousands of Christians, and
that there soon will be tens of thousands, unaffectedly anxious to
be rightly guided" in regard to subjects that concern the Church.
The belief was soon justified.

When the first forty-six Tracts were collected into a volume
towards the end of 1834, the following "advertisement" explaining their nature and objects was prefixed to it. It is a contemporary
and authoritative account of what was the mind of the leaders of
the movement; and it has a significance beyond the occasion which
prompted it.

> The following Tracts were published with the object of con-
> tributing something towards the practical revival of doctrines,
> which, although held by the great divines of our Church, at
> present have become obsolete with the majority of her members,
> and are withdrawn from public view even by the more learned
> and orthodox few who still adhere to them. The Apostolic suc-
> cession, the Holy Catholic Church, were principles of action in
> the minds of our predecessors of the seventeenth century; but, in
> proportion as the maintenance of the Church has been secured by
> law, her ministers have been under the temptation of leaning
> on an arm of flesh instead of her own divinely-provided
> discipline, a temptation increased by political events and
> arrangements which need not here be more than alluded to. A
> lamentable increase of sectarianism has followed; being occas-
> ioned (in addition to other more obvious causes), first, by the
> cold aspect which the new Church doctrines have presented to
> the religious sensibilities of the mind, next to their meagreness
> in suggesting motives to restrain it from seeking out a more
> influential discipline. Doubtless obedience to the law of the
> land, and the careful maintenance of "decency and order" (the
> topics in usage among us), are plain duties of the Gospel, and a
> reasonable ground for keeping in communion with the Estab-
> lished Church; yet, if Providence has graciously provided for our
> weakness more interesting and constraining motives, it is a sin

thanklessly to neglect them; just as it would be a mistake to rest the duties of temperance or justice on the mere law of natural religion, when they are mercifully sanctioned in the Gospel by the more winning authority of our Saviour Christ. Experience has shown the inefficacy of the mere injunctions of Church order, however scripturally enforced, in restraining from schism the awakened and anxious sinner; who goes to a dissenting preacher "because" (as he expresses it) "he gets good from him": and though he does not stand excused in God's sight for yielding to the temptation, surely the ministers of the Church are not blameless if, by keeping back the more gracious and consoling truths provided for the little ones of Christ, they indirectly lead him into it. Had he been taught as a child, that the Sacraments, not preaching, are the sources of Divine Grace; that the Apostolical ministry had a virtue in it which went out over the whole Church, when sought by the prayer of faith; that fellowship with it was a gift and privilege, as well as a duty, we could not have had so many wanderers from our fold, nor so many cold hearts within it.

This instance may suggest many others of the superior *influence* of an apostolical over a mere secular method of teaching. The awakened mind knows its wants, but cannot provide for them; and in its hunger will feed upon ashes, if it cannot obtain the pure milk of the word. Methodism and Popery are in different ways the refuge of those whom the Church stints of the gifts of grace; they are the foster-mothers of abandoned children. The neglect of the daily service, the desecration of festivals, the Eucharist scantily administered, insubordination permitted in all ranks of the Church, orders and offices imperfectly developed, the want of societies for particular religious objects, and the like deficiencies, lead the feverish mind, desirous of a vent to its feelings, and a stricter rule of life, to the smaller religious communities, to prayer and Bible meetings, and ill-advised institutions and societies, on the one hand, on the other, to the solemn and captivating services by which Popery gains its proselytes. Moreover, the multitude of men cannot teach or guide themselves; and an injunction given them to depend on their private judgment, cruel in itself, is doubly hurtful, as throwing them on such teachers as speak daringly and promise largely, and not only aid but supersede individual exertion.

These remarks may serve as a clue, for those who care to pursue it, to the views which have led to the publication of the following Tracts. The Church of Christ was intended to cope with human nature in all its forms, and surely the gifts vouch-safed it are adequate for that gracious purpose. There are zealous sons and servants of her English branch, who see with sorrow that she is defrauded of her full usefulness by particular theories and principles of the present age, which interfere with the execution of one portion of her commission; and while they consider that the revival of this portion of truth is especially adapted to break up existing parties in the Church, and to form instead a bond of union among all who love the Lord Jesus Christ in sincerity, they believe that nothing but these neglected doctrines, faithfully preached, will repress that extension of Popery, for which the ever multiplying divisions of the religious world are too clearly preparing the way.

Another publication ought to be noticed, a result of the Hadleigh meeting, which exhibited the leading ideas of the conference, and especially of the more "conservative" members of it. This was a little work in question and answer, called the "Churchman's Manual," drawn up in part some time before the meeting by Mr. Perceval, and submitted to the revision of Mr. Rose and Mr. Palmer. It was intended to be a supplement to the "Church Catechism," as to the nature and claims of the Church and its Ministers. It is a terse, clear, careful, and, as was inevitable, rather dry summary of the Anglican theory, and of the position which the English Church holds to the Roman Church, and to the Dissenters. It was further revised at the conference, and "some important suggestions were made by Froude"; and then Mr. Perceval, who had great hopes from the publication, and spared himself no pains to make it perfect, submitted it for revision and advice to a number of representative Churchmen. The Scotch Bishops whom he consulted were warm in approval, especially the venerable and saintly Bishop Jolly; as were also a number of men of weight and authority in England: Judge Allan Park, Joshua Watson, Mr. Sikes of Guilsborough, Mr. Churton of Crayke, Mr. H. H. Norris, Dr. Wordsworth, and Dr. Routh. It was then laid before the Archbishop for correction, or, if desirable, suppression; and for his sanction if approved. The answer was what might have been expected, that there was no objection to it, but that official sanction must be declined on general grounds. After all this Mr. Perceval not unnaturally claimed for it special importance. It was really, he observed, the "first Tract," systematically put forth, and its preparation "apparently gave rise" to the series; and it was the only one which received the approval of all immediately concerned in the movement. "The care bestowed on it," he says, "probably exceeds that which any theological publication in the English communion received for a long time;" and further, it shows "that the foundation of the movement with which Mr. Rose was connected, was laid with all the care and circumspection that reason could well suggest." It appears to have had a circulation, but there is no reason to think that it had any considerable influence, one way or other, on opinion in the Church. When it was referred to in after-years by Mr. Perceval in his own vindication, it was almost forgotten. More interesting, if not more important, Tracts had thrown it into the shade.

VII

The Tractarians

Thus had been started—hurriedly perhaps, yet not without counting the cost—a great enterprise, which had for its object to rouse
the Church from its lethargy, and to strengthen and purify religion, by making it deeper and more real; and they who had put
their hands to the plough were not to look back any more. It was
not a popular appeal; it addressed itself not to the many but to
the few; it sought to inspire and to teach the teachers. There was
no thought as yet of acting on the middle classes, or on the ignorance and wretchedness of the great towns, though Newman
had laid down that the Church must rest on the people, and
Froude looked forward to colleges of unmarried priests as the
true way to evangelise the crowds. There was no display about
this attempt, no eloquence, nothing attractive in the way of original speculation or sentimental interest. It was suspicious, perhaps
too suspicious, of the excitement and want of soberness, almost
inevitable in strong appeals to the masses of mankind. It brought
no new doctrine, but professed to go back to what was obvious and
old-fashioned and commonplace. It taught people to think less of
preaching than of what in an age of excitement were invidiously
called forms—of the sacraments and services of the Church. It
discouraged, even to the verge of an intended dryness, all that
was showy, all that in thought or expression or manner it condemned under the name of "flash." It laid stress on the exercise
of an inner and unseen self-discipline, and the cultivation of the
less interesting virtues of industry, humility, self-distrust, and

obedience. If from its writers proceeded works which had impressed people—a volume like the *Christian Year*, poems original in their force and their tenderness, like some of those in the *Lyra Apostolica*, sermons which arrested the hearers by their keenness and pathetic undertone—the force of all this was not the result of literary ambition and effort, but the reflexion, unconscious, unsought, of thought and feeling that could not otherwise express itself, and that was thrown into moulds shaped by habitual refinement and cultivated taste. It was from the first a movement from which, as much by instinct and temper as by deliberate intention, self-seeking in all its forms was excluded. Those whom it influenced looked not for great things for themselves, nor thought of making a mark in the world.

The first year after the Hadleigh meeting (1834) passed uneventfully. The various addresses in which Mr. Palmer was interested, the election and installation of the Duke of Wellington as Chancellor, the enthusiasm and hopes called forth by the occasion, were public and prominent matters. The Tracts were steadily swelling in number; the busy distribution of them had ceased, and they had begun to excite interest and give rise to questions. Mr. Palmer, who had never liked the Tracts, became more uneasy; yet he did not altogether refuse to contribute to them. Others gave their help, among them Mr. Perceval, Froude, the two Kebles, and Mr. Newman's friend, a layman, Mr. J. Bowden; some of the younger scholars furnished translations from the Fathers; but the bulk and most forcible of the Tracts were still the work of Mr. Newman. But the Tracts were not the most powerful instruments in drawing sympathy to the movement. None but those who remember them can adequately estimate the effect of Mr. Newman's four o'clock sermons at St. Mary's.[1] The world knows them, has heard a great deal about them, has passed its various judgments on them. But it hardly realises that without those sermons the movement might never have gone on, certainly would never have been what it was. Even people who heard them continually, and felt them to be different from any other sermons, hardly estimated their real power, or knew at the time the influence which the sermons were having upon them. Plain, direct,

1. See note at the end of this chapter.

unornamented, clothed in English that was only pure and lucid, free from any faults of taste, strong in their flexibility and perfect command both of language and thought, they were the expression of a piercing and large insight into character and conscience and motives, of a sympathy at once most tender and most stern with the tempted and the wavering, of an absolute and burning faith in God and His counsels, in His love, in His judgments, in the awful glory of His generosity and His magnificence. They made men think of the things which the preacher spoke of, and not of the sermon or the preacher. Since 1828 this preaching had been going on at St. Mary's, growing in purpose and directness as the years went on, though it could hardly be more intense than in some of its earliest examples. While men were reading and talking about the Tracts, they were hearing the sermons; and in the sermons they heard the living meaning, and reason, and bearing of the Tracts, their ethical affinities, their moral standard. The sermons created a moral atmosphere, in which men judged the questions in debate. It was no dry theological correctness and completeness which were sought for. No love of privilege, no formal hierarchical claims, urged on the writers. What they thought in danger, what they aspired to revive and save, was the very life of religion, the truth and substance of all that makes it the hope of human society.

But indeed, by this time, out of the little company of friends which a common danger and a common loyalty to the Church had brought together, one, Mr. Newman, had drawn ahead, and was now in the front. Unsought for, as the *Apologia* makes so clear— unsought for, as the contemporary letters of observing friends attest—unsought for, as the whole tenor of his life has proved— the position of leader in a great crisis came to him, because it must come. He was not unconscious that, as he had felt in his sickness in Sicily, he "had a work to do." But there was shyness and self-distrust in his nature as well as energy; and it was the force of genius, and a lofty character, and the statesman's eye, taking in and judging accurately the whole of a complicated scene, which conferred the gifts, and imposed inevitably and without dispute the obligations and responsibilities of leadership. Dr. Pusey of course was a friend of great account, but he was as yet in the background, a venerated and rather awful person, from his position not mixing in the easy intercourse of common-room life, but to be consulted on emergencies. Round Mr. Newman gathered, with a curious mixture of freedom, devotion, and awe—for, with unlimited power of sympathy, he was exacting and even austere in his friendships—the best men of his college, either Fellows— R. Wilberforce, Thomas Mozley, Frederic Rogers, J. F. Christie; or old pupils—Henry Wilberforce, R. F. Wilson, William Froude, Robert Williams, S. F. Wood, James Bliss, James Mozley; and in addition some outsiders—Woodgate of St. John's, Isaac Williams and Copeland, of his old College, Trinity. These, members of his intimate circle, were bound to him not merely by enthusiastic admiration and confidence, but by a tenderness of affection, a mixture of the gratitude and reliance of discipleship with the warm love of friendship, of which one has to go back far for examples, and which has had nothing like it in our days at Oxford. And Newman was making his mark as a writer. The *Arians*, though an imperfect book, was one which, for originality and subtlety of thought, was something very unlike the usual theological writing of the day. There was no doubt of his power, and his mind was brimming over with ideas on the great questions which were rising into view. It was clear to all who knew him that he could speak on them as no one else could.

Towards the end of 1834, and in the course of 1835, an event happened which had a great and decisive influence on the character and fortunes of the movement. This was the accession to it of Dr. Pusey. He had looked favourably on it from the first, partly from his friendship with Mr. Newman, partly from the workings of his own mind. But he had nothing to do with the starting of it, except that he early contributed an elaborate paper on "Fasting." The Oxford branch of the movement, as distinguished from that which Mr. Palmer represented, consisted up to 1834 almost exclusively of junior men, personal friends of Mr. Newman, and most of them Oriel men. Mr. Newman's deep convictions, his fiery enthusiasm, had given the Tracts their first stamp and impress, and had sent them flying over the country among the clergy on his own responsibility. They answered their purpose. They led to widespread and sometimes deep searchings of heart; to some they seemed to speak forth what had been long dormant within them, what their minds had unconsciously and vaguely thought and longed for; to some they seemed a challenge pregnant with danger. But still they were but an outburst of individual feeling and zeal, which, if nothing more came of its fragmentary displays, might blaze and come to nothing. There was nothing yet which spoke outwardly of the consistency and weight of a serious attempt to influence opinion and to produce a practical and lasting effect on the generation which was passing. Cardinal Newman, in the *Apologia,* has attributed to Dr. Pusey's unreserved adhesion to the cause which the Tracts represented a great change in regard to the weight and completeness of what was written and done.

> Dr. Pusey [he writes] gave us at once a position and a name. Without him we should have had no chance, especially at the early date of 1834, of making any serious resistance to the liberal aggression. But Dr. Pusey was a Professor and Canon of Christ Church; he had a vast influence in consequence of his deep religious seriousness, the munificence of his charities, his Professorship, his family connexions, and his easy relations with the University authorities. He was to the movement all that Mr. Rose might have been, with that indispensable addition, which was wanting to Mr. Rose, the intimate friendship and the familiar daily society of the persons who had commenced it. And he had that special claim on their attachment which lies in the living presence of a faithful and loyal affectionateness. There was henceforth a man who could be the head and centre of the zealous people in every part of the country who were adopting the new opinions, and not only so, but there was one who furnished the movement with a front to the world, and gained for it a recognition from other parties in the University.[2]

This is not too much to say of the effect of Dr. Pusey's adhesion. It gave the movement a second head, in close sympathy with its original leader, but in many ways very different from him. Dr. Pusey became, as it were, its official chief in the eyes of the world. He became also, in a remarkable degree, a guarantee for its stability and steadiness: a guarantee that its chiefs knew what they were about, and meant nothing but what was for the benefit of the English Church. "He was," we read in the *Apologia,* "a man of large designs; he had a hopeful, sanguine mind; he had no fear

2. *Apologia,* p. 136.

of others; he was haunted by no intellectual perplexities. . . . If confidence in his position is (as it is) a first essential in the leader of a party, Dr. Pusey had it." An inflexible patience, a serene composure, a meek, resolute self-possession, was the habit of his mind, and never deserted him in the most trying days. He never for an instant, as the paragraph witnesses, wavered or doubted about the position of the English Church.

He was eminently, as his friend justly observes, "a man of large designs." It is doubtless true, as the *Apologia* goes on to say, that it was due to the place which he now took in the movement that great changes were made in the form and character of the Tracts. To Dr. Pusey's mind, accustomed to large and exhaustive theological reading, they wanted fulness, completeness, the importance given by careful arrangement and abundant knowledge. It was not for nothing that he had passed an apprenticeship among the divines of Germany, and been the friend and correspondent of Tholuck, Schleiermacher, Ewald, and Sack. He knew the meaning of real learning. In controversy it was his sledge-hammer and battle-mace, and he had the strong and sinewy hand to use it with effect. He observed that when attention had been roused to the ancient doctrines of the Church by the startling and peremptory language of the earlier Tracts, fairness and justice demanded that these doctrines should be fully and carefully explained and defended against misrepresentation and mistake. Forgetfulness and ignorance had thrown these doctrines so completely into the shade that, identified as they were with the best English divinity, they now wore the air of amazing novelties; and it was only due to honest inquiries to satisfy them with solid and adequate proof. "Dr. Pusey's influence was felt at once. He saw that there ought to be more sobriety, more gravity, more careful plans, more sense of responsibility in the Tracts and in the whole movement." At the end of 1835 Dr. Pusey gave an example of what he meant. In place of the "short and incomplete papers," such as the earlier Tracts had been, Nos. 67, 68, and 69 formed the three parts of a closely-printed pamphlet of more than 300 pages.[3] It was a treatise on Baptism, perhaps the most elaborate that has yet appeared in the English language. "It is to be re-

3. It swelled in the second edition to 400 pages (in spite of the fact that in that edition the historical range of the treatise was greatly reduced).

garded," says the advertisement to the second volume of the Tracts, "not as an inquiry into a single or isolated doctrine, but as a delineation and serious examination of a modern system of theology, of extensive popularity and great speciousness, in its elementary and characteristic principles." The Tract on Baptism was like the advance of a battery of heavy artillery on a field where the battle has been hitherto carried on by skirmishing and musketry. It altered the look of things and the condition of the fighting. After No. 67 the earlier form of the Tracts appeared no more. Except two or three reprints from writers like Bishop Wilson, the Tracts from No. 70 to No. 90 were either grave and carefully worked out essays on some question arising out of the discussions of the time, or else those ponderous *catenae* of patristic or Anglican divinity, by which the historical continuity and Church authority of various points of doctrine were established.

Dr. Pusey was indeed a man of "large designs." The vision rose before him of a revived and instructed Church, earnest in purpose and strict in life, and of a great Christian University roused and quickened to a sense of its powers and responsibilities. He thought of the enormous advantages offered by its magnificent foundations for serious study and the production of works for which time and deep learning and continuous labour were essential. Such works, in the hands of single-minded students, living lives of simplicity and hard toil, had in the case of the Portroyalists, the Oratorians, and above all, the Benedictines of St. Maur, splendidly redeemed the Church of France, in otherwise evil days, from the reproach of idleness and self-indulgence. He found under his hand men who had in them something of the making of students; and he hoped to see college fellowships filled more and more by such men, and the life of a college fellow more and more recognised as that of a man to whom learning, and especially sacred learning, was his call and sufficient object, as pastoral or educational work might be the call of others. Where fellowships were not to be had, he encouraged such men to stay up in Oxford; he took them into his own house; later, he tried a kind of hall to receive them. And by way of beginning at once, and giving them something to do, he planned on a large scale a series of translations and also editions of the Fathers. It was announced, with an elaborate prospectus, in 1836, under the title, in conformity with the usage of the time, which had *Libraries of Useful Knowledge, etc.,* of a *Library of Fathers of the Holy Catholic Church Anterior to the Division of the East and West,* under the editorship of Dr. Pusey, Mr. Keble, and Mr. Newman. It was dedicated to the Archbishop of Canterbury, and had a considerable number of Bishops among its subscribers. Down to a very late date, the *Library of the Fathers,* in which Charles Marriott came to take a leading part, was a matter of much concern to Dr. Pusey. And to bring men together, and to interest them in theological subjects, he had evening meetings at his own house, where papers were read and discussed. "Some persons," writes a gossiping chronicler of the time,[4] "thought that these meetings were liable to the statute, *De conventiculis illicitis reprimendis."* Some important papers were the result of those meetings; but the meetings themselves were irresistibly sleepy, and in time they were discontinued. But indefatigable and powerful in all these beginnings Dr. Pusey stirred men to activity and saw great ground of hope. He was prepared for opposition, but he had boundless reliance on his friends and his cause. His forecast of the future, of great days in store for the Church of England, was, not unreasonably, one of great promise. Then years might work wonders. The last fear that occurred to him was that within ten years a hopeless rift, not of affection but of conviction, would have run through that company of friends, and parted irrevocably their course and work in life.

Note

The subjoined extracts record the impression made by Mr. Newman's preaching on contemporaries well qualified to judge, and standing respectively in very different relations to the movement. This is the judgment of a very close observer, and very independent critic, James Mozley. In an article in the *Christian Remembrancer,* January 1846 (p. 169), after speaking of the obvious reasons of Mr. Newman's influence, he proceeds:—

4. *Recollections of Oxford,* by G. V. Cox, p. 278.

We inquire further, and we find that this influence has been of a peculiarly ethical and inward kind; that it has touched the deepest part of our minds, and that the great work on which it has been founded is a practical, religious one—his Sermons. We speak not from our own fixed impression, however deeply felt, but from what we have heard and observed everywhere, from the natural, incidental, unconscious remarks dropped from persons' mouths, and evidently showing what they thought and felt. For ourselves, we must say, one of Mr. Newman's sermons is to us a marvellous production. It has perfect power, and perfect nature; but the latter it is which makes it so great. A sermon of Mr. Newman's enters into all our feelings, ideas, modes of viewing things. He wonderfully realises a state of mind, enters into a difficulty, a temptation, a disappointment, a grief; he goes into the different turns and incidental, unconscious symptoms of a case, with notions which come into the head and go out again, and are forgotten, till some chance recalls them. . . . To take the first instance that happens to occur to us . . . we have often been struck by the keen way in which he enters into a regular trades-man's vice—avarice, fortune-getting, amassing capital, and so on. This is not a temper to which we can imagine Mr. Newman ever having felt in his own mind even the temptation; but he under-stands it, and the temptation to it, as perfectly as any merchant could. No man of business could express it more naturally, more pungently, more *ex animo*. . . . So with the view that worldly men take of religion, in a certain sense, he quite enters into it, and the world's point of view: he sees, with a regular worldly man's eye, religion vanishing into nothing, and becoming an unreality, while the visible system of life and facts, politics and society, gets more and more solid and grows upon him. The whole influence of the world on the imagination; the weight of example; the force of repetition; the way in which maxims, rules, sentiments, by being simply sounded in the ear from day to day, seem to prove themselves, and make themselves believed by being often heard,—every part of the easy, natural, passive process by which a man becomes a man of the world is entered into, as if the preacher were going to justify or excuse him, rather than condemn him. Nay, he enters deeply into what even scepticism has to say for itself; he puts himself into the infidel's state of mind, in which the world, as a great fact, seems to give the lie to all religions, converting them into phenomena which counter-balance and negative each other, and he goes down into that

99

lowest abyss and bottom of things, at which the intellect under-cuts spiritual truth altogether. He enters into the ordinary common states of mind just in the same way. He is most consoling, most sympathetic. He sets before persons their own feelings with such truth of detail, such natural expressive touches, that they seem not to be ordinary states of mind which everybody has, but very peculiar ones; for he and the reader seem to be the only two persons in the world that have them in common. Here is the point. Persons look into Mr. Newman's sermons and see their own thoughts in them. This is, after all, what as much as anything gives a book hold upon minds. . . . Wonderful pathetic power, that can so intimately, so subtilely and kindly, deal with the soul!—and wonderful soul that can be so dealt with.

Compare with this the judgment pronounced by one of quite a different school, the late Principal Shairp:—

Both Dr. Pusey and Mr. Keble at that time were quite second in importance to Mr. Newman. The centre from which his power went forth was the pulpit of St. Mary's, with those wonderful afternoon sermons. Sunday after Sunday, year after year, they went on, each continuing and deepening the impression produced by the last. As the hour interfered with the dinner-hour of the Colleges, most men preferred a warm dinner without Newman's sermon to a cold one with it; so the audience was not crowded—the large church little more than half filled. The service was very simple, no pomp, no ritualism; for it was characteristic of the leading men of the movement that they left these things to the weaker brethren. Their thoughts, at all events, were set on great questions which touched the heart of unseen things. About the service, the most remarkable thing was the beauty, the silver intonation of Mr. Newman's voice as he read the lessons. . . . When he began to preach, a stranger was not likely to be much struck. Here was no vehemence, no declamation, no show of elaborated argument, so that one who came prepared to hear "a great intellectual effort" was almost sure to go away disappointed. Indeed, we believe that if he had preached one of his St. Mary's sermons before a Scotch town congregation, they would have thought the preacher a "silly body." . . . Those who never heard him might fancy that his sermons would generally be about apostolical succession, or rights of the Church, or against Dissenters. Nothing of the kind. You might hear him preach for weeks without an allusion to these things. What there was of High

Church teaching was implied rather than enforced. The local, the temporary, and the modern were ennobled by the presence of the Catholic truth belonging to all ages that pervaded the whole. His power showed itself chiefly in the new and unlooked-for way in which he touched into life old truths, moral or spiritual, which all Christians acknowledge, but most have ceased to feel—when he spoke of "unreal words," of the "individuality of the soul," of the "invisible world," of a "particular Providence," or again, of the "ventures of faith," "warfare the condition of victory," "the Cross of Christ the measure of the world," "the Church a Home for the lonely." As he spoke, how the old truth became new; how it came home with a meaning never felt before! He laid his finger how gently, yet how powerfully, on some inner place in the hearer's heart, and told him things about himself he had never known till then. Subtlest truths, which it would have taken philosophers pages of circumlocution and big words to state, were dropt out by the way in a sentence or two of the most transparent Saxon. What delicacy of style, yet what strength! how simple, yet how suggestive! how homely, yet how refined! how penetrating, yet how tender-hearted! If now and then there was a forlorn undertone which at the time seemed inexplicable, you might be perplexed at the drift of what he said, but you felt all the more drawn to the speaker. . . . After hearing these sermons you might come away still not believing the tenets peculiar to the High Church system; but you would be harder than most men, if you did not feel more than ever ashamed of coarseness, selfishness, worldliness, if you did not feel the things of faith brought closer to the soul.—*John Keble,* by J. C. Shairp, Professor of Humanity, St. Andrews (1866), pp. 12–17.

I venture to add the judgment of another contemporary, on the effect of this preaching, from the *Reminiscences* of Sir F. Doyle, p. 145:—

That great man's extraordinary genius drew all those within his sphere, like a magnet, to attach themselves to him and his doctrines. Nay, before he became a Romanist, what we may call his mesmeric influence acted not only on his Tractarian adherents, but even in some degree on outsiders like myself. Whenever I was at Oxford, I used to go regularly on Sunday afternoons to listen to his sermon at St. Mary's, and I have never heard such preaching since. I do not know whether it is a mere fancy of mine, or whether those who know him better will accept and endorse my belief, that one element of his wonderful power showed itself after this fashion. He always began as if he had determined to set forth his idea of the truth in the plainest and simplest language—language, as men say, "intelligible to the meanest understanding." But his ardent zeal and fine poetical imagination were not thus to be controlled. As I hung upon his words, it seemed to me as if I could trace behind his will, and pressing, so to speak, against it, a rush of thoughts, of feelings which he kept struggling to hold back, but in the end they were generally too strong for him, and poured themselves out in a torrent of eloquence all the more impetuous from having been so long repressed. The effect of these outbursts was irresistible, and carried his hearers beyond themselves at once. Even when his efforts of self-restraint were more successful, those very efforts gave a life and colour to his style which riveted the attention of all within the reach of his voice. Mr. Justin Mc-Carthy, in his *History of Our Own Times,* says of him: "In all the arts that make a great preacher or orator, Cardinal Newman was deficient. His manner was constrained and ungraceful, and even awkward; his voice was thin and weak, his bearing was not at first impressive in any way—a gaunt emaciated figure, a sharp eagle face, and cold meditative eye, rather repelled than attracted those who saw him for the first time." I do not think Mr. Mc-Carthy's phrases very happily chosen to convey his meaning. Surely a gaunt emaciated frame and a sharp eagle face are the very characteristics which we should picture to ourselves as belonging to Peter the Hermit, or Scott's Ephraim Macbriar in *Old Mortality.* However unimpressive the look of an eagle may be in Mr. McCarthy's opinion, I do not agree with him about Dr. Newman. When I knew him at Oxford, these somewhat disparaging remarks would not have been applicable. His manner, it is true, may have been self-repressed, constrained it was not. His bearing was neither awkward nor ungraceful; it was simply quiet and calm, because under strict control; but beneath that calmness, intense feeling, I think, was obvious to those who had any instinct of sympathy with him. But if Mr. McCarthy's acquaintance with him only began when he took office in an Irish Catholic university, I can quite understand that (flexibility not being one of his special gifts) he may have failed now and again to bring himself into perfect harmony with an Irish audience. He was probably too much of a typical Englishman for his place; nevertheless Mr. McCarthy, though he does not seem to have admired him in the pulpit, is fully sensible of his intellectual powers and general eminence.

Dr. Pusey, who used every now and then to take Newman's duties at St. Mary's, was to me a much less interesting person. (A learned man, no doubt, but dull and tedious as a preacher.) Certainly, in spite of the name Puseyism having been given to the Oxford attempt at a new Catholic departure, he was not the Columbus of that voyage of discovery undertaken to find a safer haven for the Church of England. I may, however, be more or less unjust to him, as I owe him a sort of grudge. His discourses were not only less attractive than those of Dr. Newman, but always much longer, and the result of this was that the learned Canon of Christ Church generally made me late for dinner at my College, a calamity never inflicted on his All Souls' hearers by the terser and swifter fellow of Oriel whom he was replacing.

VIII

Subscription at Matriculation

and

Admission of Dissenters

"Depend upon it," an earnest High Churchman of the Joshua Watson type had said to one of Mr. Newman's friends, who was a link between the old Churchmanship and the new—"depend upon it, the day will come when those great doctrines" connected with the Church, "now buried, will be brought out to the light of the day, and then the effect will be quite fearful."[1] With the publication of the *Tracts for the Times*, and the excitement caused by them, the day had come.

Their unflinching and severe proclamation of Church principles and Church doctrines coincided with a state of feeling and opinion in the country, in which two very different tendencies might be observed. They fell on the public mind just when one of these tendencies would help them, and the other be fiercely hostile. On the one hand, the issue of the political controversy with the Roman Catholics, their triumph all along the line, and the now scarcely disguised contempt shown by their political representatives for the pledges and explanations on which their relief was supposed to have been conceded, had left the public mind sore, angry, and suspicious. Orthodox and Evangelicals were alike alarmed and indignant; and the Evangelicals, always doctrinally jealous of Popery, and of anything "unsound" in that direction, had been roused to increased irritation by the proceedings of the

1. The conversation between Mr. Sikes of Guilsborough and Mr. Copeland is given in full in Dr. Pusey's *Letter to the Archbishop of Canterbury* (1842), pp. 32–34.

Reformation Society, which had made it its business to hold meetings and discussions all over the country, where fervid and sometimes eloquent and able Irishmen, like Mr. E. Tottenham, afterwards of Laura Chapel, Bath, had argued and declaimed, with Roman text-books in hand, on such questions as the Right of Private Judgment, the Rule of Faith, and the articles of the Tridentine Creed—not always with the effect which they intended on those who heard them, with whom their arguments, and those which they elicited from their opponents, sometimes left behind uncomfortable misgivings, and questions even more serious than the controversy itself. On the other hand, in quarters quite unconnected with the recognised religious schools, interest had been independently and strongly awakened in the minds of theologians and philosophical thinkers, in regard to the idea, history, and relations to society of the Christian Church. In Ireland, a recluse, who was the centre of a small knot of earnest friends, a man of deep piety and great freedom and originality of mind, Mr. Alexander Knox, had been led, partly, it may be, by his intimacy with John Wesley, to think out for himself the character and true constitution of the Church, and the nature of the doctrines which it was commissioned to teach. In England, another recluse, of splendid genius and wayward humour, had dealt in his own way, with far-reaching insight, with vast reading, and often with impressive eloquence, with the same subject; and his profound sympathy and faith had been shared and reflected by a great poet. What Coleridge and Wordsworth had put in the forefront of their speculations and poetry, as the object of their profoundest interest, and of their highest hopes for mankind, might, of course, fail to appear in the same light to others; but it could not fail, in those days at least, to attract attention, as a matter of grave and well-founded importance. Coleridge's theories of the Church were his own, and were very wide of theories recognised by any of those who had to deal practically with the question, and who were influenced, in one way or another, by the traditional doctrines of theologians. But Coleridge had lifted the subject to a very high level. He had taken the simple but all-important step of viewing the Church in its spiritual character as first and foremost and above all things essentially a religious society of divine institution, not dependent on the creation or will of man, or on the privileges and honours which man might think fit to assign to it; and he had undoubtedly familiarised the minds of many with this way of regarding it, however imperfect, or cloudy, or unpractical they might find the development of his ideas, and his deductions from them. And in Oxford the questions which had stirred the friends at Hadleigh had stirred others also, and had waked up various responses. Whately's acute mind had not missed these questions, and had given original if insufficient answers to them. Blanco White knew only too well their bearing and importance, and had laboured, not without success, to leave behind him his own impress on the way in which they should be dealt with. Dr. Hampden, the man in Oxford best acquainted with Aristotle's works and with the scholastic philosophy, had thrown Christian doctrines into a phi-losophical calculus which seemed to leave them little better than the inventions of men. On the other hand, a brilliant scholar, whose after-career was strangely full of great successes and de-plorable disasters, William Sewell of Exeter College, had opened, in a way new to Oxford, the wealth and magnificence of Plato; and his thoughts had been dazzled by seeming to find in the truths and facts of the Christian Church the counterpart and realisation of the grandest of Plato's imaginations. The subjects treated with such dogmatic severity and such impetuous earnestness in the Tracts were, in one shape or another, in all men's minds, when these Tracts broke on the University and English society with their peremptory call to men "to take their side."

There was just a moment of surprise and uncertainty—uncer-tainty as to what the Tracts meant; whether they were to be a new weapon against the enemies of the Church, or were simply ex-travagant and preposterous novelties—just a certain perplexity and hesitation at their conflicting aspects; on the one hand, the known and high character of the writers, their evident determi-nation and confidence in their cause, the attraction of their re-ligious warmth and unselfishness and nobleness, the dim con-sciousness that much that they said was undeniable; and on the other hand, the apparent wildness and recklessness of their words: and then public opinion began steadily to take its "ply," and to be agreed in condemning them. It soon went farther, and became vehement in reprobating them as scandalous and dangerous pub-

lications. They incensed the Evangelicals by their alleged Romanism, and their unsound views about justification, good works, and
the sacraments; they angered the "two-bottle orthodox" by their
asceticism—the steady men, by their audacity and strong words
—the liberals, by their dogmatic severity; their seriously practical bearing was early disclosed in a tract on "Fasting." But
while they repelled strongly, they attracted strongly; they
touched many consciences, they won many hearts, they opened
new thoughts and hopes to many minds. One of the mischiefs of
the Tracts, and of those sermons at St. Mary's which were the
commentaries on them, was that so many people seemed to like
them and to be struck by them. The gathering storm muttered and
growled for some time at a distance, and men seemed to be taking
time to make up their minds; but it began to lour from early days,
till after various threatenings it broke in a furious article in the
Edinburgh, by Dr. Arnold, on the "Oxford Malignants"; and
the Tract-writers and their friends became, what they long continued to be, the most unpopular and suspected body of men in
the Church, whom everybody was at liberty to insult, both as dishonest and absurd, of whom nothing was too cruel to say, nothing
too ridiculous to believe. It is only equitable to take into account
the unprepared state of the public mind, the surprise and novelty
of even the commonest things when put in a new light, the prejudices which the Tract-writers were thought wantonly to offend
and defy, their militant and uncompromising attitude, where principles were at stake. But considering what these men were known
to be in character and life, what was the emergency and what were
the pressing motives which called for action, and what is thought
of them now that their course is run, it is strange indeed to remember who they were, to whom the courtesies of controversy were
denied, not only by the vulgar herd of pamphleteers, but by men
of ability and position, some of whom had been their familiar
friends. Of course a nickname was soon found for them: the word
"Tractarian" was invented, and Archbishop Whately thought it
worth while, but not successfully, to improve it into "Tractites."
Archbishop Whately, always ingenious, appears to have suspected
that the real but concealed object of the movement was to propagate a secret infidelity; they were "Children of the Mist," or

"Veiled Prophets";[2] and he seriously suggested to a friend who was writing against it,—"this rapidly spreading pestilence,"— to parallel it, in its characteristics and modes of working, with Indian Thuggee.[3]

But these things were of gradual growth. Towards the end of 1834 a question appeared in Oxford interesting to numbers besides Mr. Newman and his friends, which was to lead to momentous consequences. The old, crude ideas of change in the Church had come to appear, even to their advocates, for the present impracticable, and there was no more talk for a long time of schemes which had been in favour two years before. The ground was changed, and a point was now brought forward on the Liberal side, for which a good deal might be plausibly said. This was the requirements of subscription to the Thirty-nine Articles from young men at matriculation; and a strong pamphlet advocating its abolition, with the express purpose of admitting Dissenters, was published by Dr. Hampden, the Bampton Lecturer of two years before.

Oxford had always been one of the great schools of the Church. Its traditions, its tone, its customs, its rules, all expressed or presumed the closest attachment to that way of religion which was specially identified with the Church, in its doctrinal and historical aspect. Oxford was emphatically definite, dogmatic, orthodox, compared even with Cambridge, which had largely favoured the Evangelical school, and had leanings to Liberalism. Oxford, unlike Cambridge, gave notice of its attitude by requiring every one who matriculated to subscribe the Thirty-nine Articles: the theory of its Tutorial system, of its lectures and examinations, implied

2. "Dr. Wilson was mightily pleased with my calling the traditionals the 'Children of the Mist.' The title of 'Veiled Prophets' he thought too severe" (1838), *Life,* ed. 1875, p. 167. Compare "Hints to Transcendentalists for Working Infidel Designs through Tractarianism," a *jeu d'esprit* (1840), ibid., p. 188. "As for the suspicion of secret infidelity, I have said no more than I sincerely feel," ibid., p. 181.

3. "It would be a curious thing if you (the Provost of Oriel) were to bring into your Bampton Lectures a mention of the Thugs. . . . Observe their submissive piety, their faith in long-preserved *tradition,* their regular succession of ordinations to their offices, their *faith* in the sacramental virtue of the consecrated governor; in short, compare our religion with the *Thuggee, putting out of account all those considerations which the traditionists deprecate the discussion of,* and where is the difference?" (1840), ibid., p. 194.

what of late years in the better colleges, though certainly not everywhere, had been realised in fact—a considerable amount of religious and theological teaching. And whatever might have been said originally of the lay character of the University, the colleges, which had become coextensive with the University, were for the most part, in the intention of their founders, meant to educate and support theological students on their foundations for the service of the Church. It became in time the fashion to call them lay institutions: legally they may have been so, but judged by their statutes, they were nearly all of them as ecclesiastical as the Chapter of a Cathedral. And Oxford was the fulcrum from which the theological revival hoped to move the Church. It was therefore a shock and a challenge of no light kind, when not merely the proposal was made to abolish the matriculation subscription with the express object of attracting Dissenters, and to get Parliament to force the change on the University if the University resisted, but the proposal itself was vindicated and enforced in a pamphlet by Dr. Hampden by a definite and precise theory which stopped not short of the position that all creeds and formularies—everything which represented the authority of the teaching Church—however incidentally and temporarily useful, were in their own nature the inventions of a mistaken and corrupt philosophy, and invasions of Christian liberty. This was cutting deep with a vengeance, though the author of the theory seemed alone unable to see it. It went to the root of the whole matter; and if Dr. Hampden was right, there was neither Church nor doctrine worth contending for, except as men contend about the Newtonian or the undulatory theory of light.

No one ought now to affect, as some people used to affect at the time, that the question was of secondary importance, and turned mainly on the special fitness of the Thirty-nine Articles to be offered for the proof of a young man's belief. It was a much more critical question. It was really, however disguised, the question, asked then for the first time, and since finally decided, whether Oxford was to continue to be a school of the Church of England; and it also involved the wider question, what part belief in definite religion should have in higher education. It is speciously said that you have no right to forestall a young man's inquiries and convictions by imposing on him in his early years opinions which to him become prejudices. And if the world consisted simply of individuals, entirely insulated and self-sufficing; if men could be taught anything whatever, without presuming what is believed by those who teach them; and if the attempt to exclude religious prejudice did not necessarily, by the mere force of the attempt, involve the creation of anti-religious prejudice, these reasoners, who try in vain to get out of the conditions which hem them in, might have more to say for themselves. To the men who had made such an effort to restore a living confidence in the Church, the demand implied giving up all that they had done and all that they hoped for. It was not the time for yielding even a clumsy proof of the religious character of the University. And the beginning of a long and doubtful war was inevitable.

A war of pamphlets ensued. By the one side the distinction was strongly insisted on between mere instruction and education, the distinctly religious character of the University education was not perhaps overstated in its theory, but portrayed in stronger colours than was everywhere the fact; and assertions were made, which sound strange in their boldness now, of the independent and constitutional right to self-government in the great University corporations. By the other side, the ordinary arguments were used, about the injustice and mischief of exclusion, and the hurtfulness of tests, especially such tests as the Articles applied to young and ignorant men. Two pamphlets had more than a passing interest: one, by a then unknown writer who signed himself *Rusticus*, and whose name was Mr. F. D. Maurice, defended subscription on the ground that the Articles were signed, not as tests and confessions of faith, but as "conditions of thought," the expressly stated conditions, such as there must be in all teaching, under which the learners are willing to learn and the teacher to teach: and he developed his view at great length, with great wealth of original thought and illustration and much eloquence, but with that fatal want of clearness which, as so often afterwards, came from his struggles to embrace in one large view what appeared opposite aspects of a difficult subject. The other was the pamphlet, already referred to, by Dr. Hampden: and of which the importance arose, not from its conclusions, but from its reasons. Its ground was the distinction which he had argued out at great length in his Bamp-

ton Lectures— the distinction between the "Divine facts" of revelation, and all human interpretations of them and inferences from
them. "Divine facts," he maintained, were of course binding on
all Christians, and in matter of fact were accepted by all who
called themselves Christians, including Unitarians. Human interpretations and inferences—and all Church formularies were such
—were binding on no one but those who had reason to think them
true; and therefore least of all on undergraduates who could not
have examined them. The distinction, when first put forward,
seemed to mean much; at a later time it was explained to mean
very little. But at present its value as a ground of argument against
the old system of the University was thought much of by its author
and his friends. A warning note was at once given that its significance was perceived and appreciated. Mr. Newman, in acknowledging a presentation copy, added words which foreshadowed
much that was to follow. "While I respect," he wrote, "the tone
of piety which the pamphlet displays, I dare not trust myself to
put on paper my feelings about the principles contained in it;
*tending, as they do, in my opinion, to make shipwreck of Chris-
tian faith.* I also lament that, by its appearance, the first step has
been taken towards interrupting that peace and mutual good understanding which has prevailed so long in this place, and which,
if once seriously disturbed, will be succeeded by discussions the
more intractable, because justified in the minds of those who resist innovation by a feeling of imperative duty." "Since that time,"
he goes on in the *Apologia,* where he quotes this letter, "Phaeton
has got into the chariot of the sun."[4] But they were early days
then; and when the Heads of Houses, who the year before had
joined with the great body of the University in a declaration
against the threatened legislation, were persuaded to propose to
the Oxford Convocation the abolition of subscription at matriculation in May 1835, this proposal was rejected by a majority of
five to one.

This large majority was a genuine expression of the sense
of the University. It was not specially a "Tractarian" success,
though most of the arguments which contributed to it came from
men who more or less sympathised with the effort to make a vig-

4. *Apologia,* pp. 131, 132.

orous fight for the Church and its teaching; and it showed that they who had made the effort had touched springs of thought and feeling, and awakened new hopes and interest in those around them, in Oxford, and in the country. But graver events were at hand. Towards the end of the year (1835), Dr. Burton, the Regius Professor of Divinity, suddenly died, still a young man. And Lord Melbourne was induced to appoint as his successor, and as the head of the theological teaching of the University, the writer who had just a second time seemed to lay the axe to the root of all theology; who had just reasserted that he looked upon creeds, and all the documents which embodied the traditional doctrine and collective thought of the Church, as invested by ignorance and prejudice with an authority which was without foundation, and which was misleading and mischievous.

IX

Dr. Hampden

The stage on which what is called the Oxford movement ran through its course had a special character of its own, unlike the circumstances in which other religious efforts had done their work. The scene of Jansenism had been a great capital, a brilliant society, the precincts of a court, the cells of a convent, the studies and libraries of the doctors of the Sorbonne, the council chambers of the Vatican. The scene of Methodism had been English villages and country towns, the moors of Cornwall, and the collieries of Bristol, at length London fashionable chapels. The scene of this new movement was as like as it could be in our modern world to a Greek πόλις, or an Italian self-centered city of the Middle Ages. Oxford stood by itself in its meadows by the rivers, having its relations with all England, but like its sister at Cambridge, living a life of its own, unlike that of any other spot in England, with its privileged powers, and exemptions from the general law, with its special mode of government and police, its usages and tastes and traditions, and even costume, which the rest of England looked at from the outside, much interested but much puzzled, or knew only by transient visits. And Oxford was as proud and jealous of its own ways as Athens or Florence; and like them it had its quaint fashions of polity; its democratic Convocation and its oligarchy; its social ranks; its discipline, severe in theory and usually lax in fact; its self-governed bodies and corporations within itself; its faculties and colleges, like the guilds and "arts" of Florence; its internal rivalries and discords; its "sets" and factions. Like these, too, it professed a special recognition of the supremacy of religion; it claimed to be a home of worship and religious training, *Dominus illuminatio mea*, a claim too often falsified in the habit and tempers of life. It was a small sphere, but it was a conspicuous one; for there was much strong and energetic character, brought out by the aims and conditions of University life; and though moving in a separate orbit, the influence of the famous place over the outside England, though imperfectly understood, was recognised and great. These conditions affected the character of the movement, and of the conflicts which it caused. Oxford claimed to be eminently the guardian of "true religion and sound learning"; and therefore it was eminently the place where religion should be recalled to its purity and strength, and also the place where there ought to be the most vigilant jealousy against the perversions and corruptions of religion. Oxford was a place where every one knew his neighbour, and measured him, and was more or less friendly or repellent; where the customs of life brought men together every day and all day, in converse or discussion; and where every fresh statement or every new step taken furnished endless material for speculation or debate, in common rooms or in the afternoon walk. And for this reason, too, feelings were apt to be more keen and intense and personal than in the larger scenes of life; the man who was disliked or distrusted was so close to his neighbours that he was more irritating than if he had been obscured by a crowd; the man who attracted confidence and kindled enthusiasm, whose voice was continually in men's ears, and whose private conversation and life was something ever new in its sympathy and charm, created in those about him not mere admiration, but passionate friendship, or unreserved discipleship. And these feelings passed from individuals into parties; the small factions of a limited area. Men struck blows and loved and hated in those days in Oxford as they hardly did on the wider stage of London politics or general religious controversy.

The conflicts which for a time turned Oxford into a kind of image of what Florence was in the days of Savonarola, with its nicknames, Puseyites, and Neomaniacs, and High and Dry, counterparts to the *Piagnoni* and *Arrabbiati*, of the older strife, began around a student of retired habits, interested more than was usual at Oxford in abtruse philosophy, and the last person who might be expected to be the occasion of great dissensions in the University. Dr. Hampden was a man who, with no definite intentions of innovating on the received doctrines of the Church—indeed, as his sermons showed, with a full acceptance of them—had taken a very difficult subject for a course of Bampton Lectures, without at all fathoming its depth and reach, and had got into a serious scrape in consequence. Personally he was a man of serious but cold religion, having little sympathy with others, and consequently not able to attract any. His isolation during the whole of his career is remarkable; he attached no one, as Whately or Arnold attached men. His mind, which was a speculative one, was not one, in its own order, of the first class. He had not the grasp nor the subtlety necessary for his task. He had a certain power of statement, but little of co-ordination; he seems not to have had the power of seeing when his ideas were really irreconcilable, and he thought that simply by insisting on his distinctly orthodox statements he not only balanced, but neutralised, and did away with his distinctly unorthodox ones. He had read a good deal of Aristotle and something of the Schoolmen, which probably no one else in Oxford had done except Blanco White; and the temptation of having read what no one else knows anything about sometimes leads men to make an unprofitable use of their special knowledge, which they consider their monopoly.

The creed and the dogmas of the Christian Church are at least in their broad features, not a speculation, but a fact. That not only the Apostles' Creed, but the Nicene and Constantinopolitan Creed, are assumed as facts by the whole of anything that can be called the Church, is as certain as the reception by the same body, and for the same time, of the Scriptures. Not only the Creed, but, up to the sixteenth century, the hierarchy, and not only Creed and hierarchy and Scriptures, but the sacramental idea as expressed in the liturgies, are equally in the same class of facts. Of course it is open to any one to question the genuine origin of any of these great portions of the constitution of the Church; but the Church is so committed to them that he cannot enter on his destructive criticism without having to criticise, not one only, but all these beliefs, and without soon having to face the question whether the whole idea of the Church, as a real and divinely ordained society, with a definite doctrine and belief, is not a delusion, and whether Christianity, whatever it is, is addressed solely to each individual, one by one, to make what he can of it. It need hardly be said that within the limits of what the Church is committed to there is room for very wide differences of opinion; it is also true that these limits have, in different times of the Church, been illegitimately and mischievously narrowed by prevailing opinions, and by documents and formularies respecting it. But though we may claim not to be bound by the Augsburg Confession, or by the Lambeth articles, or the Synod of Dort, or the Bull *Unigenitus,* it does not follow that, if there is a Church at all, there is no more binding authority in the theology of the Nicene and Athanasian Creeds. And it is the province of the divine who believes in a Church at all, and in its office to be the teacher and witness of religious truth, to distinguish between the infinitely varying degrees of authority with which professed representations of portions of this truth are propounded for acceptance. It may be difficult or impossible to agree on a theory of inspiration; but that the Church doctrine of some kind of special inspiration of Scripture is part of Christianity is, unless Christianity be a dream, certain. No one can reasonably doubt, with history before him, that the answer of the Christian Church was, the first time the question was asked, and has continued to be through ages of controversy, *against* Arianism, *against* Socinianism, *against* Pelagianism, *against* Zwinglianism. It does not follow that the Church has settled everything, or that there are not hundreds of questions which it is vain and presumptuous to attempt to settle by any alleged authority.

Dr. Hampden was in fact unexceptionably, even rigidly orthodox in his acceptance of Church doctrine and Church creeds. He had published a volume of sermons containing, among other things, an able statement of the Scriptural argument for the doctrine of the Trinity, and an equally able defence of the Athanasian Creed. But he felt that there are formularies which may be only the interpretations of doctrine and inferences from Scripture of a particular time or set of men; and he was desirous of putting into their proper place the authority of such formularies. His object was to put an interval between them and the Scriptures from which they professed to be derived, and to prevent them from claiming the command over faith and conscience which was due only to the authentic evidences of God's revelation. He wished to make room for a deeper sense of the weight of Scripture. He proposed to himself the same thing which was aimed at by the German divines, Arndt, Calixtus, and Spener, when they rose up against the grinding oppression which Lutheran dogmatism had raised on its *Symbolical Books,*[1] and which had come to outdo the worst extravagances of scholasticism. This seems to have been his object—a fair and legitimate one. But in arguing against investing the Thirty-nine Articles with an authority which did not belong to them, he unquestionably, without seeing what he was doing, went much farther—where he never meant to go. In fact, he so stated his argument that he took in with the Thirty-nine Articles every expression of collective belief, every document, however venerable, which the Church had sanctioned from the first. Strangely enough, without observing it, he took in —what he meant to separate by a wide interval from what he called dogma—the doctrine of the infallible authority and sufficiency of Scripture. In denying the worth of the *consensus* and immemorial judgment of the Church, he cut from under him the claim to that which he accepted as the source and witness of "divine facts." He did not mean to do this, or to do many other things; but from want of clearness of head, he certainly, in these writings which were complained of, did it. He was, in temper and habit, too desirous to be "orthodox," as Whately feared, to accept in its consequences his own theory. The theory which he put forward in his Bampton Lectures, and on which he founded his plan of comprehension in his pamphlet on Dissent, left nothing standing but the authority of the letter of Scripture. All else—right or wrong as it might be—was "speculation," "human inference," "dogma." With perfect consistency, he did not pretend to take even the Creeds out of this category. But the truth was, he did not consciously mean all that he said; and when keener and more powerful and more theological minds pointed out with relentless accuracy what he *had said,* he was profuse and overflowing with explanations, which showed how little he had perceived the drift of his words. There is not the least reason to doubt the sincerity of these explanations; but at

1. See Pusey's *Theology of Germany* (1828), p. 18 *sqq.*

the same time they showed the unfitness of a man who had so to explain away his own speculations to be the official guide and teacher of the clergy. The criticisms on his language, and the objections to it, were made before these explanations were given; and though he gave them, he was furious with those who called for them, and he never for a moment admitted that there was anything seriously wrong or mistaken in what he had said. To those who pointed out the meaning and effect of his words and theories, he replied by the assertion of his personal belief. If words mean anything he had said that neither Unitarians nor any one else could get behind the bare letter, and what he called "facts," of Scripture, which all equally accepted in good faith; and that therefore there was no reason for excluding Unitarians as long as they accepted the "facts." But when it was pointed out that this reasoning reduced all belief in the realities behind the bare letter to the level of personal and private opinion, he answered by saying that he valued supremely the Creeds and Articles and by giving a statement of the great Christian doctrines which he held, and which the Church taught. But he never explained what their authority could be with any one but himself. There might be interpretations and inferences from Scripture, by the hundred or the thousand, but no one certain and authoritative one; none that warranted an organised Church, much more a Catholic and Apostolic Church, founded on the assumption of this interpretation being the one true faith, the one truth of the Bible. The point was brought out forcibly in a famous pamphlet written by Mr. Newman, though without his name, called "Elucidations of Dr. Hampden's Theological Statements." This pamphlet was a favourite object of attack on the part of Dr. Hampden's supporters as a flagrant instance of unfairness and garbled extracts. No one, they said, ever read the Bampton Lectures, but took their estimate of the work from Mr. Newman's quotations. Extracts are often open to the charge of unfairness, and always to suspicion. But in this case there was no need of unfairness. Dr. Hampden's theory lay on the very surface of his Bampton Lectures and pamphlet; and any unbiassed judge may be challenged to read these works of his, and say whether the extracts in the "Elucidations" do not adequately represent Dr. Hampden's statements and arguments, and whether the comments on them are forced or strained. They do not represent his explanations, for the explanations had not been given; and when the explanations came, though they said many things which showed that Dr. Hampden did not mean to be unorthodox and unevangelical, but only anti-scholastic and anti-Roman, they did not unsay a word which he had said. And what this was, what had been Dr. Hampden's professed theological theory up to the time when the University heard the news of his appointment, the "Elucidations" represent as fairly as any adverse statement can represent the subject of its attack.

In quieter times such an appointment might have passed with nothing more than a paper controversy or protest, or more probably without more than conversational criticism. But these were not quiet and unsuspicious times. There was reason for disquiet. It was fresh in men's minds what language and speculation like that of the Bampton Lectures had come to in the case of Whately's intimate friend, Blanco White. The unquestionable hostility of Whately's school to the old ideas of the Church had roused alarm and a strong spirit of resistance in Churchmen. Each party was on the watch, and there certainly was something at stake for both parties. Coupled with some recent events, and with the part which Dr. Hampden had taken on the subscription question, the appointment naturally seemed significant. Probably it was not so significant as it seemed on the part at least of Lord Melbourne, who had taken pains to find a fit man. Dr. Hampden was said to have been recommended by Bishop Copleston, and not disallowed by Archbishop Howley. In the University, up to this time, there had been no authoritative protest against Dr. Hampden's writings. And there were not many Liberals to choose from. In the appointment there is hardly sufficient ground to blame Lord Melbourne. But the outcry against it at Oxford, when it came, was so instantaneous, so strong, and so unusual, that it might have warned Lord Melbourne that he had been led into a mistake, out of which it would be wise to seek at least a way of escape. Doubtless it was a strong measure for the University to protest as it did; but it was also a strong measure, at least in those days, for a Minister of the Crown to force so extremely unacceptable a Regius Professor of Divinity on a great University. Dr. Hampden offered to resign; and there would have been plenty of opportunities to compensate him for his sacrifice of a post which could only be a painful one. But the temper of both sides was up. The remonstrances from Oxford were treated with something like contempt, and the affair was hurried through till there was no retreating; and Dr. Hampden became Regius Professor.

Mr. Palmer has recorded how various efforts were made to neutralise the effect of the appointment. But the Heads of Houses, though angry, were cautious. They evaded the responsibility of stating Dr. Hampden's unsound positions; but to mark their distrust, brought in a proposal to deprive him of his vote in the choice of Select Preachers till the University should otherwise determine. It was defeated in Convocation by the veto of the two Proctors (March 1836), who exercised their right with the full approval of Dr. Hampden's friends, and the indignation of the large majority of the University. But it was not unfairly used: it could have only a suspending effect, of which no one had a right to complain; and when new Proctors came into office, the proposal was introduced again, and carried (May 1836) by 474 to 94. The liberal minority had increased since the vote on subscription, and Dr. Hampden went on with his work as if nothing had happened. The attempt was twice made to rescind the vote: first, after the outcry about the Ninetieth Tract and the contest about the Poetry Professorship, by a simple repeal, which was rejected by 334 to 219 (June 1842); and next, indirectly by a statute enlarging the Professorship's powers over Divinity degrees, which was also rejected by 341 to 21 (May 1844). From first to last, these things and others were the unfortunate incidents of an unfortunate appointment.

The "persecution of Dr. Hampden" has been an unfailing subject of reproach to the party of the Oxford movement, since the days when the *Edinburgh Review* held them up to public scorn and hatred in an article of strange violence. They certainly had their full share in the opposition to him, and in the measures by which that opposition was carried out. But it would be the greatest mistake to suppose that in this matter they stood alone. All in the University at this time, except a small minority, were of one mind, Heads of Houses and country parsons, Evangelicals and High Churchmen—all who felt that the grounds of

a definite belief were seriously threatened by Dr. Hampden's
speculations. All were angry at the appointment; all were agreed
that something ought to be done to hinder the mischief of it.
In this matter Mr. Newman and his friends were absolutely at
one with everybody round them, with those who were soon to
be their implacable opponents. Whatever deeper view they might
have of the evil which had been done by the appointment, and
however much graver and more permanent their objections to it,
they were responsible only as the whole University was responsible for what was done against Dr. Hampden. It was convenient afterwards to single them out, and to throw this responsibility and the odium of it on them alone; and when they came
under the popular ban, it was forgotten that Dr. Gilbert, the
Principal of Brasenose, Dr. Symons, the Warden of Wadham,
Dr. Faussett, afterwards the denouncer of Dr. Pusey, Mr.
Vaughan Thomas, and Mr. Hill of St. Edmund Hall, were quite
as forward at the time as Dr. Pusey and Mr. Newman in protest-
ing against Dr. Hampden, and in the steps to make their protest
effective. Mr. Palmer, in his *Narrative*,[2] anxious to dissociate
himself from the movement under Mr. Newman's influence, has
perhaps underrated the part taken by Mr. Newman and Dr.
Pusey; for they, at any rate, did most of the argumentative work.
But as far as personal action goes, it is true, as he says, that
the "movement against Dr. Hampden was not guided by the
Tract-writers." "The condemnation of Dr. Hampden, then, was
not carried by the Tract-writers; it was carried by the *independent*
body of the University. The fact is that, had those writers taken
any leading part, the measure would have been a failure, for the
number of their friends at that time was a *very small proportion*
to the University at large, and there was a general feeling of distrust in the soundness of their views."

We are a long way from those days in time, and still more
in habits and sentiment; and a manifold and varied experience
has taught most of us some lessons against impatience and violent
measures. But if we put ourselves back equitably into the ways
of thinking prevalent then, the excitement about Dr. Hampden
will not seem so unreasonable or so unjustifiable as it is some-

2. *Narrative,* pp. 29, 30, ed. 1843; p. 131, ed. 1883.

times assumed to be. The University legislation, indeed, to which it led was poor and petty, doing small and annoying things, because the University rulers dared not commit themselves to definite charges. But, in the first place, the provocation was great on the part of the Government in putting into the chief theological chair an unwelcome man who could only save his orthodoxy by making his speculations mean next to nothing—whose *prima facie* unguarded and startling statements were resolved into truisms put in a grand and obscure form. And in the next place, it was assumed in those days to be the most natural and obvious thing in the world to condemn unsound doctrine, and to exclude unsound teachers. The principle was accepted as indisputable, however slack might have been in recent times the application of it. That it was accepted, not on one side only, but on all, was soon to be shown by the subsequent course of events. No one suffered more severely and more persistently from its application than the Tractarians; no one was more ready to apply it to them than Dr. Hampden with his friends; no one approved and encouraged its vigorous enforcement against them more than Dr. Whately. The idle distinction set up, that they were not merely unsound but dishonest, was a more insolent pretext to save trouble in argument, and to heighten the charge against them; no one could seriously doubt that they wrote in good faith as much as Dr. Whately or Dr. Faussett. But unless acts like Dr. Pusey's suspension, and the long proscription that went on for years after it, were mere instances of vindictive retaliation, the reproach of persecution must be shared by all parties then, and by none more than by the party which in general terms most denounced it. Those who think the Hampden agitation unique in its injustice ought to ask themselves what their party would have done if at any time between 1836 and 1843 Mr. Newman had been placed in Dr. Hampden's seat.

People in our days mean by religious persecution what happens when the same sort of repressive policy is applied to a religious party as is applied to vaccination recusants, or to the "Peculiar People." All religious persecution, from the days of Socrates, has taken a legal form, and justified itself on legal grounds. It is the action of authority, or of strong social judgments backed by authority, against a set of opinions, or the expression of them in word or act—usually innovating opinions, but not by any means necessarily such. The disciples of M. Monod, the "Momiers" of Geneva, were persecuted by the Liberals of Geneva, not because they broke away from the creed of Calvin, but because they adhered to it. The word is not properly applied to the incidental effects in the way of disadvantage, resulting from some broad constitutional settlement—from the government of the Church being Episcopal and not Presbyterian, or its creed Nicene and not Arian—any more than it is persecution for a nation to change its government, or for a legitimist to have to live under a republic, or for a Christian to have to live in an infidel state, though persecution may follow from these conditions. But the *privilegium* passed against Dr. Hampden was an act of persecution, though a mild one compared with what afterwards fell on his opponents with his full sanction. Persecution is the natural impulse, in those who think a certain thing right and important or worth guarding, to disable those who, thinking it wrong, are trying to discredit and upset it, and to substitute something different. It implies a state of war, and the resort to the most available weapons to inflict damage on those who are regarded as rebellious and dangerous. These weapons were formidable enough once: they are not without force still. But in its mildest form—personal disqualification or proscription—it is a disturbance which only war justifies. It may, of course, make itself odious by its modes of proceeding, by meanness and shabbiness and violence, by underhand and ignoble methods of misrepresentation and slander, or by cruelty and plain injustice; and then the odium of these things fairly falls upon it. But it is very hard to draw the line between conscientious repression, feeling itself bound to do what is possible to prevent mischief, and what those who are opposed, if they are the weaker party, of course call persecution.

If persecution implies a state of war in which one side is stronger, and the other weaker, it is hardly a paradox to say that (1) no one has a right to complain of persecution as such, apart from odious accompaniments, any more than of superior numbers or hard blows in battle; and (2) that every one has a right to take advantage and make the most of being persecuted, by appeals to sympathy and the principle of doing as you would be done by. No one likes to be accused of persecution, and few people like to give up the claim to use it, if necessary. But no one can help observing in the course of events the strange way in which, in almost all cases, the "wheel comes full circle." Δράσαντι παθεῖν— *Chi la fa, l' aspetti*,[3] are some of the expressions of Greek awe and Italian shrewdness representing the experience of the world on this subject, on a large scale and a small. Protestants and Catholics, Churchmen and Nonconformists, have all in their turn made full proof of what seems like a law of action and reaction. Except in cases beyond debate, cases where no justification is possible, the note of failure is upon this mode of repression. Providence, by the visible Nemesis which it seems always to bring round, by the regularity with which it has enforced the rule that infliction and suffering are bound together and in time duly change places, seems certainly and clearly to have declared against it. It may be that no innovating party has a right to complain of persecution; but the question is not for them. It is for those who have the power, and who are tempted to think that they have the call, to persecute. It is for them to consider whether it is right, or wise, or useful for their cause; whether it is agreeable to what seems the leading of Providence to have recourse to it.

3. Δράσαντι παθεῖν Τριγέρων μῦθος τάδε φωνεῖ. Æsch. *Choeph.* 310. Italian proverb, in Landucci, *Diario Fiorentino*, 1513, p. 343.

X

Growth
of the Movement
1835–1840

By the end of 1835, the band of friends, whom great fears and great hopes for the Church had united, and others who sympathised with them both within and outside the University, had grown into what those who disliked them naturally called a party. The Hampden controversy, though but an episode in the history of the movement, was an important one, and undoubtedly gave a great impulse to it. Dr. Hampden's attitude and language seemed to be its justification—a palpable instance of what the Church had to expect. And in this controversy, though the feeling against Dr. Hampden's views was so widely shared, and though the majority which voted against him was a very mixed one, and contained some who hoped that the next time they were called to vote it might be against the Tractarians, yet the leaders of the movement had undertaken the responsibility, conspicuously and almost alone, of pointing out definitely and argumentatively the objections to Dr. Hampden's teaching. The number of Mr. Newman's friends might be, as Mr. Palmer says, insignificant, but it was they who had taken the trouble to understand and give expression to the true reasons for alarm.[1] Even in this hasty and imperfect way, the discussion revealed to many how much deeper and more serious the treatment of the subject was in the hands of Mr. Newman and Dr. Pusey compared with the ordinary criticisms on Dr. Hampden. He had learned in too subtle a school

1. "I answered, the person whom we were opposing had committed himself in writing, and we ought to commit ourselves too."—*Apologia,* p. 143.

to be much touched by the popular exceptions to his theories, however loudly expressed. The mischief was much deeper. It was that he had, unconsciously, no doubt, undermined the foundation of definite Christian belief, and had resolved it into a philosophy, so-called scholastic, which was now exploded. It was the sense of the perilous issues to which this diluted form of Blanco White's speculations, so recklessly patronised by Whately, was leading theological teaching in the University, which opened the eyes of many to the meaning of the movement, and brought some fresh friends to its side.

There was no attempt to form a party, or to proselytise; there was no organisation, no distinct and recognised party marks. "I would not have it called a party," writes Dr. Newman in the *Apologia*. But a party it could not help being: quietly and spontaneously it had grown to be what community of ideas, aims, and sympathies, naturally, and without blame, leads men to become. And it had acquired a number of recognised nicknames, to friends and enemies the sign of growing concentration. For the questions started in the Tracts and outside them became of increasing interest to the more intelligent men who had finished their University course and were preparing to enter into life, the Bachelors and younger Masters of Arts. One by one they passed from various states of mind—alienation, suspicion, fear, indifference, blank ignorance—into a consciousness that something beyond the mere commonplace of religious novelty and eccentricity, of which there had been a good deal recently, was before them; that doctrines and statements running counter to the received religious language of the day, doctrines about which, in confident prejudice, they had perhaps bandied about off-hand judgments, had more to say for themselves than was thought at first; that the questions thus raised drove them in on themselves, and appealed to their honesty and seriousness; and that, at any rate, in the men who were arresting so much attention, however extravagant their teaching might be called, there was a remarkable degree of sober and reserved force, an earnestness of conviction which could not be doubted, an undeniable and subtle power of touching souls and attracting sympathies. One by one, and in many different ways, these young men went through various stages of curiosity, of surprise, of perplexity, of doubt, of misgiving, of interest; some were frightened, and wavered, and drew back more or less reluctantly; others, in spite of themselves, in spite of opposing influences, were led on step by step, hardly knowing whither, by a spell which they could not resist, of intellectual, or still more, moral pressure. Some found their old home teaching completed, explained, lighted up, by that of the new school. Others, shocked at first at hearing the old watchwords and traditions of their homes decried and put aside, found themselves, when they least expected it, passing from the letter to the spirit, from the technical and formal theory to the wide and living truth. And thus, though many of course held aloof, and not a few became hostile, a large number, one by one, some rapidly, others slowly, some unreservedly, others with large and jealous reserves, more and more took in the leading idea of the movement, accepted the influence of its chiefs, and looked to them for instruction and guidance. As it naturally happens, when a number of minds are drawn together by a common and strong interest, some men, by circumstances, or by strength of conviction, or by the mutual affinities of tastes and character, came more and more into direct personal and intimate relations with the leaders, took service, as it were, under them, and prepared to throw themselves into their plans of work. Others, in various moods, but more independent, more critical, more disturbed about consequences, or unpersuaded on special points, formed a kind of fringe of friendly neutrality about the more thoroughgoing portion of the party. And outside of these were thoughtful and able men, to whom the whole movement, with much that was utterly displeasing and utterly perplexing, had the interest of being a break-up of stagnation and dull indolence in a place which ought to have the highest spiritual and intellectual aims; who, whatever repelled them, could not help feeling that great ideas, great prospects, a new outburst of bold thought, a new effort of moral purpose and force, had disturbed the old routine; could not help being fascinated, if only as by a spectacle, by the strange and unwonted teaching, which partly made them smile, partly perhaps permanently disgusted them, but which also, they could not deny, spoke in a language more fearless, more pathetic, more subtle, and yet more human, than they had heard from the religious teachers of the day. And thus the circle of persons interested in the Tracts, of persons who sympathised with their views, of persons who more and more gave a warm and earnest adherence to them, was gradually extended in the University—and, in time, in the country also. The truth was that the movement, in its many sides, had almost monopolised for the time both the intelligence and the highest religious earnestness of the University,[2] and either in curiosity or inquiry, in approval or in condemnation, all that was deepest and most vigorous, all that was most refined, most serious, most high-toned, and most promising in Oxford was drawn to the issues which it raised. It is hardly too much to say that wherever men spoke seriously of the grounds and prospects of religion, in Oxford, or in Vacation reading-parties, in their walks and social meetings, in their studies or in common-room, the "Tractarian" doctrines, whether assented to or laughed at, deplored or fiercely denounced, were sure to come to the front. All subjects in discussion seemed to lead up to them—art and poetry, Gothic architecture and German romance and painting, the philosophy of language, and the novels of Walter Scott and Miss Austen, Coleridge's transcendentalism and Bishop Butler's practical wisdom, Plato's ideas and Aristotle's analysis. It was difficult to keep them out of lecture-rooms and examinations for Fellowships.

But in addition to the intrinsic interest of the questions and discussions which the movement opened, personal influence played a great and decisive part in it. As it became a party, it had chiefs. It was not merely as leaders of thought but as teachers with their disciples, as friends with friends, as witnesses and examples of high self-rule and refined purity and goodness, that the chiefs whose names were in all men's mouths won the hearts and trust of so many, in the crowds that stood about them. Foremost, of course, ever since he had thrown himself into it in 1835, was Dr. Pusey. His position, his dignified office, his learning, his solidity and seriousness of character, his high standard of religious life, the charm of his charity, and the sweetness of his temper naturally gave him the first place in the movement

2. "I very much doubt between Oxford and Cambridge for my boy. Oxford, which I should otherwise prefer, on many accounts, has at present two-thirds of the steady-reading men, Rabbinists, *i.e.* Puseyites." But this was probably an exaggeration.—Whately's *Life;* letter of Oct. 1838, p. 163 (ed. 1875).

in Oxford and the world. It came to be especially associated with him. Its enemies fastened on it a nickname from his name, and this nickname, partly from a greater smoothness of sound, partly from an odd suggestion of something funny in it, came more into use than others; and the terms *Puseismus, Puséisme, Puseista* found their way into German lecture-halls and Paris salons and remote convents and police offices in Italy and Sicily; indeed, in the shape of πουζεισμός it might be lighted on in a Greek newspaper. Dr. Pusey was a person who commanded the utmost interest and reverence; he was more in communication with the great world outside than Oxford people generally, and lived much in retirement from Oxford society; but to all interested in the movement he was its representative and highest authority. He and Mr. Newman had the fullest confidence in one another, though conscious at times of not perfect agreement; yet each had a line of his own, and each of them was apt to do things out of his own head. Dr. Pusey was accessible to all who wished to see him; but he did not encourage visits which wasted time. And the person who was preeminently, not only before their eyes, but within their reach in the ordinary intercourse of man with man, was Mr. Newman. Mr. Newman, who lived in College in the ordinary way of a resident Fellow, met other university men, older or younger, on equal terms. As time went on, a certain wonder and awe gathered round him. People were a little afraid of him; but the fear was in themselves, not created by any intentional stiffness or coldness on his part. He did not try to draw men to him, he was no proselytiser; he shrank with fear and repugnance from the character—it was an invasion of the privileges of the heart.[3] But if men came to him, he was accessible; he allowed his friends to bring their friends to him, and met them more than half-way. He was impatient of mere idle worldliness, of conceit and impertinence, of men who gave themselves airs; he was very impatient of pompous and solemn emptiness. But he was very patient with those whom he believed to sympathise with what was nearest his heart; no one, probably, of his power and penetration and sense of the absurd, was ever so

3. "The sagacious and aspiring man of the world, the scrutiniser of the heart, the conspirator against its privileges and rights."—*Prophetical Office of the Church,* p. 132.

ready to comply with the two demands which a witty prelate proposed to put into the examination in the Consecration Service of Bishops: "Wilt thou answer thy letters?" "Wilt thou suffer fools gladly?" But courteous, affable, easy as he was, he was a keen trier of character; he gauged, and men left that he gauged, their motives, their reality and soundness of purpose; he let them see, if they at all came into his intimacy, that if *they* were not, *he,* at any rate, was in the deepest earnest. And at an early period, in a memorable sermon,[4] the vivid impression of which at the time still haunts the recollection of some who heard it, he gave warning to his friends and to those whom his influence touched, that no child's play lay before them; that they were making, it might be without knowing it, the "Ventures of Faith." But feeling that he had much to say, and that a university was a place for the circulation and discussion of ideas, he let himself be seen and known and felt, publicly and in private. He had his breakfast parties and his evening gatherings. His conversation ranged widely, marked by its peculiar stamp—entire ease, unstudied perfection of apt and clean-cut words, unexpected glimpses of a sure and piercing judgment. At times, at more private meetings, the violin, which he knew how to touch, came into play.

He had great gifts for leadership. But as a party chief he was also deficient in some of the qualities which make a successful one. His doctrine of the Church had the disadvantage of an apparently intermediate and ambiguous position, refusing the broad, intelligible watchwords and reasonings of popular religionism. It was not without clearness and strength; but such a position naturally often leads to what seem over-subtle modes of argument, seemingly over-subtle because deeper and more original than the common ones; and he seemed sometimes to want sobriety in his use of dialectic weapons, which he wielded with such force and effect. Over-subtlety in the leader of a party tends to perplex friends and give a handle to opponents. And with all his confidence in his cause, and also in his power and his call to use it, he had a curious shyness and self-distrust as to his own way of doing what he had to do; he was afraid of "wilfulness," of too great reliance on intellect. He had long been accustomed to

4. *Parochial Sermons,* 4: 20. Feb. 1836.

observe and judge himself, and while conscious of his force, he was fully alive to the drawbacks, moral and intellectual, which wait on the highest powers. When attacks were made on him by authorities, as in the case of the Tract No. 90, his more eager friends thought him too submissive; they would have liked a more combative temper and would not accept his view that confidence in him was lost, because it might be shaken.[5] But if he bent before official authority the disapproval of friends was a severer trouble. Most tender in his affections, most trustful in his confidence, craving for sympathy, it came like a shock and chill when things did not go right between himself and his friends. He was too sensitive under such disapproval for a successful party chief. The true party leader takes these things as part of that tiresome human stupidity and perverseness with which he must make his account. Perhaps they sting for the moment, but he brushes them away and goes forward, soon forgetting them. But with Mr. Newman, his cause was identified with his friendships and even his family affections. And as a leader, he was embarrassed by the keenness with which he sympathised with the doubts and fears of friends; want of sympathy and signs of distrust darkened the prospect of the future; they fell like a blight on his stores of hope, never over-abundant; they tempted him, not to assert himself, but to throw up the game as convicted of unfitness, and retire for good and all to his books and silence. "Let them," he seemed to say, "have their way, as they will not let me have mine; they have the right to take theirs, only not to make me take it." In spite of his enthusiasm and energy, his unceasing work, his occasional bursts of severe punishment inflicted on those who provoked him, there was always present this keen sensitiveness, the source of so much joy and so much pain. He would not have been himself without it. But he would have been a much more powerful and much more formidable combatant

5. See J. B. Mozley, *Letters,* pp. 114, 115. "Confidence in me was lost, but I had already lost confidence in myself." This, to a friend like J. B. Mozley, seemed exaggeration. "Though admiring the letter [to the Vice-Chancellor] I confess, for my own part, I think a general confession of humility was irrelevant to the present occasion, the question being simply on a point of theological interpretation. I have always had a prejudice against general confessions." Mozley plainly thought Newman's attitude too meek: he would have liked something more spirited and pugnacious.

if he had cared less for what his friends felt, and followed more unhesitatingly his own line and judgment. This keen sensitiveness made him more quickly alive than other people to all that lay round him and before; it made him quicker to discern danger and disaster; it led him to give up hope and to retire from the contest long before he had a right to do so. The experience of later years shows that he had despaired too soon. Such delicate sensitiveness, leading to impatience, was not capable of coping with the rough work involved in the task of reform, which he had undertaken.

All this time the four o'clock sermons at St. Mary's were always going on. But, besides, these, he anticipated a freedom—familiar now, but unknown then—of public lecturing. In Advent and after Easter a company, never very large, used to gather on a week-day afternoon in Adam de Brome's Chapel—the old Chapel of "Our Lady of Littlemore"—to hear him lecture on some theological subject. It is a dark, dreary appendage to St. Mary's on the north side, in which Adam de Brome, Edward II's almoner, and the founder of Oriel College, is supposed to lie, beneath an unshapely tomb, covered by a huge slab of Purbeck marble, from which the brass has been stripped. The place is called a chapel, but is more like a court or place of business, for which, indeed, it was used in the old days by one of the Faculties of the House of Convocation, which held its assemblies there. At the end is a high seat and desk for the person presiding, and an enclosure and a table for officials below him; and round the rest of the dingy walls run benches fixed to the wall, dingy as the walls themselves. But it also had another use. On occasions of a university sermon, a few minutes before it began, the Heads of Houses assembled, as they still assemble, in the chapel, ranging themselves on the benches round the walls. The Vice-Chancellor has his seat on one side, the preacher, with the two Proctors below him, sits opposite; and there all sit in their robes, more or less grand, according to the day, till the beadle comes to announce that it is time to form the procession into church. This desolate place Mr. Newman turned into his lecture-room; in it he delivered the lectures which afterwards became the volume on the *Prophetical Character of the Church,* or *Romanism and Popular Protestantism;* the lectures which formed the volume on *Justification;*

132

those on *Antichrist,* and on *Rationalism and the Canon of Scripture,* which afterwards became Nos 83 and 85 of the *Tracts for the Times.*[6] The force, the boldness, the freedom from the trammels of commonplace, the breadth of view and grasp of the subject which marked those lectures, may be seen in them still. But it is difficult to realise now the interest with which they were heard at the time by the first listeners to that clear and perfectly modulated voice, opening to them fresh and original ways of regarding questions which seemed worn out and exhausted. The volumes which grew out of the Adam de Brome lectures were some of the most characteristic portions of the theological literature of the early movement. They certainly greatly influenced the course of thought in it, and some of its most serious issues.

The movement was not one of mere opinion. It took two distinct though connected lines. It was, on the one hand, theological; on the other, resolutely practical. Theologically, it dealt with great questions of religious principle—What is the Church? Is it a reality or a mode of speech? On what grounds does it rest? How may it be known? Is it among us? How is it to be discriminated from its rivals or counterfeits? What is its essential constitution? What does it teach? What are its shortcomings? Does it need reform? But, on the other hand, the movement was marked by its deep earnestness on the practical side of genuine Christian life. Very early in the movement (1833) a series of sketches of primitive Christian life appeared in the *British Magazine*—afterwards collected under the title of the *Church of the Fathers* (1840)—to remind people who were becoming interested in ancient and patristic theology that, besides the doctrines to be found in the vast folios of the Fathers, there were to be sought in them and laid to heart the temptations and trials, the aspirations and moral possibilities of actual life, "the tone and modes of thought, the habits and manners of the early times of the Church." The note struck in the first of Mr. Newman's published sermons—"Holiness necessary for future blessedness"—was never allowed to be out of mind. The movement was, above all, a moral one; it was nothing, allowed to be nothing, if it was

6. *Romanism and Popular Protestantism,* from 1834 to 1836, published March 1837; *Justification,* after Easter 1837, published March 1838; *Canon of Scripture,* published May 1838; *Antichrist,* published June 1838.

not this.[7] Seriousness, reverence, the fear of insincere words and unsound professions, were essential in the character, which alone it would tolerate in those who made common cause with it.

Its ethical tendency was shown in two things, which were characteristic of it. One was the increased care of the Gospels, and study of them, compared with other parts of the Bible. Evangelical theology had dwelt upon the work of Christ, and laid comparatively little stress on His example, or the picture left us of His Personality and Life. It regarded the Epistles of St. Paul as the last word of the Gospel message. People who can recall the popular teaching, which was spoken of then as "sound" and "faithful," and "preaching Christ," can remember how the Epistles were ransacked for texts to prove the "sufficiency of Scripture" or the "right of private judgment," or the distinction between justification and sanctification, while the Gospel narrative was imperfectly studied and was felt to be much less interesting. The movement made a great change. The great Name stood no longer for an abstract symbol of doctrine, but for a living Master, who could teach as well as save. And not forgetting whither He had gone and what He was, the readers of Scripture now sought Him eagerly in those sacred records, where we can almost see and hear His going in and out among men. It was a change in the look and use of Scripture, which some can still look back to as an epoch in their religious history. The other feature was the increased and practical sense of the necessity of self-discipline, of taking real trouble with one's self to keep thoughts and wishes in order, to lay the foundation of habits, to acquire the power of self-control. Deeply fixed in the mind of the teachers, this serious governance of life, the direction and purification of its aims, laid strong hold on the consciences of those who accepted their teaching. This training was not showy; it was sometimes austere, even extravagantly austere; but it was true, and enduring,

7. Cf. *Lyra Apostolica*, No. 65:

> *Thou* to wax fierce
> In the cause of the Lord!
>
> .   .   .   .
>
> Anger and zeal,
> And the joy of the brave,
> Who bade *thee* to feel,
>   Sin's slave?

and it issued often a steady and unconscious elevation of the religious character. How this character was fed and nurtured and encouraged—how, too, it was frankly warned of its dangers, may be seen in those *Parochial Sermons* at St. Mary's, under whose inspiration it was developed, and which will always be the best commentary on the character thus formed. Even among those who ultimately parted from the movement, with judgment more or less unfavourable to its theology and general line, it left, as if uneffaceable, this moral stamp; this value for sincerity and simplicity of feeling and life, this keen sense of the awfulness of things unseen. There was something *sui generis* in the profoundly serious, profoundly reverent tone, about everything that touched religion in all who had ever come strongly under its influence.

Of course the party soon had the faults of a party, real and imputed.[8] Is it conceivable that there should ever have been a religious movement, which has not provoked smiles from those outside of it, and which has not lent itself to caricature? There were weaker members of it, and headstrong ones, and imitative ones; there were grotesque and absurd ones; some were deeper, some shallower; some liked it for its excitement, and some liked it for its cause; there were those who were for pushing on, and those who were for holding back; there were men of combat, and men of peace; there were those whom it made conceited and self-important, and those who it drove into seriousness, anxiety, and retirement. But, whatever faults it had, a pure and high spirit ruled in it; there were no disloyal members, and there were none who sought their own in it, or thought of high things for themselves in joining it. It was this whole-heartedness, this supreme reverence for moral goodness, more even than the great ability of the leaders, and in spite of mistakes and failures, which gave its cohesion and its momentum to the movement in its earlier stages.

The state of feeling and opinion among Churchmen towards the end of 1835, two years after the Tracts had begun, is thus sketched by one who was anxiously observing it, in the preface to the second volume of the Tracts (November 1835).

8. This weak side was portrayed with severity in a story published by Mr. Newman in 1848, after he left the English Church—*Loss and Gain.*

In completing the second volume of a publication, to which the circumstances of the day have given rise, it may be right to allude to a change which has taken place in them since the date of its commencement. At that time, in consequence of long security, the attention of members of our Church had been but partially engaged, in ascertaining the grounds of their adherence to it: but the imminent peril to all which is dear to them which has since been confessed, has naturally turned their thoughts that way, and obliged them to defend it on one or other of the principles which are usually put forward in its behalf. Discussions have thus been renewed in various quarters, on points which had long remained undisturbed; and though numbers continue undecided in opinion, or take up a temporary position in some one of the hundred middle points which may be assumed between the two main theories in which the question issues; and others, again, have deliberately entrenched themselves in the modern or ultra-Protestant alternative; yet, on the whole, there has been much hearty and intelligent adoption, and much respectful study, of those more primitive views maintained by our great Divines. As the altered state of public information and opinion has a necessary bearing on the efforts of those who desire to excite attention to the subject (in which number the writers of these Tracts are to be included), it will not be inappropriate briefly to state in this place what it is conceived is the present position of the great body of Churchmen with reference to it.

While we have to be thankful for the sounder and more accurate language, which is now very generally adopted among well-judging men on ecclesiastical subjects, we must beware of over-estimating what has been done, and so becoming sanguine in our hopes of success, or slacking our exertions to secure it. Many more persons, doubtless, have taken up a profession of the main doctrine in question, that, namely, of the one Catholic and Apostolic Church, that fully enter into it. This was to be expected, it being the peculiarity of all religious teaching, that words are imparted before ideas. A child learns his Creed or Catechism before he understands it; and in beginning any deep subject we are all but children to the end of our lives. The instinctive perception of a rightly instructed mind, the *prima facie* force of the argument, or the authority of our celebrated writers, have all their due and extensive influence in furthering the reception of the doctrine, when once it was openly maintained; to which must be added the prospect of the loss of State protection, which made it necessary to look out for other reasons for adherence to the Church besides that of obedience to the civil magistrate. Nothing which has spread quickly has been received thoroughly. Doubtless there are a number of seriously-minded persons who think that they admit the doctrine in question much more fully than they do, and who would be startled at seeing that realised in particulars which they confess in an abstract form. Many there are who do not at all feel that it is capable of a practical application; and while they bring it forward on special occasions, in formal expositions of faith, or in answer to a direct interrogatory, let it slip from their minds almost entirely in their daily conduct or their religious teaching, from the long and inveterate habit of thinking and acting without it. We must not, then, at all be surprised at finding that to modify the principles and motives on which men act is not the work of a day; nor at undergoing disappointments, at witnessing relapses, misconceptions, sudden disgusts, and, on the other hand, abuses and perversions of the true doctrine, in the case of those who have taken it up with more warmth than discernment.

From the end of 1835, or the beginning of 1836, the world outside of Oxford began to be alive to the force and the rapid growth of this new and, to the world at large, not very intelligible movement. The ideas which had laid hold so powerfully on a number of leading minds in the University began to work with a spell, which seemed to many inexplicable, on others unconnected with them. This rapidity of expansion, viewed as a feature of a party, was noticed on all sides, by enemies no less than friends. In an article in the *British Critic* of April 1839, by Mr. Newman, on the State of Religious Parties, the fact is illustrated from contemporary notices.

> There is at the present moment a reaction in the Church, and a growing reaction towards the views which it has been the endeavours [of the Tract writers] and, as it seemed at the commencement, *almost hopeless endeavours*, to advocate. The fairness of the prospect at present is proved by the attack made on them by the public journals, and is confessed by the more candid and the more violent among their opponents. Thus the amiable Mr. Bickersteth speaks of it as having manifested itself "with the *most rapid* growth of the hot-bed of these evil days." The scoffing author of the *Via Media* says: "At this moment the Via is *crowded* with young enthusiasts who never presume to argue,

except against the propriety of arguing at all." The candid Mr. Baden-Powell, who sees more of the difficulties of the controversy than the rest of their antagonists put together, says that it is clear that "these views . . . have been extensively adopted, and are daily gaining ground among a considerable and influential portion of the members, as well as the ministers of the Established Church." The author of the *Natural History of Enthusiasm* says: "The spread of these doctrines is in fact having the effect of rendering all other distinctions obsolete. Soon there will be no middle ground left, and every man, especially every clergyman, will be compelled to make his choice between the two." . . . The Bishop of Chester speaks of the subject "daily assuming a more serious and alarming aspect": a gossiping writer of the moment describes these doctrines as having insinuated themselves not only into popular churches and fashionable chapels, and the columns of newspapers, but "into the House of Commons."

And the writer of the article goes on:—

Now, if there be any truth in these remarks, it is plainly idle and perverse to refer the change of opinions which is now going on to the acts of two or three individuals, as is sometimes done. Of course every event in human affairs has a beginning; and a beginning implies a when, and a where, and a by whom, and how. But except in these necessary circumstances, the phenomenon in question is in a manner quite independent of things visible and historical. It is not here or there; it has no progress, no causes, no fortunes: it is not a movement, it is a spirit, it is a spirit afloat, neither "in the secret chambers" nor "in the desert," but everywhere. It is within us, rising up in the heart where it was least expected, and working its way, though not in secret, yet so subtly and impalpably, as hardly to admit of precaution or encounter on any ordinary human rules of opposition. It is an adversary in the air, a something one and entire, a whole wherever it is, unapproachable and incapable of being grasped, as being the result of causes far deeper than political or other visible agencies, the spiritual awakening of spiritual wants.

Nothing can show more strikingly the truth of this representation than to refer to what may be called the theological history of the individuals who, whatever be their differences from each other on important or unimportant points, yet are associated together in the advocacy of the doctrines in question. Dr. Hook and Mr. Churton represent the High Church dignitaries of the last generation; Mr. Perceval, the Tory aristocrat; Mr. Keble is of the country clergy, and comes from valleys and woods, far removed both from notoriety and noise; Mr. Palmer and Mr. Todd are of Ireland; Dr. Pusey became what he is from among the Universities of Germany, and after a severe and tedious analysis of Arabic MSS. Mr. Dodsworth is said to have begun in the study of Prophecy; Mr. Newman to have been indebted to the friendship of Archbishop Whately; Mr. Froude, if any one, gained his views from his own mind. Others have passed over from Calvinism and kindred religions.

Years afterwards, and in changed circumstances, the same writer has left the following record of what came before his experience in those years:—[9]

> From beginnings so small (I said), from elements of thought so fortuitous, with prospects so unpromising, the Anglo-Catholic party suddenly became a power in the National Church, and an object of alarm to her rulers and friends. Its originators would have found it difficult to say what they aimed at of a practical kind: rather, they put forth views and principles, for their own sake, because they were true, as if they were obliged to say them; and, as they might be themselves surprised at their earnestness in uttering them, they had as great cause to be surprised at the success which attended their propagation. And, in fact, they could only say that those doctrines were in the air; that to assert was to prove, and that to explain was to persuade; and that the movement in which they were taking part was the birth of a crisis rather than of a place. In a very few years a school of opinion was formed, fixed in its principles, indefinite and progressive in their range; and it extended itself into every part of the country. If we inquire what the world thought of it, we have still more to raise our wonder; for, not to mention the excitement it caused in England, the movement and its party-names were known to the police of Italy and to the backwoodsmen of America. And so it proceeded, getting stronger and stronger every year, till it came into collision with the Nation and that Church of the Nation, which it began by professing especially to serve.

9. *Apologia*, p. 156.

XI

The Roman Question

The Hampden controversy had contributed to bring to the front
a question, which from the first starting of the Tracts had made
itself felt, but which now became a pressing one. If the Church
of England claimed to be part of the Catholic Church, what was
the answer of the Church of England to the claims and charges of
the Church of Rome? What were the true distinctions between
the doctrines of the two Churches on the great points on which
they were supposed to be at issue? The vague outcry of Popery
had of course been raised both against the general doctrine of the
Church, enforced in the Tracts, and against special doctrines and
modes of speaking, popularly identified with Romanism; and the
answer had been an appeal to the authority of the most learned
and authoritative of our writers. But, of course, to the general
public this learning was new; and the cry went on with a dreary
and stupid monotony. But the charges against Dr. Hampden led
his defenders to adopt as their best weapon an aggressive policy.
To the attack on his orthodoxy, the counter buffet was the charge
against his chief opponents of secret or open Romanising. In its
keenest and most popular form it was put forth in a mocking
pamphlet written probably under Whately's inspiration by his
most trusted confidant, Dr. Dickinson, in which, in the form of a
"Pastoral Epistle from his Holiness the Pope to some Members of
the University of Oxford," the Tract-writers are made to appear
as the emissaries and secret tools of Rome, as in a *jeu d'esprit* of
Whately's they are made to appear as the veiled prophets of in-

fidelity.[1] It was clever, but not clever enough to stand, at least in Oxford, against Dr. Pusey's dignified and gravely earnest *Remonstrance* against its injustice and trifling. But the fire of all Dr. Hampden's friends had been drawn on the leaders of the movement. With them, and almost alone with them, the opposition to him was made a personal matter. As time went on, those who had been as hot as they against Dr. Hampden managed to get their part in the business forgotten. Old scores between Orthodox, Evangelicals, and Liberals were wiped out, and the Tractarians were left to bear alone the odium of the "persecution" of Dr. Hampden. It must be said that they showed no signs of caring for it.

But the Roman controversy was looming in earnest, and it was idle to expect to keep it long out of sight. The Tracts had set forth with startling vehemence the forgotten claims of the Church. One reason why this had been done was the belief, as stated in the first volume of them, "that nothing but these neglected doctrines, faithfully preached, will repress the extension of Popery, for which the ever-multiplying divisions of the religious world are too clearly preparing the way."[2] The question, What *is* the Church? was one which the conditions of the times would not permit men any longer to leave alone. It had become urgent to meet it clearly and decisively. "We could not move a step in comfort till this was done."[3] "The controversy with the Romanists," writes Mr. Newman in No. 71 of the Tracts, about the end of 1835, "has overtaken us 'like a summer's cloud.' We find ourselves in various parts of the country preparing for it, yet, when we look back, we cannot trace the steps by which we arrived at our present position. We do not recollect what our feelings were this time last year on the subject; what was the state of our apprehensions and anticipations. All we know is, that here we are, from long scrutiny ignorant why we are not Roman Catholics, and they on the other side are said to be spreading and strengthening on all sides of us, vaunting of their success, real or apparent, and taunting us with our inability to argue with them."

The attitude taken by Mr. Newman at this time, as regards the

1. Whately's *Life,* ed. 1875, pp. 187–190.
2. Advertisement to vol. 1, 1 Nov. 1834.
3. *Apologia,* p. 139.

Roman Church, both in the Tracts and in his book on *Romanism and Popular Protestantism*, published in the early months of 1836, was a new one. He had started, as he tells us, with the common belief that the Pope was Antichrist, and that the case was so clear against the whole system, doctrinal and practical, of the Church of Rome, that it scarcely needed further examination. His feeling against Rome had been increased by the fierce struggle about Emancipation, and by the political conduct of the Roman Catholic party afterwards; and his growing dissatisfaction with the ordinary Protestantism had no visible effect in softening this feeling. Hurrell Froude's daring questions had made his friends feel that there might be more to be known about the subject than they yet knew; yet what the fellow-travellers saw of things abroad in their visit to the South in 1832 did not impress them favourably. "They are wretched Tridentines everywhere," was Froude's comment. But attention had been drawn to the subject, and its deep interest and importance and difficulty recognised. Men began to read with new eyes. Froude's keen and deep sense of shortcomings at home disposed him to claim equity and candour in judging of the alleged faults and corruptions of the Church abroad. It did more, it disposed him—naturally enough, but still unfairly, and certainly without adequate knowledge—to treat Roman shortcomings with an indulgence which he refused to English. Mr. Newman, knowing more, and more comprehensive in his view of things, and therefore more cautious and guarded than Froude, was much less ready to allow a favourable interpretation of the obvious allegations against Rome. But thought and reading, and the authority of our own leading divines, had brought him to the conviction that whatever was to be said against the modern Roman Church—and the charges against it were very heavy—it was still, amid serious corruption and error, a teacher to the nations of the Christian creed and hope; it had not forfeited, any more than the English Church, its title to be a part of that historic body which connects us with the Apostles of our Lord. It had a strong and consistent theory to oppose to its assailants; it had much more to say for itself than the popular traditions supposed. This was no new idea in Anglican divinity, however ill it might sort with the current language of Protestant controversy. But our old divines, more easily satisfied than we with the course of things at home under the protection of the Stuart kings, and stung to bitter recrimination by the insults and the unscrupulous political intrigues of Roman Catholic agents, had exhausted the language of vituperation against a great aggressive rival, which was threatening everything that they held dear. They had damaged their own character for fairness, and overlaid their substantial grounds of objection and complaint, by this unbalanced exaggeration. Mr. Newman, in his study of these matters, early saw both the need and the difficulty of discrimination in the Roman controversy. It had to be waged, not as of old, with penal legislation behind, but against adversaries who could now make themselves listened to, and before a public sufficiently robust in its Protestantism, to look with amused interest on a dialectical triumph of the Roman over the Anglican claims. Romanism, he thought, was fatal both to his recent hopes for the English Church, and to the honour and welfare of Christianity at large. But in opposing it, ground loosely taken of old must be carefully examined, and if untenable, abandoned. Arguments which proved too much, which availed against any Church at all, must be given up. Popular objections, arising from ignorance or misconception, must be reduced to their true limits or laid aside. The controversy was sure to be a real one, and nothing but what was real and would stand scrutiny was worth anything in it.

Mr. Newman had always been impressed with the greatness of the Roman Church. Of old it had seemed to him great with the greatness of Antichrist. Now it seemed great with the strange weird greatness of a wonderful mixed system, commanding from its extent of sway and its imperial authority, complicated and mysterious in its organisation and influence, in its devotion and its superstitions, and surpassing every other form of religion both in its good and its evil.[4] What now presented itself to Mr. Newman's thoughts, instead of the old notion of a pure Church on one

---

4. Vide *Lyra Apostolica,* Nos. 170, 172:
　　How shall I name thee, Light of the wide West,
　　　Or heinous error-seat? . . .
　　Oh, that thy creed were sound!
　　For thou dost sooth the heart, thou Church of Rome,
　　By thy unwearied watch and varied round
　　Of service, in thy Saviour's holy home.
And comp. No. 171, *The Cruel Church.*

side, and a corrupt Church on the other, sharply opposed to one another, was the more reasonable supposition of two great portions of the divided Church, each with its realities of history and fact and character, each with its special claims and excellences, each with its special sins and corruptions, and neither realising in practice and fact all it professed to be on paper; each of which further, in the conflicts of past days, had deeply, almost unpardonably, wronged the other. The Church of England was in possession, with its own call and its immense work to do, and striving to do it. Whatever the Church of Rome was abroad, it was here an intruder and a disturber. That to his mind was the fact and the true position of things; and this ought to govern the character and course of controversy. The true line was not to denounce and abuse wholesale, not to attack with any argument, good or bad, not to deny or ignore what was solid in the Roman ground, and good and elevated in the Roman system, but admitting all that fairly ought to be admitted, to bring into prominence, not for mere polemical denunciation, but for grave and reasonable and judicial condemnation, all that was extravagant and arrogant in Roman assumptions, and all that was base, corrupt, and unchristian in the popular religion, which, with all its claims to infallibility and authority, Rome not only permitted but encouraged. For us to condemn Rome wholesale, as was ordinarily the fashion, even in respectable writers, was as wrong, as unfair, as unprofitable to the cause of truth and Christianity, as the Roman charges against us were felt by us to be ignorant and unjust. Rome professes like England to continue the constitution, doctrine, traditions, and spirit of the ancient and undivided Church: and so far as she does so—and she does so in a great degree—we can have no quarrel with her. But in a great degree also, she does this only in profession and as a theory: she claims the witness and suffrage of antiquity, but she interprets it at her own convenience and by her own authority. We cannot claim exemption from mistakes, from deviations from our own standard and principles, any more than Rome; but while she remains as she is, and makes the monstrous claims of infallibility and supremacy, there is nothing for English Churchmen but to resist her. Union is impossible. Submission is impossible. What we have to beware of for our own sake, as well as for our cause, are false arguments, unreal objections, ignorant allegations. There is enough on the very surface, in her audacious assertions and high-handed changes, for popular arguments against her, without having recourse to exaggeration and false-hood; she may be a very faulty Church, without being Babylon and Antichrist. And in the higher forms of argument, there is abundance in those provinces of ancient theology and ecclesiastical history and law, which Protestant controversialists have commonly surrendered and left open to their opponents, to supply a more telling weapon than any which these controversialists have used.

This line, though substantially involved in the theory of our most learned divines, from Andrewes to Wake, was new in its moderation and reasonable caution; in its abstention from insult and vague abuse, in its recognition of the *prima facie* strength of much of the Roman case, in its fearless attempt, in defiance of the deepest prejudices, to face the facts and conditions of the question. Mr. Newman dared to know and to acknowledge much that our insular self-satisfaction did not know, and did not care to know, of real Christian life in the Church of Rome. He dared to admit that much that was popularly held to be Popish was ancient, Catholic, edifying; he dared to warn Churchmen that the loose unsifted imputations, so securely hazarded against Rome, were both discreditable and dangerous. All this, from one whose condemnation of Rome was decisive and severe, was novel. The attempt, both in its spirit and its ability, was not unworthy of being part of the general effort to raise the standard of thought and teaching in the English Church. It recalled men from slovenly prejudices to the study of the real facts of the living world. It narrowed the front of battle, but it strengthened it enormously. The volume on *Romanism and Popular Protestantism* is not an exhaustive survey of the controversy with Rome or of the theory of the Church. There are great portions of the subject, both theological and historical, which it did not fall within the scope of the book to touch. It was unsystematic and incomplete. But so far as its argument extended, it almost formed an epoch in this kind of controversial writing. It showed the command of a man of learning over all the technical points and minutiae of a question highly scholastical in its conceptions and its customary treatment, and it presented this question in its bearings and consequences on life and practice with the freedom and breadth of the most vigorous popular writing. The indictment against Rome was no vague or general one. It was one of those arguments which cut the ground from under a great established structure of reasonings and proofs. And its conclusions, clear and measured, but stern, were the more impressive, because they came from one who did not disguise his feeling that there was much in what was preserved in the Roman system to admire and to learn from.

The point which he chose for his assault was indeed the key of the Roman position—the doctrine of Infallibility. He was naturally led to this side of the question by the stress which the movement had laid on the idea of the Church as the witness and teacher of revealed truth: and the immediate challenge given by the critics or opponents of the movement was, how to distinguish this lofty idea of the Church, with its claim to authority, if it was at all substantial, from the imposing and consistent theory of Romanism. He urged against the Roman claim of Infallibility two leading objections. One was the way in which the assumed infallibility of the present Church was made to override and supersede, in fact, what in words was so ostentatiously put forward, the historical evidence of antiquity to doctrine, expressed by the phrase, the "consent of the Fathers." The other objection was the inherent contradiction of the notion of infallibility to the conditions of human reception of teaching and knowledge, and its practical uselessness as an assurance of truth, its partly delusive, partly mischievous, working. But he felt, as all deep minds must feel, that it is easier to overthrow the Roman theory of Church authority than to replace it by another, equally complete and commanding, and more unassailable. He was quite alive to the difficulties of the Anglican position; but he was a disciple in the school of Bishop Butler, and had learned as a first principle to recognise the limitations of human knowledge, and the unphilosophical folly of trying to round off into finished and pretentious schemes our fragmentary yet certain notices of our own condition and of God's dealings with it. He followed his teacher in insisting on the reality and importance of moral evidence as opposed to demonstrative proof; and he followed the great Anglican divines in asserting that there was a true authority, varying in its degrees, in the historic Church; that on the most fundamental points of religion this authority was trustworthy and supreme; that on many other questions, it was clear and weighty, though it could not decide everything. This view of the "prophetical office of the Church" had the dialectical disadvantage of appearing to be a compromise, to many minds a fatal disadvantage. It got the name of the *Via Media*; a satisfactory one to practical men like Dr. Hook, to whom it recommended itself for use in popular teaching; but to others, in aftertimes, an ill-sounding phrase of dislike, which summed up the weakness of the Anglican case. Yet it only answered to the certain fact, that in the early and undivided Church there was such a thing as authority, and there was no such thing known as Infallibility. It was an appeal to the facts of history and human nature against the logical exigencies of a theory. Men must transcend the conditions of our experience if they want the certainty which the theory of Infallibility speaks of.

There were especially two weak points in this view of Anglicanism. Mr. Newman felt and admitted them, and of course they were forced on his attention by controversialists on both sides; by the Ultra-Protestant school, whose modes of dealing with Scripture he had exposed with merciless logic, and by the now eager Roman disputants, of whom Dr. Wiseman was the able and not over-scrupulous chief. The first of these points was that the authority of the undivided Church, which Anglicanism invoked, though it completely covered the great foundations of Christian doctrine, our faith as to the nature of God, did not cover with equal completeness other important points of controversy, such as those raised at the Reformation as to the Sacraments, and the justification of the sinner. The Anglican answer was that though the formal and conciliar authority was not the same in each case, the patristic literature of the time of the great councils, all that it took for granted and preserved as current belief and practice, all that resulted from the questions and debates of the time, formed a body of proof, which carried with it moral evidence only short of authoritative definition, and was so regarded in the Anglican formularies. These formularies implied the authority of the Church to speak; and what was defined on this authority was based on good evidence, though there were portions of its teaching which had even better. The other point was more serious. "Your theory," was the objection, "is nothing but a paper theory," it never was a reality; it never can be. There may be an ideal halting-place, there is neither a logical nor an actual one, between Romanism and the ordinary negations of Protestantism." The answer to the challenge then was, "Let us see if it cannot be realised. It has recognised foundations to build upon, and the impediments and interruptions which have hindered it are well known. Let us see if it will not turn out something more than a paper theory." That was the answer given at the time, abandoned ten years afterwards. But this at least may be said, that the longer experience of the last fifty years has shown that the Church of England has been working more and more on such a theory, and that the Church of England, whatever its faults may be, is certainly not a Church only on paper.

But on the principles laid down in this volume, the Roman controversy, in its varying forms, was carried on—for the time by Mr. Newman, permanently by the other leaders of the movement. In its main outlines, the view has become the accepted Anglican view. Many other most important matters have come into the debate. The publicly altered attitude of the Papacy has indefinitely widened the breach between England and Rome. But the fundamental idea of the relations and character of the two Churches remains the same as it was shadowed forth in 1836.

One very important volume on these questions ought not to be passed by without notice. This was the *Treatise on the Church of Christ*, 1838, by Mr. W. Palmer, who had already by his *Origines* of the English Ritual, 1832, done much to keep up that interest of Churchmen in the early devotional language of the Church, which had first been called forth by Bishop Lloyd's lectures on the Prayer Book. The *Treatise on the Church* was an honour to English theology and learning; in point of plan and structure we have few books like it.[5] It is comprehensive, methodical, well-com-

5. "The most important theological work which has lately appeared is Mr. Palmer's *Treatise on the Church.* . . . Whatever judgement may be formed of the conclusions to which he has come on the variety of points which he had to consider, we cannot contemplate without admiration, and (if it were right) without envy, the thorough treatment which his subject has received at his hands. It is indeed a work quite in character with the religious movement which has commenced in various parts of the Church, displaying a magnificence of design similar to that of the Bishop of London's plan of fifty new churches, and Dr. Pusey, of Oxford's projected translation of the Fathers."—*Brit. Crit.,* July 1838, Short Notices.

pacted, and, from its own point of view, exhaustive. It is written with full knowledge of the state of the question at the time, both on the Anglican side and on the Roman. Its author evades no objection, and is aware of most. It is rigorous in form, and has no place for anything but substantial argument. It is a book which, as the *Apologia* tells us, commanded the respect of such an accomplished controversialist as Perrone; and, it may be added, of a theologian of an opposite school, Dr. Döllinger. It is also one on which the highest value has been set by Mr. Gladstone. It is remarkable that it did not exercise more influence on religious thought in Oxford at the critical time when it appeared. But it had defects, and the moment was against it. It was dry and formal —inevitably so, from the scientific plan deliberately adopted for it; it treated as problems of the theological schools, to be discussed by the rules of severe and passionless disputation, questions which were once more, after the interval of more than a century, beginning to touch hearts and consciences, and were felt to be fraught with the gravest practical issues. And Mr. Newman, in his mode of dealing with them, unsystematic, incomplete, unsatisfactory in many ways as it was, yet saw in them not abstract and scholastic inquiries, however important, but matters in which not only sound argument, but sympathy and quick intelligence of the conditions and working of the living minds around him, were needed to win their attention and interest. To persons accustomed to Mr. Newman's habit of mind and way of writing, his ease, his frankness, his candour, his impatience of conventionality, his piercing insight into the very centre of questions, his ever-ready recognition of nature and reality, his range of thought, his bright and clear and fearless style of argument, his undisplayed but never unfelt consciousness of the true awfulness of anything connected with religion, any stiff and heavy way of treating questions which he had treated would have seemed unattractive and unpersuasive. He had spoiled his friends for any mere technical handling, however skilful, of great and critical subjects. He himself pointed out in a review the unique merit and the real value of Mr. Palmer's book, pointing out also, significantly enough, where it fell short, both in substance and in manner. Observing that the "scientific" system of the English Church is not yet "sufficiently cleared and adjusted," and adding a variety of instances of this deficiency, he lets us see what he wanted done, where difficulties most pressed upon himself, and where Mr. Palmer had missed the real substance of such difficulties. Looking at it by the light of after-events, we can see the contradiction and reaction produced by Mr. Palmer's too optimist statements. Still, Mr. Newman's praise was sincere and discriminating. But Mr. Palmer's book, though never forgotten, scarcely became, what it at another time might well have become, an English text-book.

XII

Changes

The first seven years of the movement, as it is said in the *Apologia*, had been years of prosperity. There had been mistakes; there had been opposition; there had been distrust and uneasiness. There was in some places a ban on the friends of Mr. Newman; men like Mr. James Mozley and Mr. Mark Pattison found their connexion with him a difficulty in the way of fellowships. But on the whole, things had gone smoothly, without any great breakdown, or any open collision with authority. But after 1840 another period was to begin of trouble and disaster. The seeds of this had been partially sown before in the days of quiet, and the time was come for their development. Differences in the party itself had been growing sharper; differences between the more cautious and the more fearless, between the more steady-going and the more subtle thinkers. The contrast between the familiar and customary, and the new—between the unknown or forgotten, and a mass of knowledge only recently realised—became more pronounced. Consequences of a practical kind, real or supposed, began to show themselves, and to press. And above all, a second generation, without the sobering experience of the first, was starting from where the first had reached to, and, in some instances, was rising up against their teachers' caution and patience. The usual dangers of all earnest and aggressive assertions of great principles appeared: contempt for everything in opinion and practice that was not advanced, men vying with each other in bold inferences, in the pleasure of "talking strong." With this grew

151

fear and exasperation on the other side, misunderstanding, mis-givings, strainings of mutual confidence, within. Dr. Hook alter-nated between violent bursts of irritation and disgust, and equally strong returns of sympathy, admiration, and gratitude; and he represented a large amount of feeling among Churchmen. It was but too clear that storms were at hand. They came perhaps quicker than they were anticipated.

Towards the end of 1838, a proposal was brought forward for which in its direct aspect much might plausibly be said, but which was in intention and indirectly a test question, meant to put the Tractarians in a difficulty, and to obtain the weight of authority in the University against them. It was proposed to raise a subscrip-tion, and to erect a monument in Oxford, to the martyrs of the Reformation, Cranmer, Ridley, and Latimer. Considering that the current and popular language dated the Church of England from the Reformation of the sixteenth century, and cited the Re-formers as ultimate and paramount authorities on its doctrine, there was nothing unreasonable in such a proposal. Dr. Hook, strong Churchman as he was, "called to union on the principles of the English Reformation." But the criticism which had been set afloat by the movement had discovered and realised, what de-fenders of the English Church had hitherto felt it an act of piety to disbelieve, when put before them by Romanists like Lingard, and radicals like Cobbett, that the Reformers had been accomp-lices in many indefensible acts, and had been inconsistent and untrustworthy theologians. Providentially, it was felt, the force of old convictions and tradition and the historical events of the time had obliged them to respect the essentials of Catholic truth and polity and usage; we owned to them much that was beautiful and devotional in the Prayer Book; and their Articles, clear in all mat-ters decided by the early theology, avoided foreign extremes in dealing with later controversies. But their own individual lan-guage was often far in advance of the public and official language of formularies, in the direction of the great Protestant authorities of Geneva and Zurich. There were still, even among the move-ment party, many who respected the Reformers for the work which they had attempted, and partly and imperfectly done, to be more wisely and soberly carried on by their successors of the sev-enteenth century. But the charges against their Calvinistic and even Zwinglian language were hard to parry; even to those who respected them for their connexion with our present order of things, their learning, their soundness, their authority appeared to be greatly exaggerated; and the reaction from excessive veneration made others dislike and depreciate them. This was the state of feeling when the Martyrs' Memorial was started. It was eagerly pressed with ingenious and persevering arguments by Mr. Golightly, the indefatigable and long-labouring opponent of all that savoured of Tractarianism. The appeal seemed so specious that at first many even of the party gave in their adhesion. Even Dr. Pusey was disposed to subscribe to it. But Mr. Newman, as was natural, held aloof; and his friends for the most part did the same. It was what was expected and intended. They were either to commit themselves to the Reformation as understood by the promoters of the Memorial; or they were to be marked as showing their disloyalty to it. The subscription was successful. The Memorial was set up, and stood, a decisive though unofficial sign of the judgment of the University against them.

But the "Memorial" made little difference to the progress of the movement. It was an indication of hostility in reserve, but this was all; it formed an ornament to the city, but failed as a religious and effective protest. Up to the spring of 1839, Anglicanism, placed on an intellectual basis by Mr. Newman, developed practically in different ways by Dr. Pusey and Dr. Hook, sanctioned in theory by divines who represented the old divinity of the English Church, like Bishop Phillpotts and Mr. H. J. Rose, could speak with confident and hopeful voice. It might well seem that it was on its way to win over the coming generations of the English clergy. It had on its side all that gives interest and power to a cause,—thought, force of character, unselfish earnestness; it had unity of idea and agreement in purpose, and was cemented by the bonds of warm affection and common sympathies. It had the promise of a nobler religion, as energetic and as spiritual as Puritanism and Wesleyanism, while it drew its inspiration, its canons of doctrine, its moral standards, from purer and more venerable sources;—from communion, not with individual teachers and partial traditions, but with the consenting teaching and authoratative documents of the continuous Catholic Church.

Anglicanism was agreed, up to this time—the summer of 1839

—as to its general principles. Charges of an inclination to Roman views had been promptly and stoutly met; nor was there really anything but the ignorance or ill-feeling of the accusers to throw doubt on the sincerity of these disavowals. The deepest and strongest mind in the movement was satisfied; and his steadiness of conviction could be appealed to if his followers talked wildly and rashly. He had kept one unwavering path; he had not shrunk from facing with fearless honesty the real living array of reasons which the most serious Roman advocates could put forward. With a frankness new in controversy, he had not been afraid to state them with a force which few of his opponents could have put forth. With an eye ever open to that supreme Judge of all our controversies, who listens to them on His throne on high, he had with conscientious fairness admitted what he saw to be good and just on the side of his adversaries, conceded what in the confused wrangle of conflicting claims he judged ought to be conceded. But after all admissions and all concessions, the comparative strength of his own case appeared all the more undeniable. He had stripped it of its weaknesses, its incumbrances, its falsehoods; and it did not seem the weaker for being presented in its real aspect and on its real grounds. People felt that he had gone to the bottom of the question as no one had yet dared to do. He was yet staunch in his convictions; and they could feel secure.

But a change was at hand. In the course of 1839, the little cloud showed itself in the outlook of the future; the little rift opened, small and hardly perceptible, which was to widen into an impassable gulf. Anglicanism started with undoubted confidence in its own foundations and its own position, as much against Romanism as against the more recent forms of religion. In the consciousness of its strength, it could afford to make admissions and to refrain from tempting but unworthy arguments in controversy with Rome; indeed the necessity of such controversy had come upon it unexpectedly and by surprise. With English frankness, in its impatience of abuses and desire for improvement within, it had dwelt strongly on the faults and shortcomings of the English Church which it desired to remedy; but while allowing what was undeniably excellent in Rome, it had been equally outspoken and emphatic in condemnation of the evils of Rome. What is there to wonder at in such a position? It is the position of every honest reforming movement, at least in England. But Anglican self-reliance was unshaken, and Anglican hope waxed stronger as the years went on, and the impression made by Anglican teaching became wider and deeper. Outside attacks, outside persecution, could now do little harm; the time was past for that. What might have happened had things gone on as they began, it is idle to inquire. But at the moment when all seemed to promise fair, the one fatal influence, the presence of internal uncertainty and doubt, showed itself. The body of men who had so far acted together began to show a double aspect. While one portion of it continued on the old lines, holding the old ground, defending the old principles, and attempting to apply them for the improvement of the practical system of the English Church, another portion had asked the question, and were pursuing the anxious inquiry, whether the English Church was a true Church at all, a true portion of the one uninterrupted Catholic Church of the Redeemer. And the question had forced itself with importunate persistence on the leading mind of the movement. From this time the fate of Tractarianism, as a party, was decided.

In this overthrow of confidence, two sets of influences may be traced.

1. One, which came from above, from the highest leading authority in the movement, was the unsettlement of Mr. Newman's mind. He has told the story, the story as he believed of his enfranchisement and deliverance; and he has told the story, though the story of a deliverance, with so keen a feeling of its pathetic and tragic character,—as it is indeed the most tragic story of a conversion to peace and hope on record,—that it will never cease to be read where the English language is spoken. Up to the summer of 1839, his view of the English position had satisfied him—satisfied him, that is, as a tenable one in the anomalies of existing Christendom. All seemed clear and hopeful, and the one thing to be thought of was to raise the English Church to the height of its own standard. But in the autumn of that year (1839), as he has told us, a change took place. In the summer of 1839, he had set himself to study the history of the Monophysite controversy. "I have no reason," he writes, "to suppose that the thought of Rome came across my mind at all. . . . It was during this course of reading that for the first time a doubt came across

me of the tenableness of Anglicanism. I had seen the shadow of a hand on the wall. He who has seen a ghost cannot be as if he had never seen it. The heavens had opened and closed again." To less imaginative and slower minds this seems an overwrought description of a phenomenon, which must present itself sometime or other to all who search the foundations of conviction; and by itself he was for the time proof against its force. "The thought for the moment had been, The Church of Rome will be found right after all; and then it had vanished. My old convictions remained as before." But another blow came, and then another. An article by Dr. Wiseman on the Donatists greatly disturbed him. The words of St. Augustine about the Donatists, *securus judicat orbis terrarum*, rang continually in his ears, like words out of the sky. He found the threatenings of the Monophysite controversy renewed in the *Arian*: "the ghost had come a second time." It was a "most uncomfortable article," he writes in his letters; "the first real hit from Romanism which has happened to me"; it gave him, as he says, "a stomach-ache." But he still held his ground, and returned his answer to the attack in an article in the *British Critic*, on the "Catholicity of the English Church." He did not mean to take the attack for more than it was worth, an able bit of *ex parte* statement. But it told on him, as nothing had yet told on him. What it did, was to "open a vista which was closed before, and of which he could not see the end"; "we are not at the bottom of things," was the sting it left behind. From this time, the hope and exultation with which, in spite of checks and misgivings, he had watched the movement, gave way to uneasiness and distress. A new struggle was beginning, a long struggle with himself, a long struggle between rival claims which would not be denied, each equally imperious, and involving fatal consequences if by mistake the wrong one was admitted. And it was not only the effect of these thoughts on his own mind which filled him with grief and trouble. He always thought much for others; and now there was the misery of perhaps unsettling others—others who had trusted him with their very souls—others, to whom it was impossible to explain the conflicts which were passing in his own mind. It was so bitter to unsettle their hope and confidence. All through this time, more trying than his own difficulties, were the perplexities and sorrows which he foresaw for those whom he loved. Very illogical and inconsecutive, doubtless; if only he had had the hard heart of a proselytiser, he would have seen that it was his duty to undermine and shatter their old convictions. But he cared more for the tempers and beliefs in which he was at one with his Anglican friends, than for those in which they could not follow him. But the struggle came on gradually. What he feared at first was not the triumph of Rome, but the break-up of the English Church; the apparent probability of a great schism in it. "I fear I see more clearly that we are working up to a schism in the English Church, that is, a split between Peculiars and Apostolicals. . . . I never can be surprised at individuals going off to Rome, but that is not my chief fear, but a schism; that is, those two parties, which have hitherto got on together as they could, from the times of Puritanism downwards, gathering up into clear, tangible, and direct forces, and colliding. Our Church it not at one with itself, there is no denying it." That was at first the disaster before him. His thought for himself began to turn, not to Rome, but to a new life without office and authority, but still within the English Church. "You see, if things come to the worst, I should turn brother of charity in London." And he began to prepare for a move from Oxford, from St. Mary's, from his fellowship. He bought land at Littlemore, and began to plant. He asks his brother-in-law for plans for building what he calls a μονή. He looks forward to its becoming a sort of Monastic school, but still connected with the University.

In Mr. Newman's view of the debate between England and Rome, he had all along dwelt on two broad features, *Apostolicity* and *Catholicity*, likeness to the Apostolic teaching, and likeness to the uninterrupted unity and extent of the undivided Church; and of those two features he found the first signally wanting in Rome, and the second signally wanting in England. When he began to distrust his own reasonings, still the disturbing and repelling element in Rome was the alleged defect of Apostolicity, the contrast between primitive and Roman religion; while the attractive one was the apparent widely extended Catholicity in all lands, East and West, continents and isles, of the world-wide spiritual empire of the Pope. It is these two great points which may be traced in their action on his mind at this crisis. The contrast between early and Roman doctrine and practice, in a variety of ways, some of them most grave and important, was long a great difficulty in the way of attempting to identify the Roman Church, absolutely and exclusively, with the Primitive Church. The study of antiquity indisposed him, indeed, more and more to the existing system of the English Church; its claims to model itself on the purity and simplicity of the Early Church seemed to him, in the light of its documents, and still more of the facts of history and life, more and more questionable. But modern Rome was just as distant from the Early Church though it preserved many ancient features, lost or unvalued by England. Still, Rome was not the same thing as the Early Church; and Mr. Newman ultimately sought a way out of his difficulty—and indeed there was no other—in the famous doctrine of Development. But when the difficulty about *Apostolicity* was thus provided for, then the force of the great vision of the Catholic Church came upon him, unchecked and irresistible. That was a thing present, visible, undeniable as a fact of nature; that was a thing at once old and new; it belonged as truly, as manifestly, to the recent and modern world of democracy and science, as it did to the Middle Ages and the Fathers, to the world of Gregory and Innocent, to the world of Athanasius and Augustine. The majesty, the vastness of an imperial polity, outlasting all states and kingdoms, all social changes and political revolutions, answered at once to the promises of the prophecies, and to the antecedent idea of the universal kingdom of God. Before this great idea, embodied in concrete form, and not a paper doctrine, partial scandals and abuses seemed to sink into insignificance. Objections seemed petty and ignoble; the pretence of rival systems impertinent and absurd. He resented almost with impatience anything in the way of theory or explanation which seemed to him narrow, technical, dialectical. He would look at nothing but what had on it the mark of greatness and largeness which befitted the awful subject, and was worthy of arresting the eye and attention of an ecclesiastical statesman, alive to mighty interests, compared to which even the most serious human affairs were dwarfed and obscured.

But all this was gradual in coming. His recognition of the claims of the English Church, faulty and imperfect as he thought it, did not give way suddenly and at once. It survived the rude shock of 1839. From first to almost the last she was owned as his "mother"—owned in passionate accents of disappointment and despair as a Church which knew not how to use its gifts; yet still, even though life seemed failing her, and her power of teaching and ruling seemed paralysed, his mother; and as long as there seemed to him a prospect of restoration to health, it was his duty to stay by her.[1] This was his first attitude for three or four years after 1839. He could not speak of her with the enthusiasm and triumph of the first years of the movement. When he fought her battles, it was with the sense that her imperfections made his task the harder. Still he clung to the belief that she held a higher standard than she had yet acted up to, and discouraged and perplexed he yet maintained her cause. But now two things happened. The Roman claims, as was natural when always before him, seemed to him more and more indisputable. And in England his interpretation of Anglican theology seemed to be more and more contradicted, disavowed, condemned, by all that spoke with any authority in the Church. The University was not an ecclesiastical body, yet it had practically much weight in matters of theology; it informally, but effectually, declared against him. The Bishops, one by one, of course only spoke as individuals; but they were the official spokesmen of the Church, and their consent, though not the act of a Synod, was weighty—they too had declared against him. And finally that vague but powerful voice of public opinion, which claims to represent at once the cool judgment of the unbiassed, and the passion of the zealous—it too declared against him. Could he claim to understand the mind of the Church better than its own organs?

Then at length a change came; and it was marked outwardly by a curious retraction of his severe language about Rome, published in a paper called the *Conservative Journal*, in January 1843; and more distinctly, by his resignation of St. Mary's in September 1843, a step contemplated for some time, and by his announcement that he was preparing to resign his fellowship. From this time he felt that he could no longer hold office, or be a champion of the English Church; from this time, it was only a matter of waiting, waiting to make quite certain that he was right and was under no delusion, when he should leave her for the Roman Communion. And to his intimate friends, to his sisters,

---

1. See Sermons on *Subjects of the Day*, 1843.

he gave notice that this was now impending. To the world out-side, all that was known was that he was much unsettled and dis-tressed by difficulties.

It may be asked why this change was not at this time commu-nicated, not to a few intimates, but to the world? Why did he not at this time hoist his quarantine flag and warn every one that he was dangerous to come near? So keen a mind must, it was said, have by this time foreseen how things would end; he ought to have given earlier notice. His answer was that he was sincerely desirous of avoiding, as far as possible, what might prejudice the Church in which he had ministered, even at the moment of leav-ing her. He saw his own way becoming clearer and clearer; but he saw it for himself alone. He was not one of those who forced the convictions of others; he was not one of those who think it a great thing to be followed in a serious change by a crowd of disciples. Whatever might be at the end, it was now an agonising wrench to part from the English body, to part from the numbers of friends whose loyalty was immovable, to part from numbers who had trusted and learned from him. Of course, if he was in the right way, he could wish them nothing better than that they should follow him. But they were in God's hands; it was not his business to unsettle them; it was not his business to ensnare and coerce their faith. And so he tried for this time to steer his course alone. He wished to avoid observation. He was silent on all that went on round him, exciting as some of the incidents were. He would not be hurried; he would give himself full time; he would do what he could to make sure that he was not acting under the influence of a delusion.

The final result of all this was long in coming; there was, we know, a bitter agony of five years, a prolonged and obstinate and cruel struggle between the deepest affections and ever-growing convictions. But this struggle, as has been said, did not begin with the conviction in which it ended. It began and long continued with the belief that though England was wrong, Rome was not right; that though the Roman argument seemed more and more unanswerable, there were insuperable difficulties of certain fact which made the Roman conclusion incredible; that there was so much good and truth in England, with all its defects and faults, which was unaccountable and unintelligible on the Roman hypothesis; that the real upshot was that the whole state of things in Christendom was abnormal; that to English Churchmen the English Church had immediate and direct claims which nothing but the most irresistible counterclaims could overcome or neutral-ise—the claims of a shipwrecked body cut off from country and home; yet as a shipwrecked body still organised, and with much saved from the wreck, and not to be deserted, as long as it held together, in an uncertain attempt to rejoin its lost unity. Resigna-tion, retirement, silence, lay communion, the hope of ultimate, though perhaps long-deferred reunion—these were his first thoughts. Misgivings could not be helped, would not be denied, but need not be paraded, were to be kept at arm's-length as long as possible. This is the picture presented in the autobiography of these painful and dreary years; and there is every evidence that it is a faithful one. It is conceivable, though not very probable, that such a course might go on indefinitely. It is conceivable that under different circumstances he might, like other perplexed and doubt-ing seekers after truth, have worked round through doubt and perplexity to his first conviction. But the actual result, as it came, was natural enough; and it was accelerated by provocation, by op-ponents without, and by the pressure of advanced and impatient followers and disciples in the party itself.

2. This last was the second of the two influences spoken of above. It worked from below, as the first worked from above.

Discussion and agitations, such as accompanied the movement, however much under the control of the moral and intellectual ascendancy of the leaders, could not of course be guaranteed from escaping from that control. And as the time went on, men joined the movement who had but qualified sympathy with that passion-ate love and zeal for the actual English Church, that acquaintance with its historical theology, and that temper of discipline, sobriety, and self-distrust, which marked its first representatives. These younger disciples shared in the growing excitement of the society round them. They were attracted by visible height of character, and brilliant intellectual power. They were alive to vast and origi-nal prospects, opening a new world which should be a contrast to the worn-out interest of the old. Some of these were men of wide and abtruse learning; quaint and eccentric scholars both in habit and look, students of the ancient type, who even fifty years ago seemed out of date to their generation. Some were men of considerable force of mind, destined afterwards to leave a mark on their age as thinkers and writers. To the former class belonged Charles Seager, and John Brande Morris, of Exeter College, both learned Orientalists, steeped in recondite knowledge of all kinds; men who had worked their way to knowledge through hardship and grinding labour, and not to be outdone in Germany itself for devouring love of learning and a scholar's plainness of life. In the other class may be mentioned Frederic Faber, J. D. Dalgairns, and W. G. Ward, men who have all since risen to eminence in their different spheres. Faber was a man with a high gift of imagination, remarkable powers of assimilating knowledge, and a great richness and novelty and elegance of thought, which with much melody of voice made him ultimately a very attractive preacher. If the promise of his powers has not been adequately fulfilled, it is partly to be traced to a want of severity of taste and self-restraint, but his name will live in some of his hymns, and in some very beautiful portions of his devotional writings. Dalgairn's mind was of a different order. "That man has an eye for theology," was the remark of a competent judge on some early paper of Dalgairn's which came before him. He had something of the Frenchman about him. There was in him, in his Oxford days, a bright and frank briskness, a mixture of modesty and arch daring, which gave him an almost boyish appearance; but beneath this boyish appearance there was a subtle and powerful intellect, alive to the problems of religious philosophy, and impatient of any but the most thorough solutions of them; while, on the other hand, the religious affections were part of his nature, and mind and will and heart yielded an unreserved and absolute obedience to the leading and guidance of faith. In his later days, with his mind at ease, Father Dalgairns threw himself into the great battle with unbelief; and few men have commanded more the respect of opponents not much given to think well of the arguments for religion, by the freshness and the solidity of his reasoning. At this time, enthusiastic in temper, and acute and exacting as a thinker, he found the Church movement just, as it were, on the turn of the wave. He was attracted to it at first by its reaction against what was unreal and shallow, by its affinities with what was deep in idea and earnest in life; then, and fianally, he was repelled from it, by its want of completeness, by its English acquiescence in compromise, by its hesitations and clinging to insular associations and sympathies, which had little interest for him.

Another person, who was at this time even more prominent in the advanced portion of the movement party, and whose action had more decisive influence on its course, was Mr. W. G. Ward, Fellow of Balliol. Mr. Ward, who was at first at Christ Church, had distinguished himself greatly at the Oxford Union as a vigorous speaker, at first on the Tory side; he came afterwards under the influence of Arthur Stanley, then fresh from Rugby, and naturally learned to admire Dr. Arnold; but Dr. Arnold's religious doctrines did not satisfy him; the movement, with its boldness and originality of idea and ethical character, had laid strong hold on him, and he passed into one of the most thoroughgoing adherents of Mr. Newman. There was something to smile at in his person, and in some of his ways—his unbusiness-like habits, his joyousness of manner, his racy stories; but few more powerful intellects passed through Oxford in his time, and he has justified his University reputation by his distinction since, both as a Roman Catholic theologian and professor, and as a profound metaphysical thinker, the equal antagonist on their own ground of J. Stuart Mill and Herbert Spencer. But his intellect at that time was as remarkable for its defects as for its powers. He used to divide his friends, and thinking people in general, into those who had facts and did not know what to do with them, and those who had in perfection the logical faculties, but wanted the facts to reason upon. He belonged himself to the latter class. He had, not unnaturally, boundless confidence in his argumentative powers; they were subtle, piercing, nimble, never at a loss, and they included a power of exposition which, if it was not always succinct and lively, was always weighty and impressive. Premises in his hands were not long in bringing forth their conclusions; and if abstractions always corresponded exactly to their concrete embodiments, and ideals were fulfilled in realities, no one could point out more perspicuously and decisively the practical judgments on them which reason must sanction. But that knowledge of things and of men which mere power of reasoning will not give was not one of his special endowments. The study of facts, often in their complicated and perplexing reality, was not to his taste. He was apt to accept them on what he considered adequate authority, and his argumentation, formidable as it always was, recalled, even when most unanswerable at the moment, the application of pure mathematics without allowance for the actual forces, often difficult to ascertain except by experiment, which would have to be taken account of in practice.

The tendency of this section of able men was unquestionably Romewards, almost from the beginning of their connexion with the movement. Both the theory and the actual system of Rome, so far as they understood it, had attractions for them which nothing else had. But with whatever perplexity and perhaps impatience, Mr. Newman's power held them back. He kept before their minds continually those difficulties of fact which stood in the way of their absolute and peremptory conclusions, and of which they were not much inclined to take account. He insisted on those features, neither few nor unimportant nor hard to see, which proved the continuity of the English Church with the Church Universal. Sharing their sense of anomaly in the Anglican theory and position, he pointed out with his own force and insight that anomaly was not in England only, but everywhere. There was much to regret, there was much to improve, there were many unwelcome and dangerous truths, *invidiosi veri*, to be told and defended at any cost. But patience, as well as honesty and courage, was a Christian virtue; and they who had received their Christianity at the hands of the English Church had duties towards it from which neither dissatisfaction nor the idea of something better could absolve them. *Spartam nactus es, hanc exorna* is the motto for every one whose lot is cast in any portion of Christ's Church. And as long as he could speak with this conviction, the strongest of them could not break away from his restraint. It was when the tremendous question took shape, Is the English Church a true Church, a real part of the Church Catholic?—when the question became to his mind more and more doubtful, at length desperate —that they, of course, became more difficult to satisfy, more confident in their own allegations, more unchecked in their sympathies, and, in consequence, in their dislikes. And in the continued effort—for it did continue—to make them pause and wait and hope, they reacted on him; they asked him questions which he found it hard to answer; they pressed him with inferences which he might put by, but of which he felt the sting; they forced on him all the indications, of which every day brought its contribution, that the actual living system of the English Church was against what he had taught to be Catholic, that its energetic temper and spirit condemned and rejected him. What was it that private men were staunch and undismayed? What was it that month by month all over England hearts and minds were attracted to his side, felt the spell of his teaching, gave him their confidence? Suspicion and disapprobation, which had only too much to ground itself upon, had taken possession of the high places of the Church. Authority in all its shapes had pronounced as decisively as his opponents could wish; as decisively as they too could wish, who desired no longer a barrier between themselves and Rome.

Thus a great and momentous change had come over the movement, over its action and prospects. It had started in a heroic effort to save the English Church. The claims, the blessings, the divinity of the English Church, as a true branch of Catholic Christendom, had been assumed as the foundation of all that was felt and said and attempted. The English Church was the one object to which English Christians were called upon to turn their thoughts. Its spirit animated the *Christian Year*, and the teaching of those whom the *Christian Year* represented. Its interests were what called forth the zeal and the indignation recorded in Froude's *Remains*. No one seriously thought of Rome, except as a hopelessly corrupt system, though it had some good and Catholic things, which it was Christian and honest to recognise. The movement of 1833 started out of the Anti-Roman feelings of the Emancipation time. It was Anti-Roman as much as it was Anti-Sectarian and Anti-Erastian. It was to avert the danger of people becoming Romanists from ignorance of Church principles. This was all changed in one important section of the party. The fundamental conceptions and assumptions were reversed. It was not the Roman Church, but the English Church, which was put on its trial; it was not the Roman Church, but the English, which was to be, if possible, apologised for perhaps borne with for a time, but which was to be regarded as deeply fallen, holding an untenable position, and incomparably, unpardonably, below both the standard and the practical system of the Roman Church. From this point of view the object of the movement was no longer to elevate and improve an independent English Church, but to approximate it as far as possible to what was assumed to be undeniable—the perfect Catholicity of Rome. More almost than ideas and assumptions, the tone of feeling changed. It had been, towards the English Church, affectionate, enthusiastic, reverential, hopeful. It became contemptuous, critical, intolerant, hostile with the hostility not merely of alienation but disgust. This was not of course the work of a moment, but it was of very rapid growth. "How I hate these Anglicans!" was the expression of one of the younger men of this section, an intemperate and insolent specimen of it. It did not represent the tone or the language of the leader to whom the advanced section deferred, vexed as he often was with the course of his own thoughts, and irritated and impatient at the course of things without. But it expressed but too truly the difference between 1833 and 1840.

XIII

*The Authorities
and the Movement*

While the movement was making itself felt as a moral force, without a parallel in Oxford for more than two centuries, and was impressingly deeply and permanently some of the most promising men in the rising generation in the University, what was the attitude of the University authorities? What was the attitude of the Bishops?

At Oxford it was that of contemptuous indifference, passing into helpless and passionate hostility. There is no sadder passage to be found in the history of Oxford than the behaviour and policy of the heads of this great Christian University towards the religious movement which was stirring the interest, the hopes, the fears of Oxford. The movement was, for its first years at least, a loyal and earnest effort to serve the cause of the Church. Its objects were clear and reasonable; it aimed at creating a sincere and intelligent zeal for the Church, and at making the Church itself worthy of the great position which her friends claimed for her. Its leaders were men well known in the University, in the first rank in point of ability and character; men of learning, who knew what they were talking about; men of religious and pure, if also severe lives. They were not men merely of speculation and criticism, but men ready to forego anything, to devote everything for the practical work of elevating religious thought and life. All this did not necessarily make their purposes and attempts wise and good; but it did entitle them to respectful attention. If they spoke language new to the popular mind or the "religious world," it was not new—at least it ought not to have been new—to orthodox Churchmen, with opportunities of study and acquainted with our best divinity. If their temper was eager and enthusiastic, they alleged the presence of a great and perilous crisis. Their appeal was mainly not to the general public, but to the sober and the learned; to those to whom was entrusted the formation of faith and character in the future clergy of the Church; to those who were responsible for the discipline and moral tone of the first University of Christendom, and who held their conspicuous position on the understanding of that responsibility. It behoved the heads of the University to be cautious, even to be suspicious; movements might be hollow or dangerous things. But it behoved them also to become acquainted with so striking a phenomenon as this; to judge it by what it appealed to—the learning of English divines, the standard of a high and generous moral rule; to recognise its aims at least, with equity and sympathy, if some of its methods and arguments seemed questionable. The men of the movement were not mere hostile innovators; they were fighting for what the University and its chiefs held dear and sacred, the privileges and safety of the Church. It was the natural part of the heads of the University to act as moderators; at any rate, to have shown, with whatever reserve, that they appreciated what they needed time to judge of. But while on the one side there was burning and devouring earnestness, and that power of conviction which doubles the strength of the strong, there was on the other a serene ignoring of all that was going on, worthy of a set of dignified French *abbés* on the eve of the Revolution. This sublime or imbecile security was occasionally interrupted by bursts of irritation at some fresh piece of Tractarian oddness or audacity, or at some strange story which made its way from the gossip of common-rooms to the society of the Heads of Houses. And there was always ready a stick to beat the offenders; everything could be called Popish. But for the most part they looked on, with smiles, with jokes, sometimes with scolding.[1] Thus the men who by their

1. Fifty years ago there was much greater contrast than now between old and young. There was more outward respect for the authorities, and among the younger men, graduates and undergraduates, more inward amusement at foibles and eccentricities. There still lingered the survivals of a more old-fashioned

place ought to have been able to gauge and control the movement, who might have been expected to meet half-way a serious attempt to brace up the religious and moral tone of the place, so incalculably important in days confessed to be anxious ones, simply set their faces steadily to discountenance and discredit it. They were good and respectable men, living comfortably in a certain state and ease. Their lives were mostly simple compared with the standard of the outer world, though Fellows of Colleges thought them luxurious. But they were blind and dull as tea-table gossips as to what was the meaning of the movement, as to what might come of it, as to what use might be made of it by wise and just and generous recognition, and, if need be, by wise and just criticism and repression. There were points of danger in it; but they could only see what *seemed* to be dangerous, whether it was so or not; and they multiplied these points of danger by all that was good and hopeful in it. It perplexed and annoyed them; they had not imagination nor moral elevation to take in what it aimed at; they were content with the routine which they had inherited; and, so that men read for honours and took first classes, it did not seem to them strange or a profanation that a whole mixed crowd of undergraduates should be expected to go

---

type of University life and character, which, quite apart from the movements of religious opinion, provoked those νεανιεύματα ἰδιωτῶν εἰς τοὺς ἄρχοντας (Plato R. P. 3. 390), *impertinences of irresponsible juniors towards superiors*, which Wordsworth, speaking of a yet earlier time, remembered at Cambridge—

> "In serious mood, but oftener, I confess,
> With playful zest of fancy, did we note
> (How could we less?) the manners and the ways
> Of those who lived distinguished by the badge
> Of good or ill report; or those with whom
> By frame of Academic discipline
> We were perforce connected, men whose sway
> And known authority of office served
> To set our minds on edge, and did no more.
> Nor wanted we rich pastime of this kind,
> Found everywhere, but chiefly in the ring
> Of the grave Elders, men unscoured, grotesque
> In character, tricked out like aged trees
> Which through the laspe of their infirmity
> Gave ready place to any random seed
> That chooses to be reared upon their trunks."

Prelude, bk. 3

on a certain Sunday in term, willing or unwilling, fit or unfit, to the Sacrament, and be fined if they did not appear. Doubtless we are all of us too prone to be content with the customary, and to be prejudiced against the novel, nor is this condition of things without advantage. But we must bear our condemnation if we stick to the customary too long, and so miss our signal opportunities. In their apathy, in their self-satisfied ignorance, in their dulness of apprehension and forethought, the authorities of the University let pass the great opportunity of their time. As it usually happens, when this posture of lofty ignoring what is palpable and active, and the object of everybody's thought, goes on too long, it is apt to turn into impatient dislike and bitter antipathy. The Heads of Houses drifted insensibly into this position. They had not taken the trouble to understand the movement, to discriminate between its aspects, to put themselves frankly into communication with its leading persons, to judge with the knowledge and justice of scholars and clergymen of its designs and ways. They let themselves be diverted from this, their proper though troublesome task, by distrust, by the jealousies of their position, by the impossibility of conceiving that anything so strange could really be true and sound. And at length they found themselves going along with the outside current of uninstructed and ignoble prejudice, in a settled and pronounced dislike, which took for granted that all was wrong in the movement, which admitted any ill-natured surmise and foolish misrepresentation, and really allowed itself to acquiesce in the belief that men so well known in Oxford, once so admired and honoured, had sunk down to deliberate corrupters of the truth, and palterers with their own intellects and consciences. It came in a few years to be understood on both sides, that the authorities were in direct antagonism to the movement; and though their efforts in opposition to it were feeble and petty, it went on under the dead weight of official University disapproval. It would have been a great thing for the English Church—though it is hard to see how, things being as they were, it could have come about—if the movement had gone on, at least with the friendly interest, if not with the support, of the University rulers. Instead of that, after the first two or three years there was one long and bitter fight in Oxford, with the anger on one side created by the belief of vague but growing dangers, and a sense of incapacity in resisting them, and with deep resentment at injustice and stupidity on the other.

The Bishops were farther from the immediate scene of the movement, and besides, had other things to think of. Three or four of them might be considered theologians—Archbishop Howley, Phillpotts of Exeter, Kaye of Lincoln, Marsh of Peterborough. Two or three belonged to the Evangelical school, Ryder of Lichfield, and the two Sumners at Winchester and Chester. The most prominent among them, and next to the Bishop of Exeter the ablest, alive to the real dangers of the Church, anxious to infuse vigour into its work, and busy with plans for extending its influence, was Blomfield, Bishop of London. But Blomfield was not at his best as a divine, and, for a man of his unquestionable power, singularly unsure of his own mind. He knew, in fact, that when the questions raised by the Tracts came before him he was unqualified to deal with them; he was no better furnished by thought or knowledge or habits to judge of them than the average Bishop of the time, appointed, as was so often the case, for political or personal reasons. At the first start of the movement, the Bishops not unnaturally waited to see what would come of it. It was indeed an effort in favour of the Church, but it was in irresponsible hands, begun by men whose words were strong and vehement and of unusual sound, and who, while they called on the clergy to rally round their fathers the Bishops, did not shrink from wishing for the Bishops the fortunes of the early days: "we could not wish them a more blessed termination of their course than the spoiling of their goods and martyrdom."[2] It may reasonably be supposed that such good wishes were not to the taste of all of them. As the movement developed, besides that it would seem to them extravagant and violent, they would be perplexed by its doctrine. It took strong ground for the Church; but it did so in the teeth of religious opinions and prejudices, which were popular and intolerant. For a moment the Bishops were in a difficulty; on the one hand, no one for generations had so exalted the office of a Bishop as the Tractarians; no one had claimed for it so high and sacred an origin; no one had urged with such practical earnestness the duty of Churchmen to recog-

2. *Tracts for the Times,* No. I, 9th September 1833.

nise and maintain the unique authority of the Episcopate against its despisers or oppressors. On the other hand, this was just the time when the Evangelical party, after long disfavour, was beginning to gain recognition, for the sake of its past earnestness and good works, with men in power, and with ecclesiastical authorities of a different and hitherto hostile school; and in the Tractarian movement the Evangelical party saw from the first its natural enemy. The Bishops could not have anything to do with the Tractarians without deeply offending the Evangelicals. The result was that, for the present, the Bishops held aloof. They let the movement run on by itself. Sharp sarcasms, worldly-wise predictions, kind messages of approval, kind cautions, passed from mouth to mouth, or in private correspondence from high quarters, which showed that the movement was watched. But for some time the authorities spoke neither good nor bad of it publicly. In his Charge at the close of 1836, Bishop Phillpotts spoke in clear and unfaltering language—language remarkable for its bold decision—of the necessity of setting forth the true ideas of the Church and the sacraments; but he was silent about the call of the same kind which had come from Oxford. It would have been well if the other Bishops later on, in their charges, had followed his example. The Bishop of Oxford, in his Charge of 1838, referred to the movement in balanced terms of praise and warning. The first who condemned the movement was the Bishop of Chester, J. Bird Sumner; in a later Charge he came to describe it as the work of Satan; in 1838 he only denounced the "undermining of the foundations of our Protestant Church by men who dwell within her walls," and the bad faith of those "who sit in the Reformers' seat, and traduce the Reformation."

These were grave mistakes on the part of those who were responsible for the government of the University and the Church. They treated as absurd, mischievous, and at length traitorous, an effort, than which nothing could be more sincere, to serve the Church, to place its claims on adequate grounds, to elevate the standard of duty in its clergy, and in all its members. To have missed the aim of the movement and to have been occupied and irritated by obnoxious details and vulgar suspicions was a blunder which gave the measure of those who made it, and led to great evils. They alienated those who wished for nothing better than to help them in their true work. Their "unkindness" was felt to be, in Bacon's phrase,[3] *injuriae potentiorum.* But on the side of the party of the movement there were mistakes also.

1. The rapidity with which the movement had grown, showing that some deep need had long been obscurely felt, which the movement promised to meet,[4] had been too great to be altogether wholesome. When we compare what was commonly received before 1833, in teaching, in habits of life, in the ordinary assumptions of history, in the ideas and modes of worship, public and private—the almost sacramental conception of preaching, the neglect of the common prayer of the Prayer Book, the slight regard to the sacraments—with what the teaching of the Tracts and their writers had impressed for good and all, five years later, on numbers of earnest people, the change seems astonishing. The change was a beneficial one and it was a permanent one. The minds which it affected, it affected profoundly. Still it was but a short time, for young minds especially, to have come to a decision on great and debated questions. There was the possibility, the danger, of men having been captivated and carried away by the excitement and interest of the time; of not having looked all round and thought out the difficulties before them; of having embraced opinions without sufficiently knowing their grounds or counting the cost or considering the consequences. There was the danger of precipitate judgment, of ill-balanced and disproportionate views of what was true and all-important. There was an inevitable feverishness in the way in which the movement was begun, in the way in which it went on. Those affected by it were themselves surprised at the swiftness of the pace. When a cause so great and so sacred seemed thus to be flourishing, and carrying along with it men's assent and sympathies, it was hardly wonderful that there should often be exaggeration, impatience at resistance, scant consideration for the slowness or the scruples or the alarms of others. Eager and sanguine men talked as if their work was accomplished, when in

3. *An Advertisement touching the Controversies of the Church of England:* printed in the *Resuscitatio,* p. 138 (ed. 1671).

4. See Mr. Newman's article, "The State of Religious Parties," in the *British Critic,* April 1839, reprinted in his *Essays Historical and Critical,* 1871, vol. 1, essay 6.

truth it was but beginning. No one gave more serious warnings against this and other dangers than the leaders; and their warnings were needed.[5]

2. Another mistake, akin to the last, was the frequent forgetfulness of the apostolic maxim, "All things are lawful for me, but all things are not expedient." In what almost amounted to a revolution in many of the religious ideas of the time, it was especially important to keep distinct the great central truths, the restoration of which to their proper place justified and made it necessary, and the many subordinate points allied with them and naturally following from them, which yet were not necessary to their establishment or acceptance. But it was on these subordinate points that the interest of a certain number of followers of the movement was fastened. Conclusions which they had a perfect right to come to, practices innocent and edifying to themselves, but of secondary account, began to be thrust forward into prominence, whether or not these instances of self-will really helped the common cause, whether or not they gave a handle to ill-nature and ill-will. Suspicion must always have attached to such a movement as this; but a great deal of it was provoked by indiscreet defiance, which was rather glad to provoke it.

3. Apart from these incidents—common wherever a number of men are animated with zeal for an inspiring cause—there were what to us now seem mistakes made in the conduct itself of the movement. Considering the difficulties of the work, it is wonderful that there were not more; and none of them were discreditable,

5. "It would not be at all surprising, though, in spite of the earnestness of the principal advocates of the views in question, for which every one seems to give them credit, there should be among their followers much that is enthusiastic, extravagant, or excessive. All these aberrations will be and are imputed to the doctrines from which they proceed; nor unnaturally, but hardly fairly, for aberrations there must be, whatever the doctrine is, while the human heart is sensitive, capricious, and wayward. . . . There will ever be a number of persons professing the opinions of a movement party, who talk loudly and strangely, do odd and fierce things, display themselves unnecessarily, and disgust other people; there will ever be those who are too young to be wise, too generous to be cautious, too warm to be sober, or too intellectual to be humble; of whom human sagacity cannot determine, only the event, and perhaps not even that, whether they feel what they say, or how far; whether they are to be encouraged or discountenanced."—*British Critic*, April 1839, "State of Religious Parties," p. 405.

none but what arose from the limitation of human powers matched against confused and baffling circumstances.

In the position claimed for the Church of England, confessedly unique and anomalous in the history of Christendom, between Roman authority and infallibility on one side, and Protestant freedom of private judgment on the other, the question would at once arise as to the grounds of belief. What, if any, are the foundations of conviction and certitude, apart from personal inquiry, and examination of opposing arguments on different sides of the case, and satisfactory logical conclusions? The old antithesis between Faith and Reason, and the various problems connected with it, could not but come to the front, and require to be dealt with. It is a question which faces us from a hundred sides, and, subtly and insensibly transforming itself, looks different from them all. It was among the earliest attempted to be solved by the chief intellectual leader of the movement, and it has occupied his mind to the last.[6] However near the human mind seems to come to a solution, it only, if so be, comes near; it never arrives. In the early days of the movement it found prevailing the specious but shallow view that everything in the search for truth was to be done by mere producible and explicit argumentation; and yet it was obvious that of this two-thirds of the world are absolutely incapable. Against this Mr. Newman and his followers pressed, what was as manifestly certain in fact as it accorded with any deep and comprehensive philosophy of the formation and growth of human belief, that not arguments only, but the whole condition of the mind to which they were addressed—and not the reasonings only which could be stated, but those which went on darkly in the mind, and which "there was not at the moment strength to bring forth," real and weighty reasons which acted like the obscure rays of the spectrum, with their proper force, yet eluding distinct observation—had their necessary and inevitable and legitimate place in determining belief. All this was perfectly true; but it is obvious how easily it might be taken hold of, on very opposite sides, as a ground for saying that Tractarian or Church views did not care about argu-

6. Cardinal Newman, *Grammar of Assent*.

ment, or, indeed, rather preferred weak arguments to strong ones in the practical work of life. It was ludicrous to say it in a field of controversy, which, on the "Tractarian" side, was absolutely bristling with argument, keen, subtle, deep, living argument, and in which the victory in argument was certainly not always with those who ventured to measure swords with Mr. Newman or Dr. Pusey. Still, the scoff could be plausibly pointed at the "young enthusiasts who crowded the Via Media, and who never presumed to argue, except against the propriety of arguing at all." There was a good deal of foolish sneering at reason; there was a good deal of silly bravado about not caring whether the avowed grounds of opinions taken up were strong or feeble. It was not merely the assent of a learner to his teacher, of a mind without means of instruction to the belief which it has inherited, or of one new to the ways and conditions of life to the unproved assertions and opinions of one to whom experience had given an open and sure eye. It was a positive carelessness, almost accounted meritorious, to inquire and think, when their leaders called them to do so. "The Gospel of Christ is not a matter of mere argument." It is not, indeed, when it comes in its full reality, in half a hundred different ways, known and unsearchable, felt and unfelt, moral and intellectual, on the awakened and quickened soul. But the wildest fanatic can take the same words into his mouth. Their true meaning was variously and abundantly illustrated, especially in Mr. Newman's sermons. Still, the adequate, the emphatic warning against their early abuse was hardly pressed on the public opinion and sentiment of the party of the movement with the force which really was requisite. To the end there were men who took up their belief avowedly on insufficient and precarious grounds, glorying in the venturesomeness of their faith and courage, and justifying their temper of mind and their intellectual attitude by alleging misinterpreted language of their wiser and deeper teachers. A recoil from Whately's hard and barren dialectics, a sympathy with many tender and refined natures which the movement had touched, made the leaders patient with intellectual feebleness when it was joined with real goodness and Christian temper; but this also sometimes made them less impatient than they might well have been with that curious form of conceit and affectation which veils itself under an intended and supposed humility, a supposed distrust of self and its own powers.

Another difficult matter, not altogether successfully managed—at least from the original point of view of the movement, and of those who saw in it a great effort for the good of the English Church—was the treatment of the Roman controversy. The general line which the leaders proposed to take was the one which was worthy of Christian and truth-loving teachers. They took a new departure; and it was not less just than it was brave, when, recognising to the full the overwhelming reasons why "we should not be Romanists," they refused to take up the popular and easy method of regarding the Roman Church as apostate and antichristian; and declined to commit themselves to the vulgar and indiscriminate abuse of it was the discreditable legacy of the old days of controversy. They did what all the world was loudly professing to do, they looked facts in the face; they found, as any one would find who looked for himself into the realities of the Roman Church, that though the bad was often as bad as could be, there was still, and there had been all along, goodness of the highest type, excellence both of system and of personal life which it was monstrous to deny, and which we might well admire and envy. To ignore all this was to fail in the first duty, not merely of Christians, but of honest men; and we at home were not so blameless that we could safely take this lofty tone of contemptuous superiority. If Rome would only leave us alone, there would be estrangement, lamentable enough among Christians, but there need be no bitterness. But Rome would not leave us alone. The moment that there were signs of awakening energy in England, that moment was chosen by its agents, for now it could be done safely, to assail and thwart the English Church. Doubtless they were within their rights, but this made controversy inevitable, and for controversy the leaders of the movement prepared themselves. It was an obstacle which they seemed hardly to have expected, but which the nature of things placed in their way. But the old style of controversy was impossible; impossible because it was so coarse, impossible because it was so hollow.

If the argument (says the writer of Tract 71, in words which are applicable to every controversy) is radically unreal, or (what may be called) rhetorical or sophistical, it may serve the purpose of encouraging those who are really convinced, though scarcely without doing mischief to them, but certainly it will offend and alienate the more acute and sensible; while those who are in doubt, and who desire some real and substantial ground for their faith, will not bear to be put off with such shadows. The arguments [he continues] which we use must be such as are likely to convince serious and earnest minds, which are really seeking for the truth, not amusing themselves with intellectual combats, or desiring to support an existing opinion anyhow. However popular these latter methods may be, however long standing, however easy both to find and to use, they are a scandal; and while they lower our religious standard from the first, they are sure of hurting our cause in the end.

And on this principle the line of argument in *The Prophetical Office of the Church* was taken by Mr. Newman. It was certainly no make-believe, or unreal argument. It was a forcible and original way of putting part of the case against Rome. It was part of the case, a very important part; but it was not the whole case, and it ought to have been evident from the first that in this controversy we could not afford to do without the whole case. The argument from the claim of infallibility said nothing of what are equally real parts of the case—the practical working of the Roman Church, its system of government, the part which it and its rulers have played in the history of the world. Rome has not such a clean record of history, it has not such a clean account of what is done and permitted in its dominions under an authority supposed to be irresistible, that it can claim to be the one pure and perfect Church, entitled to judge and correct and govern all other Churches. And if the claim is made, there is no help for it, we must not shrink from the task of giving the answer.[7] And, as experience has shown, the more that rigid good faith is kept to in giving the answer, the more strictness and severity of even understatement are observed, the more convincing will be the result that the Roman Church cannot be that which it is alleged to be in its necessary theory and ideal.

But this task was never adequately undertaken. It was one of

7. The argument from history is sketched fairly, but only sketched in *The Prophetic Office*, Lect. 14.

no easy execution.[8] Other things, apparently more immediately pressing, intervened. There was no question for the present of perfect and unfeigned confidence in the English Church, with whatever regrets for its shortcomings, and desires for its improvement. But to the outside world it seemed as if there were a reluctance to face seriously the whole of the Roman controversy; a disposition to be indulgent to Roman defects, and unfairly hard on English faults. How mischievously this told in the course of opinion outside and inside of the movement; how it was misinterpreted and misrepresented; how these misinterpretations and misrepresentations, with the bitterness and injustice which they engendered, helped to realise themselves, was seen but too clearly at a later stage.

4. Lastly, looking back on the publications, regarded as characteristic of the party, it is difficult not to feel that some of them gave an unfortunate and unnecessary turn to things.

The book which made most stir and caused the greatest outcry was Froude's *Remains*. It was undoubtedly a bold experiment; but it was not merely boldness. Except that it might be perverted into an excuse by the shallow and thoughtless for merely "strong talk," it may fairly be said that it was right and wise to let the world know the full measure and depth of conviction which gave birth to the movement; and Froude's *Remains* did that in an unsuspiciously genuine way that nothing else could have done. And, besides, it was worth while for its own sake to exhibit with fearless honesty such a character, so high, so true, so refined, so heroic. So again, Dr. Pusey's Tract on Baptism was a bold book, and one which brought heavy imputations and misconstructions on the party. In the teaching of his long life, Dr. Pusey has abundantly dispelled the charges of harshness and over-severity which were urged, not always very scrupulously, against the doctrine of the Tract on Post-baptismal Sin. But it was written to redress the balance against the fatally easy doctrines then in fashion; it was

8. In the Roman controversy it is sometimes hard to be just without appearing to mean more than is said: for the obligation of justice sometimes forces one who wishes to be a fair judge to be apparently an apologist or advocate. Yet the supreme duty in religious controversy is justice. But for the very reason that these controversialists wished to be just to Rome, they were bound to be just against her. They meant to be so; but events passed quickly, and leisure never came for a work which involved a serious appeal to history.

like the Portroyalist protest against the fashionable Jesuits; it was one-sided, and sometimes, in his earnestness, unguarded; and it wanted as yet the complement of encouragement, consolation, and tenderness which his future teaching was to supply so amply. But it was a blow struck, not before it was necessary, by a strong hand; and it may safely be said that it settled the place of the sacrament of baptism in the living system of the English Church, which the negations and vagueness of the Evangelical party had gravely endangered. But two other essays appeared in the Tracts, most innocent in themselves, which ten or twenty years later would have been judged simply on their merits, but which at the time became potent weapons against Tractarianism. They were the productions of two poets—of two of the most beautiful and religious minds of their time; but in that stage of the movement it is hardly too much to say that they were out of place. The cause of the movement needed clear explanations; definite statements of doctrines which were popularly misunderstood; plain, convincing reasoning on the issues which were raised by it; a careful laying out of the ground on which English theology was to be strengthened and enriched. Such were Mr. Newman's *Lectures on Justification,* a work which made its lasting mark on English theological thought; Mr. Keble's masterly exposition of the meaning of Tradition; and not least, the important collections which were documentary and historical evidence of the character of English theology, the so-called laborious *Catenas.* These were the real tasks of the hour, and they needed all that labour and industry could give. But the first of these inopportune Tracts was an elaborate essay, by Mr. Keble, on the "Mysticism of the Fathers in the use and interpretation of Scripture." It was hardly what the practical needs of the time required, and it took away men's thoughts from them; the prospect was hopeless that in that state of men's minds it should be understood, except by a very few; it merely helped to add another charge, the vague but mischievous charge of mysticism, to the list of accusations against the Tracts. The other, to the astonishment of every one, was like the explosion of a mine. That it should be criticised and objected to was natural; but the extraordinary irration caused by it could hardly have been anticipated. Written in the most devout and reverent spirit by one of the gentlest and most refined of scholars, and full of deep Scriptural knowledge, it furnished for some years the material for the most savage attacks and the bitterest sneers to the opponents of the movement. It was called "On Reserve in communicating Religious Knowledge"; and it was a protest against the coarseness and shallowness which threw the most sacred words about at random in loud and declamatory appeals, and which especially dragged in the awful mystery of the Atonement, under the crudest and most vulgar conception of it, as a ready topic of excitement in otherwise commonplace and helpless preaching. The word "Reserve" was enough. It meant that the Tract-writers avowed the principle of keeping back part of the counsel of God. It meant, further, that the real spirit of the party was disclosed; its love of secret and crooked methods, its indifference to knowledge, its disingenuous professions, its deliberate concealments, its holding doctrines and its pursuit of aims which it dared not avow, its *disciplina arcani,* its conspiracies, its Jesuitical spirit. All this kind of abuse was flung plentifully on the party as the controversy became warm; and it mainly justified itself by the Tract on "Reserve." The Tract was in many ways a beautiful and suggestive essay, full of deep and original thoughts, though composed in that spirit of the recluse which was characteristic of the writer, and which is in strong contrast with the energetic temper of to-day.[9] But it could well have been spared at the moment, and it certainly offered itself to an unfortunate use. The suspiciousness which so innocently it helped to awaken and confirm was never again allayed.

9. See a striking review in the *British Critic,* April 1839, partly correcting and guarding the view given in the Tract.

XIV

No. 90

The formation of a strong Romanising section in the Tractarian party was obviously damaging to the party and dangerous to the Church. It was *pro tanto* a verification of the fundamental charge against the party, a charge which on paper they had met successfully, but which acquired double force when this paper defence was traversed by facts. And a great blow was impending over the Church, if the zeal and ability which the movement had called forth and animated were to be sucked away from the Church, and not only lost to it, but educated into a special instrument against it. But the divergence became clear only gradually, and the hope that after all it was only temporary and would ultimately disappear was long kept up by the tenacity with which Mr. Newman, in spite of misgivings and disturbing thoughts, still recognised the gifts and claims of the English Church. And on the other hand, the bulk of the party, and its other Oxford leaders, Dr. Pusey, Mr. Keble, Mr. Isaac Williams, Mr. Marriott, were quite unaffected by the disquieting apprehensions which were beginning to beset Mr. Newman. With a humbling consciousness of the practical shortcomings of the English Church, with a ready disposition to be honest and just towards Rome, and even to minimise our differences with it, they had not admitted for a moment any doubt of the reality of the English Church. The class of arguments which specially laid hold of Mr. Newman's mind did not tell upon them—the peculiar aspect of early precedents, about which, moreover, a good deal of criticism was possible; or the large and sweeping conception of a vast, ever-growing, imperial Church, great enough to make flaws and imperfections of no account, which appealed so strongly to his statesmanlike imagination. Their content with the Church in which they had been brought up, in which they had been taught religion, and in which they had taken service, their deep and affectionate loyalty and piety to it, in spite of all its faults, remained unimpaired; and unimpaired, also, was their sense of vast masses of practical evil in the Roman Church, evils from which they shrank both as Englishmen and as Christians, and which seemed as incurable as they were undeniable. Beyond the hope which they vaguely cherished that some day or other, by some great act of Divine mercy, these evils might disappear, and the whole Church become once more united, there was nothing to draw them towards Rome; submission was out of the question, and they could only see in its attitude in England the hostility of a jealous and unscrupulous disturber of their Master's work. The movement still went on, with its original purpose, and on its original lines, in spite of the presence in it, and even the cooperation, of men who might one day have other views, and serious and fatal differences with their old friends.

The change of religion when it comes on a man gradually— when it is not welcomed from the first, but, on the contrary, long resisted, must always be a mysterious and perplexing process, hard to realise and follow by the person most deeply interested, veiled and clouded to lookers-on, because naturally belonging to the deepest depths of the human conscience, and inevitably, and without much fault on either side, liable to be misinterpreted and misunderstood. And this process is all the more tangled when it goes on, not in an individual mind, travelling in its own way on its own path, little affected by others, and little affecting them, but in a representative person, with the responsibilities of a great cause upon him, bound by closest ties of every kind to friends, colleagues, and disciples, thinking, feeling, leading, pointing out the way for hundreds who love and depend on him. Views and feelings vary from day to day, according to the events and conditions of the day. How shall he speak, and how shall he be silent? How shall he let doubts and difficulties appear, yet how shall he suppress them?—Doubts which may grow and become hopeless, but which, on the other hand, may be solved and disappear. How shall he go on as if nothing had happened, when all the foundations of the world seem to have sunk from under him? Yet how shall he disclose the dreadful secret, when he is not yet quite sure whether his mind will not still rally from its terror and despair? He must in honesty, in kindness, give some warning, yet how much? and how to prevent it being taken for more than it means? There are counter-considerations, to which he cannot shut his eyes. There are friends who will not believe his warnings. There are watchful enemies who are on the look-out for proofs of disingenuousness and bad faith. He could cut through his difficulties at once by making the plunge in obedience to this or that plausible sign or train of reasoning, but his conscience and good faith will not let him take things so easily; and yet he knows that if he hangs on, he will be accused by and by, perhaps speciously, of having been dishonest and deceiving. So subtle, so shifting, so impalpable are the steps by which a faith is disintegrated; so evanescent, and impossible to follow, the shades by which one set of convictions pass into others wholly opposite; for it is not knowledge and intellect alone which come into play, but all the moral tastes and habits of the character, its likings and dislikings, its weakness and its strength, its triumphs and its vexations, its keenness and its insensibilities, which are in full action, while the intellect alone seems to be busy with its problems. A picture has been given us, belonging to this time, of the process, by a great master of human nature, and a great sufferer under the process; it is, perhaps, the greatest attempt ever made to describe it; but it is not wholly successful. It tells us much, for it is written with touching good faith, but the complete effect as an intelligible whole is wanting.

"In the spring of 1839," we read in the *Apologia,* "my position in the Anglican Church was at its height. I had a supreme confidence in my controversial *status,* and I had a great and still growing success in recommending it to others."[1] This, then, may be taken as the point from which, in the writer's own estimate, the change is to be traced. He refers for illustration of his state of mind to the remarkable article on the "State of Religious

1. *Apologia,* p. 180.

Parties," in the April number of the *British Critic* for 1839, which
he has since republished under the title of "Prospects of the
Anglican Church."[2] "I have looked over it now," he writes in
1864, "for the first time since it was published; and have been
struck by it for this reason; it contains *the last words I ever spoke
as an Anglican to Anglicans. . . .* It may now be read as my
parting address and valediction, made to my friends. I little knew
it at the time." He thus describes the position which he took in
the article referred to:—

> Conscious as I was that my opinions in religious matters were
> not gained, as the world said, from Roman sources, but were, on
> the contrary, the birth of my own mind and of the circumstances
> in which I had been placed, I had a scorn of the imputations
> which were heaped upon me. It was true that I held a large, bold
> system of religion, very unlike the Protestantism of the day, but
> it was the concentration and adjustment of the statements of
> great Anglican authorities, and I had as much right to do so as
> the Evangelical party had, and more right than the Liberal, to hold
> their own respective doctrines. As I spoke on occasion of Tract 90,
> I claimed, on behalf of the writer, that he might hold in the
> Anglican Church a comprecation of the Saints with Bramhall;
> and the Mass, all but Transubstantiation, with Andrewes; or with
> Hooker that Transubstantiation itself is not a point for Churches
> to part communion upon; or with Hammond that a General
> Council, truly such, never did, never shall err in a matter of
> faith; or with Bull that man lost inward grace by the Fall; or with
> Thorndike that penance is a propitiation for post-baptismal sin;
> or with Pearson that the all-powerful name of Jesus is no other-
> wise given than in the Catholic Church. "Two can play at that
> game" was often in my mouth, when men of Protestant senti-
> ments appealed to the Articles, Homilies, and Reformers, in the
> sense that if they had a right to speak loud I had both the liberty
> and the means of giving them tit for tat. I thought the the Angli-
> can Church had been tyrannised over by a Party, and I aimed at
> bringing into effect the promise contained in the motto to the
> *Lyra*: " They shall know the difference now." I only asked to be
> allowed to show them the difference.
>
> I have said already [he goes on] that though the object of the
> movement was to withstand the Liberalism of the day, I found

2. *Essays Critical and Historical,* 1871.

and felt that this could not be done by negatives. It was necessary for me to have a positive Church theory erected on a definite basis. This took me to the great Anglican divines; and then, of course, I found at once that it was impossible to form any such theory without cuttting across the teaching of the Church of Rome. Thus came in the Roman controversy. When I first turned myself to it I had neither doubt on the subject, nor suspicion that doubt would ever come on me. It was in this state of mind that I began to read up Bellarmine on the one hand, and numberless Anglican writers on the other.[3]

And he quotes from the article the language which he used, to show the necessity of providing some clear and strong basis for religious thought in view of the impending conflict of principles, religious and anti-religious, "Catholic and Rationalist," which to far-seeing men, even at that comparatively early time, seemed inevitable:—

> Then indeed will be the stern encounter, when two real and living principles, simple, entire, and consistent, one in the Church, the other out of it, at length rush upon each other, contending not for names and words, a half view, but for elementary notions and distinctive moral characters. Men will not keep standing in that very attitude which you call sound Church-of-Englandism or orthodox Protestantism. They will take one view or another, but it will be a consistent one . . . it will be real. . . . Is it sensible, sober, judicious, to be so very angry with the writers of the day who point to the fact, that our divines of the seventeenth century have occupied a ground which is the true and intelligible mean between extremes? . . . Would you rather have your sons and your daughters members of the Church of England or of the Church of Rome?[4]

"The last words that I spoke as an Anglican to Anglicans,"— so he describes this statement of his position and its reasons; so it seems to him, as he looks back. And yet in the intimate and frank disclosures which he makes, he has shown us much that indicates both that his Anglicanism lasted much longer and that his Roman sympathies began to stir much earlier. This only shows the enor-

3. *Apologia,* pp. 181, 182. Comp. *Letter to Jelf,* p. 18.
4. *British Critic,* April 1839, pp. 419–426. Condensed in the *Apologia,* pp. 192–194.

mous difficulties of measuring accurately the steps of a transition state. The mind, in such a strain of buffeting, is never in one stay. The old seems impregnable, yet it has been undermined; the new is indignantly and honestly repelled, and yet leaves behind it its never-to-be-forgotten and unaccountable spell. The story, as he tells it, goes on, how, in the full swing and confidence of his Anglicanism, and in the course of his secure and fearless study of antiquity, appearance after appearance presented itself, un-expected, threatening, obstinate, in the history of the Early Church, by which this confidence was first shaken and then utterly broken down in the summer of 1839. And he speaks as though all had been over after two years from that summer: "From the end of 1841 I was on my death-bed, as regards my membership with the Anglican Church, though at the time I became aware of it only by degrees." In truth, it was only the end which showed that it was a "death-bed." He had not yet died to allegiance or "to hope, then or for some time afterwards." He speaks in later years of the result, and reads what was then in the light of what followed. But after all that had happened, and much, of course, disturbing happened in 1841, he was a long way off from what then could have been spoken of as "a death-bed." Deep and painful misgivings may assail the sincerest faith; they are not fatal signs till faith has finally given way.

What is true is, that the whole state of religion, and the whole aspect of Christianity in the world, had come to seem to him por-tentously strange and anomalous. No theory would take in and suit all the facts, which the certainties of history and experience presented. Neither in England, nor in Rome, and much less any-where else, did the old, to which all appealed, agree with the new; it might agree variously in this point or in that, in others there were contrarieties which it was vain to reconcile. Facts were against the English claim to be a Catholic Church—how could Catholicity be shut up in one island? How could England assert its continuity of doctrine? Facts were against the Roman claim to be an infallible, and a perfect, and the whole Church—how could that be perfect which was marked in the face of day with enormous and undeniable corruptions? How could that be infallible which was irreconcilable with ancient teaching? How could that be the whole Church, which, to say nothing of the break-up in the West, ignored, as if it had no existence, the ancient and uninterrupted Eastern Church? Theory after theory came up and was tried, and was found wanting. Each had much to say for itself, its strong points, its superiority over its rivals in dealing with the difficulties of the case, its plausibilities and its imaginative attractions. But all had their tender spot, and flinched when they were touched in earnest. In the confusions and sins and divisions of the last fifteen centuries, profound disorganisation had fastened on the Western Church. Christendom was not, could not be pretended to be, what it had been in the fourth century; and whichever way men looked the reasons were not hard to see. The first and characteristic feeling of the movement, one which Mr. Newman had done so much to deepen, was that of shame and humiliation at the disorder at home, as well as in every part of the Church. It was not in Rome only, or in England only; it was everywhere. What had been peculiar to Anglicanism among all its rivals, was that it had emphatically and without reserve confessed it.

With this view of the dislocation and the sins of the Church, he could at once with perfect consistency recognise the short-comings of the English branch of the Church, and yet believe and maintain that it was a true and living branch. The English frag-ment was not what it should be, was indeed much that it should not be; the same could be said of the Roman, though in different respects. This, as he himself reminds us, was no new thing to his mind when the unsettlement of 1839 began. "At the end of 1835, or the beginning of 1836, I had the whole state of the question before me, on which, to my mind, the decision between the Churches depended." It did not, he says, depend on the claims of the Pope, as centre of unity; "it turned on the Faith of the Church"; "there was a contrariety of *claims* between the Roman and Anglican religions"; and up to 1839, with the full weight of Roman arguments recognised, with the full conscious-ness of Anglican disadvantages, he yet spoke clearly for Anglican-ism. Even when misgivings became serious, the balance still inclined without question the old way. He hardly spoke stronger in 1834 than he did in 1841, after No. 90.

> And now [he writes in his Letter to the Bishop of Oxford] having said, I trust, as much as your Lordship requires on the sub-

ject of Romanism, I will add a few words, to complete my explanation, in acknowledgment of the inestimable privilege I feel in being a member of that Church over which your Lordship, with others, presides. Indeed, did I not feel it to be a privilege which I am able to seek nowhere else on earth, why should I be at this moment writing to your Lordship? What motive have I for an unreserved and joyful submission to your authority, but the feeling that the Church in which your Lordship rules is a divinely-ordained channel of supernatural grace to the souls of her members? Why should I not prefer my own opinion, and my own way of acting, to that of the Bishop's, except that I know full well that in matters indifferent I should be acting lightly towards the Spouse of Christ and the awful Presence which dwells in her, if I hesitated a moment to put your Lordship's will before my own? I know full well that your Lordship's kindness to me personally would be in itself quite enough to win any but the most insensible heart, and, did a clear matter of conscience occur in which I felt bound to act for myself, my feelings towards your Lordship would be a most severe trial to me, independently of the higher considerations to which I have alluded; but I trust I have shown my dutifulness to you prior to the influence of personal motives; and this I have done because I think that to belong to the Catholic Church is the first of all privileges here below, as involving in it heavenly privileges, and because I consider the Church over which your Lordship presides to be the Catholic Church in this country. Surely then I have no need to profess in words, I will not say my attachment, but my deep reverence towards the Mother of Saints, when I am showing it in action; yet that words may not be altogether wanting, I beg to lay before your Lordship the following extract from a defence of the English Church, which I wrote against a Roman controversialist in the course of the last year.

"The Church is emphatically a living body, and there can be no greater proof of a particular communion being part of the Church than the appearance in it of a continued and abiding energy, nor a more melancholy proof of its being a corpse than torpidity. We say an energy continued and abiding, for accident will cause the activity of a moment, and an external principle give the semblance of self-motion. On the other hand, even a living body may for a while be asleep.

. . . . . .

"It concerns, then, those who deny that we are the true Church because we have not at present this special note, intercommunion with other Christians, to show cause why the Roman Church in the tenth century should be so accounted, with profligates, or rather the profligate mothers of profligate sons for her supreme rulers. And still notwithstanding life *is* a note of the Church; she alone revives, even if she declines; heretical and schismatical bodies cannot keep life; they gradually became cold, stiff, and insensible.

.   .   .   .   .   .

"Now if there ever were a Church on whom the experiment has been tried, whether it had life in it or not, the English is that one. For three centuries it has endured all vicissitudes of fortune. It has endured in trouble and prosperity, under seduction, and under oppression. It has been practised upon by theorists, browbeaten by sophists, intimidated by princes, betrayed by false sons, laid waste by tyranny, corrupted by wealth, torn by schism, and persecuted by fanaticism. Revolutions have come upon it sharply and suddenly, to and fro, hot and cold, as if to try what it was made of. It has been a sort of battlefield on which opposite principles have been tried. No opinion, however extreme any way, but may be found, as the Romanists are not slow to reproach us, among its Bishops and Divines. Yet what has been its career upon the whole? Which way has it been moving for 300 years? Where does it find itself at the end? Lutherans have tended to Rationalism; Calvinists have become Socinians; but what has it become? As far as its Formularies are concerened, it may be said all along to have grown towards a more perfect Catholicism than that with which it started at the time of its estrangement; every act, every crisis which marks its course, has been upward.

.   .   .   .   .   .

"What a note of the Church is the mere production of a man like Butler, a pregnant fact much to be meditated on! and how strange it is, if it be as it seems to be, that the real influence of his work is only just now beginning! and who can prophesy in what it will end? Thus our Divines grow with centuries, expanding after their death in the minds of their readers into more and more exact Catholicism as years roll on.

.   .   .   .   .   .

"Look across the Atlantic to the daughter Churches of England in the States: 'Shall one that is barren bear a child in her old age?' yet 'the barren hath borne seven.' Schismatic branches put out their leaves at once, in an expiring effort; our Church has waited three centuries, and then blossoms like Aaron's rod, budding and blooming and yielding fruit, while the rest are dry. And lastly, look at the present position of the Church at home; there, too, we shall find a note of the true City of God, the Holy Jerusalem. She is in warfare with the world, as the Church Militant should be; she is rebuking the world, she is hated, she is pillaged by the world.

.   .   .   .   .

"Much might be said on this subject. At all times, since Christianity came into the world, an open contest has been going on between religion and irreligion; and the true Church, of course, has ever been on the religious side. This, then, is a sure test in every age *where* the Christian should stand. . . . Now, applying this simple criterion to the public Parties of this day, it is very plain that the English Church is at present on God's side, and therefore, so far, God's Church; we are sorry to be obliged to add that there is as little doubt on which side English Romanism is.

.   .   .   .   .

"As for the English Church, surely she has notes enough, 'the signs of an Apostle in all patience, and signs and wonders and mighty deeds.' She has the note of possession, the note of freedom from party-titles; the note of life, a tough life and a vigorous; she has ancient descent, unbroken continuance, agreement in doctrine with the ancient Church. Those of Bellarmine's Notes, which she certainly has not, are inter-communion with Christendom, the glory of miracles, and the prophetical light, but the question is, whether she has not enough of Divinity about her to satisfy her sister Churches on their own principles, that she is one body with them."

This may be sufficient to show my feelings towards my Church, as far as Statements on paper can show them.[5]

How earnestly, how sincerely he clung to the English Church, even after he describes himself on his "death-bed," no one can doubt. The charm of the *Apologia* is the perfect candour with which he records fluctuations which to many are inconceivable and unintelligible, the different and sometimes opposite and irreconcilable states of mind through which he passed, with no

5. *Letter to the Bishop of Oxford* (29th March 1841), pp. 33–40. Comp. *Letter to Jelf*, pp. 7, 8.

attempt to make one fit into another. It is clear, from what he tells us, that his words in 1839 were not his *last* words as an Anglican to Anglicans. With whatever troubles of mind, he strove to be a loyal and faithful Anglican long after that. He spoke as an Anglican. He fought for Anglicanism. The theory, as he says, may have gone by the board, in the intellectual storms raised by the histories of the Monophysites and Donatists. "By these great words of the ancient father—*Securus judicat orbis terrarum*"—the theory of the *Via Media* was "absolutely pulverised." He was "sore," as he says in 1840, "about the great Anglican divines, as if they had taken me in, and made me say strong things against Rome, which facts did not justify."[6] Yes, he felt, as other men do not feel, the weak points of even a strong argument, the exaggerations and unfairness of controversialists on his own side, the consciousness that you cannot have things in fact, or in theory, or in reasoning, smoothly and exactly as it would be convenient, and as you would like to have them. But his conclusion, on the whole, was unshaken. There was enough, and amply enough, in the English Church to bind him to its allegiance, to satisfy him of its truth and its life, enough in the Roman to warn him away. In the confusions of Christendom, in the strong and obstinate differences of schools and parties in the English Church, he, living in days of inquiry and criticism, claimed to take and recommend a theological position on many controverted questions, which many might think a new one, and which might not be exactly that occupied by any existing school or party.[7] "We are all," he writes to an intimate friend on 22d April 1842, a year after No. 90, "much quieter and more resigned than we were, and are remarkably desirous of building up a position, and proving that the English theory is tenable, or rather the English state of things. If the Bishops would leave us alone, the fever would subside."

He wanted, when all other parties were claiming room for their speculations, to claim room for his own preference for ancient doctrine. He wished to make out that no branch of the Church had authoritatively committed itself to language which was hopelessly and fatally irreconcilable with Christian truth.

6. *Apologia,* pp. 212, 221.
7. *Letter to Jelf* (especially p. 19).

But he claimed nothing but what he could maintain to be fairly within the authorised formularies of the English Church. He courted inquiry, he courted argument. If his claim seemed a new one, if his avowed leaning to ancient and Catholic views seemed to make him more tolerant than had been customary, not to Roman abuses, but to Roman authoritative language, it was part of the more accurate and the more temperate and charitable thought of our day compared with past times. It was part of the same change which has brought Church opinions from the unmitigated Calvinism of the Lambeth Articles to what the authorities of those days would have denounced, without a doubt, as Arminianism. Hooker was gravely and seriously accused to the Council for saying that a Papist could be saved, and had some difficulty to clear himself; it was as natural as it is amazing now.[8]

But with this sincere loyalty to the English Church, as he believed it to be, there was, no doubt, in the background the haunting and disquieting misgiving that the attempt to connect more closely the modern Church with the ancient, and this widened theology in a direction which had been hitherto specially and jealously barred, was putting the English Church on its trial. Would it bear it? Would it respond to the call to rise to a higher and wider type of doctrine, to a higher standard of life? Would it justify what Mr. Newman had placed in the forefront among the notes of the true Church, the note of Sanctity? Would the *Via Media* make up for its incompleteness as a theory by developing into reality and fruitfulness of actual results? Would the Church bear to be told of its defaults? Would it allow to the maintainers of Catholic and Anglican principles the liberty which others claimed, and which by large and powerful bodies of opinion was denied to Anglicans? Or would it turn out on trial, that the *Via Media* was an idea without substance, a dialectical fiction, a mere theological expedient for getting out of difficulties, unrecognised, and when put forward, disowned? Would it turn out that the line of thought and teaching which connected the modern with the ancient Church was but the private and accidential opinion of Hooker and Andrewes and Bull and Wilson,

8. *Walton's Life,* i. 59 (Oxford: 1845).

unauthorised in the English Church, uncongenial to its spirit, if
not contradictory to its formularies? It is only just to Mr. Newman to say, that even after some of his friends were frightened,
he long continued to hope for the best; but undoubtedly, more
and more, his belief in the reality of the English Church was
undergoing a very severe, and as time went on, discouraging
testing.

In this state of things he published the Tract No. 90. It was
occasioned by the common allegation, on the side of some of the
advanced section of the Tractarians, as well as on the side of their
opponents, that the Thirty-nine Articles were hopelessly irreconcilable with that Catholic teaching which Mr. Newman had
defended on the authority of our great divines, but which both
the parties above mentioned were ready to identify with the teaching of the Roman Church. The Tract was intended, by a rigorous
examination of the language of the Articles, to traverse this allegation. It sought to show that all that was clearly and undoubtedly
Catholic, this language left untouched:[9] that it was doubtful
whether even the formal definitions of the Council of Trent were
directly and intentionally contradicted; and that what were really
aimed at were the abuses and perversions of a great popular
and authorised system, tyrannical by the force of custom and the
obstinate refusal of any real reformation.

> It is often urged [says the writer], and sometimes felt and
> granted, that there are in the Articles propositions or terms in-
> consistent with the Catholic faith; or, at least, if persons do not
> go so far as to feel the objection as of force, they are perplexed
> how best to answer it, or how most simply to explain the pas-
> sages on which it is made to rest. The following Tract is drawn
> up with the view of showing how groundless the objection is,
> and further, of approximating towards the argumentative answer
> to it, of which most men have an implicit apprehension, though
> they may have nothing more. That there are real difficulties to a
> Catholic Christian in the ecclesiastical position of our Church at
> this day, no one can deny; but the statements of the Articles are
> not in the number, and it may be right at the present moment to
> insist upon this.

9. No. 90, p.24.

When met by the objection that the ideas of the framers of the Articles were well known, and that it was notorious that they had meant to put an insuperable barrier between the English Church and everything that savoured of Rome, the writer replied that the actual English Church received the Articles not from them but from a much later authority, that we are bound by their words not by their private sentiments either as theologians or ecclesiastical politicans, and that in fact they had intended the Articles to comprehend a great body of their countrymen, who would have been driven away by any extreme and anti-Catholic declarations even against Rome. The temper of compromise is characteristic of the English as contrasted with the foreign Reformation. It is visible, not only in the Articles, but in the polity of the English Church, which clung so obstinately to the continuity and forms of the ancient hierarchical system. It is visible in the sacramental offices of the Prayer Book, which left so much out to satisfy the Protestants, and left so much in to satisfy the Catholics.

The Tract went in detail through the Articles which were commonly looked upon as either anti-Catholic or anti-Roman. It went through them with a dry logical way of interpretation, such as a professed theologian might use, who was accustomed to all the niceties of language and the distinctions of the science. It was the way in which they would be likely to be examined and construed by a purely legal court. The effect of it, doubtless, was like that produced on ordinary minds by the refinements of a subtle advocate, or by the judicial interpretation of an Act of Parliament which the judges do not like; and some of the interpretations undoubtedly seemed far-fetched and artificial. Yet some of those which were pointed to at the time as flagrant instances of extravagant misinterpretation have now come to look different. Nothing could exceed the scorn poured on the interpretation of the Twenty-second Article, that it condemns the *"Roman"* doctrine of Purgatory, but not *all* doctrine of purgatory as a place of gradual purification beyond death. But in our days a school very far removed from Mr. Newman's would require and would claim to make the same distinction. And so with the interpretation of the "Sacrifices of Masses" in the same article. It was the fashion in 1841 to see in this the condemnation of all doctrine of a sacrifice in the Eucharist; and when Mr. Newman confined the phrase to the gross abuses connected with the Mass, this was treated as an affront to common sense and honesty. Since then we have become better acquainted with the language of the ancient liturgies; and no instructed theologian could now venture to treat Mr. Newman's distinction as idle. There was in fact nothing new in his distinctions on these two points. They had already been made in two of the preceding Tracts, the reprint of Archbishop Ussher on Prayers for the Dead, and the Catena on the Eucharistic Sacrifice; and in both cases the distinctions were supported by a great mass of Anglican authority.[10]

But the Tract had sufficient novelty about it to account for most of the excitement which it caused. Its dryness and negative curtness were provoking. It was not a positive argument, it was not an appeal to authorities; it was a paring down of language, alleged in certain portions of the Articles to be somewhat loose, to its barest meaning; and to those to whom that language had always seemed to speak with fulness and decision, it seemed like sapping and undermining a cherished bulwark. Then it seemed to ask for more liberty than the writer in his position at that time needed; and the object of such an indefinite claim, in order to remove, if possible, misunderstandings between two long-alienated branches of the Western Church, was one to excite in many minds profound horror and dismay. That it maintained without flinching and as strongly as ever the position and the

---

10. The following letter of Mr. James Mozley (8th March 1841) gives the first impression of the Tract:—"A new Tract has come out this week, and is beginning to make a sensation. It is on the Articles, and shows that they bear a highly Catholic meaning; and that many doctrines, of which the Romanist are corruptions, may be held consistently with them. This is no more than what we know as a matter of history, for the Articles were expressly worded to bring in Roman Catholics. But people are astonished and confused at the idea now, as if it were quite new. And they have been so accustomed for a long time to look at the Articles as on a par with the Creed, that they think, I suppose, that if they subscribe to them they are bound to hold whatever doctrines (not positively stated in them) are merely not condemned. So if they will have a Tractarian sense, they are thereby all Tractarians. . . . It is, of course, highly complimentary to the whole set of us to be so very much surprised that we should think what we held to be consistent with the Articles which we have subscribed." See also a clever Whateleian pamphlet, "The Controversy between Tract No. 90. and the Oxford Tutors." (How and Parsons, 1841.)

claim of the English Church was nothing to the purpose; the admission, both that Rome, though wrong, might not be as wrong as we thought her, and that the language of the Articles, though unquestionably condemnatory of much, was not condemnatory of as much as people thought, and might possibly be even harmonised with Roman authoritative language, was looked upon as incompatible with loyalty to the English Church.

The question which the Tract had opened, what the Articles meant and to what men were bound by accepting them, was a most legitimate one for discussion; and it was most natural also that any one should hesitate to answer it as the Tract answered it. But it was distinctly a question for discussion. It was not so easy for any of the parties in the Church to give a clear and consistent answer, as that the matter ought at once to have been carried out of the region of discussion. The Articles were the Articles of a Church which had seen as great differences as those between the Church of Edward VI and the Church of the Restoration. Take them broadly as the condemnation—strong but loose in expression, as, for instance, in the language on the "five, commonly called Sacraments"—of a powerful and well-known antagonist system, and there was no difficulty about them. But take them as scientific and accurate and precise enunciations of a systematic theology, and difficulties begin at once, with every one who does not hold the special and well-marked doctrines of the age when the German and Swiss authorities ruled supreme. The course of events from that day to this has shown more than once, in surprising and even startling examples, how much those who at the time least thought that they needed such strict construing of the language of the Articles, and were fierce in denouncing the "kind of interpretation" said to be claimed in No. 90, have since found that they require a good deal more elasticity of reading than even it asked for. The "whirligig of time" was thought to have brought "its revenges," when Mr. Newman, who had called for the exercise of authority against Dr. Hampden, found himself, five years afterwards, under the ban of the same authority. The difference between Mr. Newman's case and Dr. Hampden's, both as to the alleged offence and the position of the men, was considerable. But the "whirligig of time" brought about even stranger "revenges," when not only Mr. Gorham and Mr.

H. B. Wilson in their own defence, but the tribunals which had to decide on their cases, carried the strictness of reading and the latitude of interpretation, quite as far, to say the least, as anything in No. 90.

Unhappily Tract 90 was met at Oxford, not with argument, but with panic and wrath.[11] There is always a sting in every charge, to which other parts of it seem subordinate. No. 90 charged of course with false doctrine, with false history, and with false reasoning; but the emphatic part of the charge, the short and easy method which dispensed from the necessity of theological examination and argument, was that it was dishonest and immoral. Professors of Divinity, and accomplished scholars, such as there were in Oxford, might very well have considered it an occasion to dispute both the general principle of the Tract, if it was so dangerous, and the illustrations, in the abundance of which the writer had so frankly thrown open his position to searching criticism. It was a crisis in which much might have been usefully said, if there had been any one to say it; much too, to make any one feel, if he was competent to feel, that he had a good deal to think about in his own position, and that it would be well to ascertain what was tenable and what untenable in it. But it seemed as if the opportunity must not be lost for striking a blow. The Tract was published on 27th February. On the 8th of March four Senior Tutors, one of whom was Mr. H. B. Wilson, of St. John's, and another Mr. Tait, of Balliol, addressed the Editor of the Tract, charging No. 90 with suggesting and opening a way, by which men might, at least in the case of Roman views, violate their solemn engagements to their University. On the 15th of March, the Board of Heads of Houses, refusing to wait for Mr. Newman's defence, which was known to be coming, and which bears date 13th March, published their judgment. They declared that in No. 90 "modes of interpretation were suggested, and have since been advocated in other publications purporting to be written by members of the University, by which subscription to the Articles might be reconciled with the adoption of Roman Catholic error." And they announced their resolution, "That modes of interpretation, such as are suggested in the said Tract, evading

11. See J. B. Mozley's *Letters*, 13th March 1841.

rather than explaining the sense of the Thirty-nine Articles, and reconciling subscription to them with the adoption of errors which they are designed to counteract, defeat the object, and are inconsistent with the due observance of the above-mentioned statutes."[12]

It was an ungenerous and stupid blunder, such as men make, when they think or are told that "something must be done," and do not know what. It gave the writer an opportunity, of which he took full advantage, of showing his superiority in temper, in courtesy, and in reason, to those who had not so much condemned as insulted him. He was immediately ready with his personal expression of apology and regret, and also with his reassertion in more developed argument of the principle of the Tract; and this was followed up by further explanations in a letter to the Bishop. And in spite of the invidious position in which the Board had tried to place him, not merely as an unsound divine, but as a dishonest man teaching others to palter with their engagements, the crisis drew forth strong support and sympathy where they were not perhaps to be expected. It rallied to him, at least for the time, some of the friends who had begun to hold aloof. Mr. Palmer, of Worcester, Mr. Perceval, Dr. Hook, with reserves according to each man's point of view, yet came forward in his defence. The Board was made to feel that they had been driven by violent and partisan instigations to commit themselves to a very foolish as well as a very passionate and impotent step; that they had by very questionable authority simply thrown an ill-sounding and ill-mannered word at an argument on a very difficult question, to which they themselves certainly were not prepared with a clear and satisfactory answer; that they had made the double mistake of declaring war against a formidable antagonist, and of beginning it by creating the impression that they had treated him shabbily, and were really afraid to come to close quarters with him. As the excitement of hasty counsels subsided, the sense of this began to awake in some of them; they tried to represent the off-hand and ambiguous words of the condemnation as not meaning all that they had been taken to mean. But the seed of bitterness had been sown. Very little light was thrown, in the strife of pamphlets

12. Viz., those cited in the preamble to this resolution.

199

which ensued, on the main subject dealt with in No. 90, the authority and interpretation of such formularies as our Articles. The easier and more tempting and very fertile topic of debate was the honesty and good faith of the various disputants. Of the four Tutors, only one, Mr. H. B. Wilson, published an explanation of their part in the matter; it was a clumsy, ill-written and laboured pamphlet, which hardly gave promise of the intellectual vigour subsequently displayed by Mr. Wilson, when he appeared, not as the defender, but the assailant of received opinions. The more distinguished of the combatants were Mr. Ward and Mr. R. Lowe. Mr. Ward, with his usual dialectical skill, not only defended the Tract, but pushed its arguments yet further, in claiming tolerance for doctrines alleged to be Roman. Mr. Lowe, not troubling himself either with theological history or the relation of other parties in the Church to the formularies, threw his strength into the popular and plausible topic of dishonesty, and into a bitter and unqualified invective against the bad faith and immorality manifested in the teaching of which No. 90 was the outcome. Dr. Faussett, as was to be expected, threw himself into the fray with his accustomed zest and violence, and caused some amusement at Oxford, first by exposing himself to the merciless wit of a reviewer in the *British Critic*, and then by the fright into which he was thrown by a rumour that his re-election to his professorship would be endangered by Tractarian votes.[13] But the storm, at Oxford at least, seemed to die out. The difficulty which at one moment threatened of a strike among some of the college Tutors passed; and things went back to their ordinary course. But an epoch and a new point of departure had come into the movement. Things after No. 90 were never the same as to language and hopes and prospects as they had been before; it was the date from which a new set of conditions in men's thoughts and attitude had to be reckoned. Each side felt that a certain liberty had been claimed and had been peremptorily denied. And this was more than confirmed by the public language of the greater part of the Bishops. The charges against the Tractarian party of Romanising, and of flagrant dishonesty, long urged by irresponsible opponents, were now formally adopted by the University authorities, and specially

13. J. B. Mozley's *Letters*, 13th July 1841.

directed against the foremost man of the party. From that time the fate of the party at Oxford was determined. It must break up. Sooner or later, there must be a secession more or less discrediting and disabling those who remained. And so the break-up came, and yet, so well grounded and so congenial to the English Church were the leading principles of the movement, that not even that disastrous and apparently hopeless wreck prevented them from again asserting their claim and becoming once more active and powerful. The *Via Media*, whether or not logically consistent, was a thing of genuine English growth, and was at least a working theory.

XV

After No. 90

The proceedings about No. 90 were a declaration of war on the part of the Oxford authorities against the Tractarian party. The suspicions, alarms, antipathies, jealousies, which had long been smouldering among those in power, had at last taken shape in a definite act. And it was a turning-point in the history of the movement. After this it never was exactly what it had been hitherto. It had been so far a movement within the English Church, for its elevation and reform indeed, but at every step invoking its authority with deep respect, acknowledging allegiance to its rulers in unqualified and even excessive terms, and aiming loyally to make it in reality all that it was in its devotional language and its classical literature. But after what passed about No. 90 a change came. The party came under an official ban and stigma. The common consequences of harsh treatment on the tendencies and thought of a party, which considers itself unjustly proscribed, showed themselves more and more. Its mind was divided; its temper was exasperated; while the attitude of the governing authorities hardened more into determined hostility. From the time of the censure, and especially after the events connected with it,—the contest for the Poetry Professorship and the renewed Hampden question,—it may be said that the characteristic tempers of the Corcyrean sedition were reproduced on a small scale in Oxford.[1] The scare of Popery, not without foundation—the reaction

---

1. Τόλμα ἀλόγιστος **ἀνδρία** φιλέταιρος ἐνομίσθη . . . τὸ δὲ σῶφρον τοῦ ἀνάνδρου πρόσχημα, καὶ τὸ πρὸς ἅπαν ξυνετὸν ἐπὶ πᾶν ἀργόν. τὸ δὲ ἐμπλήκτως

against it, also not without foundation—had thrown the wisest off their balance; and what of those who were not wise? In the heat of those days there were few Tractarians who did not think Dr. Wynter, Dr. Faussett, and Dr. Symons heretics in theology and persecutors in temper, despisers of Christian devotion and self-denial. There were few of the party of the Heads who did not think every Tractarian a dishonest and perjured traitor, equivocating about his most solemn engagements, the ignorant slave of childish superstitions which he was conspiring to bring back. It was the day of the violent on both sides: the courtesies of life were forgotten; men were afraid of being weak in their censures, their dislike, and their opposition; old friendships were broken up, and men believed the worst of those whom a few years back they had loved and honoured.

It is not agreeable to recall these long extinct animosities, but they are part of the history of that time, and affected the course in which things ran. And it is easy to blame, it is hard to do justice to, the various persons and parties who contributed to the events of that strange and confused time. All was new, and unusual, and without precedent in Oxford; a powerful and enthusiastic school reviving old doctrines in a way to make them seem novelties, and creating a wild panic from a quarter where it was the least expected; the terror of this panic acting on authorities not in the least prepared for such a trial of their sagacity, patience, and skill, driving them to unexampled severity, and to a desperate effort to expel the disturbing innovators—among them some of the first men in Oxford in character and ability—from their places in the University.[2] In order to do justice on each side at

---

ὀξὺ ἀνδρὸς μοίρᾳ προσετέθη . . . καὶ ὁ μὲν χαλεπαίνων πιστὸς ἀεί, ὁ δὲ ἀντιλέγων αὐτῷ ὕποπτος.—Thuc. 3. 82. "Reckless daring was held to be loyal courage; moderation was the disguise of unmanly weakness; to know everything was to do nothing; frantic energy was in the true character of a man; the lover of violence was always trusted, and his opponent suspected."—Jowett's translation.

2. One of the strangest features in the conflict was the entire misconception shown of what Mr. Newman was—the blindness to his real character and objects—the imputation to him not merely of grave faults, but of small and mean ones. His critics could not rise above the poorest measure of his intellect and motives. One of the ablest of them, who had once been his friend, in a farewell letter of kindly remonstrance, specifies certain Roman errors, which he hopes that Mr. Newman will not fall into—adoring images and worshipping

this distance of time, we are bound to make allowance—both for the alarm and the mistaken violence of the authorities, and for the disaffection, the irritation, the strange methods which grew up in the worried and suspected party—for the difficulties which beset both sides in the conflict, and the counter-influences which drew hither and thither. But the facts are as they are; and even then a calmer temper was possible to those who willed it; and in the heat of the strife there were men among the authorities, as well as in the unpopular party, who kept their balance, while others lost it.

Undoubtedly the publication of No. 90 was the occasion of the aggravated form which dissension took, and not unnaturally. Yet it was anything but what it was taken to mean by the authorities, an intentional move in favour of Rome. It was intended to reconcile a large and growing class of minds, penetrated and disgusted with the ignorance and injustice of much of the current controversial assumptions against Rome, to a larger and more defensible view of the position of the English Church. And this was done by calling attention to that which was not now for the first time observed—to the loose and unguarded mode of speaking visible in the later controversial Articles, and to the contrast between them and the technical and precise theology of the first five Articles. The Articles need not mean all which they were supposed popularly to mean against what was Catholic in Roman doctrine. This was urged in simple good faith; it was but the necessary assumption of all who held with the Catholic theology, which the Tractarians all along maintained that they had a right to teach; it left plenty of ground of difference with unreformed and usurping Rome. And we know that the storm which No. 90 raised took the writer by surprise. He did not expect that he should give such

---

saints—as if the pleasure and privilege of worshipping images and saints were to Mr. Newman the inducement to join Rome and break the ties of a lifetime. And so of his moral qualities. A prominent Evangelical leader, Dr. Close of Cheltenham, afterwards Dean of Carlisle, at a complimentary dinner, in which he himself gloried in the "foul, personal abuse to which he had been subjected in his zeal for truth," proceeded to give his judgment on Mr. Newman: "When I first read No. 90, I did not then know the author; but I said then, and I repeat here, *not with any personal reference to the author,* that I should be sorry to trust the author of that Tract with my purse."—Report of Speech in *Cheltenham Examiner,* 1st March 1843.

deep offence. But if he thought of the effect on one set of minds, he forgot the probable effect on another; and he forgot, or under-estimated, the effect not only of the things said, but of the way in which they were said.[3] No. 90 was a surprise, in the state of ordinary theological knowledge at the time. It was a strong thing to say that the Articles left a great deal of formal Roman language untouched; but to work this out in dry, bald, technical logic, on the face of it, narrow in scope, often merely ingenious, was even a greater stumbling block. It was, undoubtedly, a great miscalculation, such as men of keen and far-reaching genius sometimes make. They mistake the strength and set of the tide; they imagine that minds round them are going as fast as their own. We can see, looking back, that such an interpretation of the Articles, with the view then taken of them in Oxford as the theological text-book, and in the condition of men's minds, could not but be a great shock.

And what seemed to give a sinister significance to No. 90 was that, as has been said, a strong current was beginning to set in the direction of Rome. It was not yet of the nature, nor of the force, which was imagined. The authorities suspected it where it was not. They accepted any contemptible bit of gossip collected by ignorance or ill-nature as a proof of it. The constitutional frank-ness of Englishmen in finding fault with what is their own—disgust at pompous glorification—scepticism as to our insular claims against all the rest of Christendom to be exactly right, to be alone, "pure and apostolic"; real increase and enlargement of knowledge, theological and historical; criticism on portions of our Reformation history; admiration for characters in mediaeval times; eagerness, over-generous it might be, to admit and repair wrong to an opponent unjustly accused; all were set down to-gether with other more unequivocal signs as "leanings to Rome." It was clear that there was a current setting towards Rome; but it was as clear that there was a much stronger current in the party as a whole, setting in the opposite direction. To those who chose to see and to distinguish, the love, the passionate loyalty of the bulk of the Tractarians to the English Church was as evident and unquestionable as any public fact could be. At this time there was

3. οὐ γὰρ ἀπόχρη τὸ ἔχειν ἅ δεῖ λέγειν, ἀλλ' ἀνάγκη καὶ ταῦτα ὡς δεῖ εἰπεῖν. —Arist. *Rhet.* iii. 1.

no reason to call in question the strong assurances given by the writer of No. 90 himself of his yet unshaken faith in the English Church. But all these important features of the movement—witnessing, indeed, to deep searchings of heart, but to a genuine desire to serve the English Church—were overlooked in the one overwhelming fear which had taken possession of the authorities. Alarming symptoms of a disposition to acknowledge and even exaggerate the claims and the attractions of the Roman system were indeed apparent. No doubt there were reasons for disquiet and anxiety. But the test of manliness and wisdom, in the face of such reasons, is how men measure their proportion, and how they meet the danger.

The Heads saw a real danger before them; but they met it in a wrong and unworthy way. They committed two great errors. In the first place, like the Jesuits in their quarrel with Portroyal and the Jansenists, they entirely failed to recognise the moral elevation and religious purpose of the men whom they opposed. There was that before them which it was to their deep discredit that they did not see. The movement, whatever else it was, or whatever else it became, was in its first stages a movement for deeper religion, for a more real and earnest self-discipline, for a loftier morality, for more genuine self-devotion to a serious life, than had ever been seen in Oxford. It was an honest attempt to raise Oxford life, which by all evidence needed raising, to something more laborious and something more religious, to something more worthy of the great Christian foundations of Oxford than the rivalry of colleges and of schools, the mere literary atmosphere of the tutor's lecture-room, and the easy and gentlemanly and somewhat idle fellowship of the common-rooms. It was the effort of men who had all the love of scholarship, and the feeling for it of the Oxford of their day, to add to this the habits of Christian students and the pursuit of Christian learning. If all this was dangerous and uncongenial to Oxford, so much the worse for Oxford, with its great opportunities and great professions—*Dominus illuminatio mea.* But certainly this mark of moral purpose and moral force was so plain in the movement that the rulers of Oxford had no right to mistake it. When the names come back to our minds of those who led and most represented the Tractarians, it must be a matter of surprise to any man who has not almost parted with the idea of

Christian goodness, that this feature of the movement could escape or fail to impress those who had known well all their lives long what these leaders were. But amid the clamour and the telltale gossip, and, it must be admitted, the folly round them, they missed it. Perhaps they were bewildered. But they must have the blame, the heavy blame, which belongs to all those who, when good is before them, do not recognise it according to its due measure.[4]

In the next place, the authorities attacked and condemned the Tractarians teaching at once violently and ignorantly; and in them ignorance of the ground on which the battle was fought was hardly pardonable. Doubtless the Tractarians language was in many respects novel and strange. But Oxford was not only a city of libraries, it was the home of what was especially accounted Church theology; and the Tractarian teaching, in its foundation and main outlines, had little but what ought to have been perfectly familiar to any one who chose to take the trouble to study the great Church of England writers. To one who, like Dr. Routh of Magdalen, had gone below the surface, and was acquainted with the questions debated by those divines, there was nothing startling in what so alarmed his brethren, whether he agreed with it or not; and to him the indiscriminate charge of Popery meant nothing. But Dr. Routh stood alone among his brother Heads in his knowledge of what English theology was. To most of them it was an unexplored and misty region; some of the ablest, under the influence of Dr. Whately's vigorous and scornful discipline, had learned to slight it. But there it was. Whether it was read or not, its great names were pronounced with honour, and quoted on occasion. From Hooker to Van Mildert, there was an unbroken thread of common principles giving continuity to a line of Church teachers. The Puritan line of doctrine, though it could claim much sanction among the divines of the Reformation—the Latitudinarian idea, though it had the countenance of famous names and powerful intellects—never could aspire to the special title of Church theology. And the teaching which had that name, both in praise, and often in disprase, as technical, scholastic, unspiritual, transcendental, nay, even Popish, countenanced the Tractarians.

4. Dr. Richards, the Rector of Exeter, seems to have stood apart from his brother heads.—Cf. *Letters of the Rev. J. B. Mozley*, p. 113.

They were sneered at for their ponderous *Catenae* of authorities; but on the ground on which this debate raged, the appeal was a pertinent and solid one. Yet to High Church Oxford and its rulers, all this was strange doctrine. Proof and quotation might lie before their eyes, but their minds still ran in one groove, and they could not realise what they saw. The words meant no harm in the venerable folio; they meant perilous heresy in the modern Tract. When the authorities had to judge of the questions raised by the movement, they were unprovided with the adequate knowledge; and this was knowledge which they ought to have possessed for its own sake, as doctors of the Theological Faculty of the University.

And it was not only for their want of learning, manifest all through the controversy, that they were to blame. Their most telling charge against the Tractarians, which was embodied in the censure of No. 90, was the charge of dishonesty. The charge is a very handy one against opponents, and it may rest on good grounds; but those who think right to make it ought, both as a matter of policy and as a matter of conscience, to be quite assured of their own position. The Articles are a public, common document. It is the differing interpretations of a common document which create political and religious parties; and only shallowness and prejudice will impute to an opponent dishonesty without strong and clear reason. Mr. Newman's interpretation in No. 90, —new, not claiming for the Articles a Catholic meaning, but in *limiting*, though it does not deny, their anti-Roman scope, was fairly open to criticism. It might be taken as a challenge, and as a challenge might have to be met. But it would have been both fair and wise in the Heads, before proceeding to unusual extremities, to have shown that they had fully considered their own theological doctrines in relation to the Church formularies. They all had obvious difficulties, and in some cases formidable ones. The majority of them were what would have been called in older controversial days frank Arminians, shutting their eyes by force of custom to the look of some of the Articles, which, if of Lutheran origin, had been claimed from the first by Calvinists. The Evangelicals had long confessed difficulties, at least, in the Baptismal Service and the Visitation Office; while the men most loud in denunciation of dishonesty were the divines of Whately's school,

who had been undermining the authority of all creeds and articles,
and had never been tired of proclaiming their dislike of that
solemn Athanasian Creed to which Prayer Book and Articles alike
bound them. Men with these difficulties daily before them had no
right to ignore them. Doubtless they all had their explanations
which they *bona fide* believed in. But what was there that excluded Mr. Newman from the claim to *bona fides*? He had attacked no foundation of Christianity; he had denied or doubted
no article of the Creed. He gave his explanations, certainly not
more far-fetched than those of some of his judges. In a Church
divided by many conflicting views, and therefore bound to all possible tolerance, he had adopted one view which certainly was unpopular and perhaps was dangerous. He might be confuted, he
might be accused, or, if so be, convicted of error, perhaps of
heresy. But nothing of this kind was attempted. The incompatibil-
ity of his view, not merely with the Articles, but with morality in
signing what all, of whatever party, had signed, was asserted in a
censure, which evaded the responsibility of specifying the point
which it condemned. The alarm of treachery and conspiracy is
one of the most maddening of human impulses. The Heads of
Houses, instead of moderating and sobering it, with the authority
of instructed and sagacious rulers, blew it into a flame. And they
acted in such a hurry that all sense of proportion and dignity was
lost. They peremptorily refused to wait even a few days, as the
writer requested, and as was due to his character, for explanation.
They dared not risk an appeal to the University at large. They
dared not abide the effect of discussion on the blow which they
were urged to strike. They chose, that they might strike without
delay, the inexpressibly childish step of sticking up at the Schools'
gates, and at College butteries, without trial, or conviction, or sentence, a notice declaring that certain modes of signing the Articles
suggested in a certain Tract were dishonest. It was, they said, to
protect undergraduates; as if undergraduates would be affected by
a vague assertion on a difficult subject, about which nothing was
more certain than that those who issued the notice were not agreed
among themselves.

The men who acted thus were good and conscientious men,
who thought themselves in the presence of a great danger. It is
only fair to remember this. But it is also impossible to be fair to

the party of the movement without remembering this deplorable failure in consistency, in justice, in temper, in charity, on the part of those in power in the University. The drift towards Rome had not yet become an unmanageable rush; and though there were cases in which nothing could have stopped its course, there is no reason to doubt that generous and equitable dealing, a more considerate reasonableness, a larger and more comprehensive judgment of facts, and a more patient waiting for strong first impressions to justify and verify themselves, would have averted much mischief. There was much that was to be regretted from this time forward in the temper and spirit of the movement party. But that which nourished and strengthened impatience, exaggeration of language and views, scorn of things as they were, intolerable of everything moderate, both in men and in words, was the consciousness with which every man got up in the morning and passed the day, of the bitter hostility of those foremost in place in Oxford—of their incompetence to judge fairly—of their incapacity to apprehend what was high and earnest in those whom they condemned—of the impossibility of getting them to imagine that Tractarians could be anything but fools or traitors—of their hopeless blindness to any fact or any teaching to which they were not accustomed. If the authorities could only have stopped to consider whether after all they were not dealing with real thought and real wish to do right, they might after all have disliked the movement, but they would have seen that which would have kept them from violence. They would not listen, they would not inquire, they would not consider. Could such ignorance, could such wrong possibly be without mischievous influence on those who were the victims of it, much more on friends and disciples who knew and loved them? The Tractarians had been preaching that the Church of England, with all its Protestant feeling and all its Protestant acts and history, was yet, as it professed to be, part and parcel of the great historic Catholic Church, which had framed the Creeds, which had continued the Sacraments, which had given us our immemorial prayers. They had spared no pains to make out this great commonplace from history and theology: nor had they spared pains, while insisting on this dominant feature in the English Church, to draw strongly and broadly the lines which distinguished it from Rome. Was it wonderful, when all guarding and explanatory limitations were contemptuously tossed aside by "all-daring ignorance," and all was lumped together in the indiscriminate charge of "Romanising," that there should have been some to take the authorities at their word? Was it wonderful when men were told that the Church of England was no place for them, that they were breaking their vows and violating solemn engagements by acting as its ministers, and that in order to preserve the respect of honest men they should leave it—that the question of change, far off as it had once seemed, came within "measurable distance"? The generation to which they belonged had been brought up with strong exhortations to be real, and to hate shams; and now the question was forced on them whether it was not a sham for the English Church to call itself Catholic; whether a body of teaching which was denounced by its authorities, however it might look on paper and be defended by learning, could be more than a plausible literary hypothesis in contrast to the great working system of which the head was Rome. When we consider the singular and anomalous position on any theory, including the Roman, of the English Church; with what great differences its various features and elements have been prominent at different times; how largely its history has been marked by contradictory facts and appearances; and how hard it is for anyone to keep all, according to their real importance, simultaneously in view; when we remember also what are the temptations of human nature in great collisions of religious belief, the excitement and passion of the time, the mixed character of all religious zeal, the natural inevitable anger which accompanies it when resisted, the fervour which welcomes self-sacrifice for the truth; and when we think of all this kept aglow by the continuous provocation of unfair and harsh dealing from persons who were scarcely entitled to be severe judges; the wonder is, human nature being what it is, not that so many went, but that so many stayed.

XVI

The Three Defeats:
Isaac Williams,
Macmullen, Pusey

The year 1841, though it had begun in storm, and though signs were not wanting of further disturbance, was at Oxford, outwardly at least, a peaceable one. A great change had happened; but, when the first burst of excitement was over, men settled down to their usual work, their lectures, or their reading, or their parishes, and by Easter things seemed to go on as before. The ordinary habits of University life resumed their course with a curious quietness. There was, no doubt, much trouble brooding underneath. Mr. Ward and others continued a war of pamphlets; and in June Mr. Ward was dismissed from his Mathematical Lectureship at Balliol. But faith in the great leader was still strong. No. 90, if it had shocked or disquieted some, had elicited equally remarkable expressions of confidence and sympathy from others who might have been, at least, silent. The events of the spring had made men conscious of what their leader was, and called forth warm and enthusiastic affection. It was not in vain that, whatever might be thought of the wisdom or the reasonings of No. 90, he had shown the height of his character and the purity and greatness of his religious purpose; and that being what he was, in the eyes of all Oxford, he had been treated with contumely, and had borne it with patience and loyal submission. There were keen observers, to whom that patience told of future dangers; they would have liked him to show more fight. But he gave no signs of defeat, nor, outwardly, of disquiet; he forbore to retaliate at Oxford: and the sermons at St. Mary's continued, penetrating and searching as ever, perhaps with something more pathetic and anxious in their undertone than before.

But if he forbore at Oxford, he did not let things pass outside. Sir Robert Peel, in opening a reading-room at Tamworth, had spoken loosely, in the conventional and pompous way then fashionable, of the all-sufficing and exclusive blessings of knowledge. While Mr. Newman was correcting the proofs of No. 90, he was also writing to the *Times* the famous letters of *Catholicus*; a warning to eminent public men of the danger of declaiming on popular commonplaces without due examination of their worth. But all seemed quiet. "In the summer of 1841," we read in the *Apologia*, "I found myself at Littlemore without any harass or anxiety on my mind. I had determined to put aside all controversy, and set myself down to my translation of St. Athanasius." Outside of Oxford there was a gathering of friends in the summer at the consecration of one of Mr. Keble's district churches, Ampfield—an occasion less common and more noticeable then than now. Again, what was a new thought then, a little band of young Oxford men, ten or twelve, taxed themselves to build a new church, which was ultimately placed at Bussage, in Mr. Thomas Keble's parish. One of Mr. Keble's curates, Mr. Peter Young, had been refused Priest's orders by the Bishop of Winchester, for alleged unsoundness on the doctrine of the Eucharist. Mr. Selwyn, not without misgivings on the part of the Whig powers, had been appointed Bishop of New Zealand. Dr. Arnold had been appointed to the Chair of Modern History at Oxford. In the course of the year there passed away one who had had a very real though unacknowledged influence on much that had happened—Mr. Blanco White. And at the end of the year, 29th October, Mr. Keble gave his last lecture on Poetry, and finished a course the most original and memorable ever delivered from his chair.

Towards the end of the year two incidents, besides some roughly-worded Episcopal charges, disturbed this quiet. They were only indirectly connected with theological controversy at Oxford; but they had great ultimate influence on it, and they helped to marshal parties and consolidate animosities. One was the beginning of the contest for the Poetry Professorship which Mr. Keble had vacated. There was no one of equal eminence to succeed him; but there was in Oxford a man of undoubted po-

etical genius, of refined taste and subtle thought, though of unequal power, who had devoted his gifts to the same great purpose
for which Mr. Keble had written the *Christian Year*. No one who
has looked into the *Baptistery*, whatever his feeling towards the
writer, can doubt whether Mr. Isaac Williams was a poet and
knew what poetry meant. He was an intimate friend of Mr. Keble
and Mr. Newman, and so he was styled a Tractarian; but no name
offered itself so obviously to the electors as his, and in due time
his friends announced their intention of bringing him forward.
His competitor was Mr. (afterwards Archdeacon) Garbett of
Brasenose, the college of Heber and Milman, an accomplished
gentleman of high culture, believed to have an acquaintance, not
common then in Oxford, with foreign literature, whose qualifications stood high in the opinion of his University friends, but
who had given no evidence to the public of his claims to the office. It was inevitable, it was no one's special fault, that the question of theological opinions should intrude itself; but at first it
was only in private that objections were raised or candidatures
recommended on theological grounds. But rumours were abroad
that the authorities of Brasenose were canvassing their college on
these grounds: and in an unlucky moment for Mr. Williams, Dr.
Pusey, not without the knowledge, but without the assenting
judgment of Mr. Newman, thought it well to send forth a circular
in Christ Church first, but soon with wider publicity, asking support for Mr. Williams as a person whose known religious views
would ensure his making his office minister to religious truth.
Nothing could be more innocently meant. It was the highest purpose to which that office could be devoted. But the mistake was
seen on all sides as soon as made. The Principal of Mr. Garbett's
college, Dr. Gilbert, like a general jumping on his antagonist
whom he has caught in the act of a false move, put forth a dignified counter-appeal, alleging that he had not raised this issue, but
adding that as it had been raised and avowed on the other side,
he was quite willing that it should be taken into account, and the
dangers duly considered of that teaching with which Dr. Pusey's
letter had identified Mr. Williams. No one from that moment
could prevent the contest from becoming almost entirely a theological one, which was to try the strength of the party of the
movement. Attempts were made, but in vain, to divest it of this

character. The war of pamphlets and leaflets dispersed in the common-rooms, which usually accompanied these contests, began, and the year closed with preparations for a severe struggle when the University met in the following January.

The other matter was the establishment of the Anglo-Prussian bishopric at Jerusalem. It was the object of the ambition of M. Bunsen to pave the way for a recognition, by the English Church, of the new State Church of Prussia, and ultimately for some closer alliance between the two bodies; and the plan of a Protestant Bishop of Jerusalem, nominated alternately by England and Prussia, consecrated by English Bishops, and exercising jurisdiction over English and German Protestants in Palestine, was proposed by him to Archbishop Howley and Bishop Blomfield, and somewhat hastily and incautiously accepted by them. To Mr. Newman, fighting a hard battle, as he felt it, for the historical and constitutional catholicity of the English Church, this step on their part came as a practical and even ostentatious contradiction of his arguments. England, it seemed, which was out of communion with the East and with Rome, could lightly enter into close communion with Lutherans and Calvinists against them both. He recorded an indignant and even bitter protest; and though the scheme had its warm apologists, such as Dr. Hook and Mr. F. Maurice, it had its keen-sighted critics, and it was never received with favour by the Church at large. And, indeed, it was only active for mischief. It created irritation, suspicion, discord in England, while no German cared a straw about it. Never was an ambitious scheme so marked by impotence and failure from its first steps to its last. But it was one, as the *Apologia* informs us,[1] in the chain of events which destroyed Mr. Newman's belief in the English Church. "It was one of the blows," he writes, "which broke me."

The next year, 1842, opened with war; war between the University authorities and the party of the movement, which was to continue in various forms and with the little intermission till the strange and pathetic events of 1845 suspended the fighting and stunned the fighters, and for a time hushed even anger in feelings of amazement, sorrow, and fear. Those events imposed

1. Pp. 243, 253.

stillness on all who had taken part in the strife, like the blowing up of the *Orient* at the battle of the Nile.

As soon as the University met in January 1842, the contest for the Poetry Professorship was settled. There was no meeting of Convocation, but a comparison of votes gave a majority of three to two to Mr. Garbett,[2] and Mr. Williams withdrew. The Tractarians had been distinctly beaten; it was their first defeat as a party. It seems as if this encouraged the Hebdomadal Board to a move, which would be felt as a blow against the Tractarians, and which, as an act of reparation to Dr. Hampden, would give satisfaction to the ablest section of their own supporters, the theological Liberals. They proposed to repeal the disqualification which had been imposed on Dr. Hampden in 1836. But they had miscalculated. It was too evidently a move to take advantage of the recent Tractarian discomfiture to whitewash Dr. Hampden's Liberalism. The proposal, and the way in which it was made, roused a strong feeling among the residents; a request to withdraw it received the signatures not only of moderate Anglicans and independent men, like Mr. Francis Faber of Magdalen, Mr. Sewell, the Greswells, and Mr. W. Palmer of Worcester, but of Mr. Tait of Balliol, and Mr. Golightly. Dr. Hampden's own attitude did not help it. There was great want of dignity in his ostentatious profession of orthodoxy and attachment to the Articles, in his emphatic adoption of Evangelical phraseology, and in his unmeasured denunciation of his opponents, and especially of those whom he viewed as most responsible for the censure of 1836—the "Tractarians" or "Romanisers." And the difficulty with those who had passed and who now proposed to withdraw the censure, was that Dr. Hampden persistently and loudly declared that he had nothing to retract, and retracted nothing; and if it was right to pass it in 1836, it would not be right to withdraw it in 1842. At the last moment, Mr. Tait and Mr. Piers Claughton of University made an attempt to get something from Dr. Hampden which might pass as a withdrawal of what was supposed to be dangerous in his Bampton Lectures; and there were some even among Mr. Newman's friends, who, disliking from the first the form of the censure, might have found in such a withdrawal a reason for

2. Garbett, 921. Williams, 623.

voting for its repeal. But Dr. Hampden was obdurate. The measure was pressed, and in June it was thrown out in Convocation by a majority of three to two[3]—the same proportion, though in smaller numbers, as in the vote against Mr. Williams. The measure was not an honest one on the part of the Hebdomadal Board, and deserved to be defeated. Among the pamphlets which the discussion produced, two by Mr. James Mozley gave only evidence, by their force of statement and their trenchant logic, of the power with which he was to take part in the questions which agitated the University.

Dr. Hampden took his revenge, and it was not a noble one. The fellows of certain colleges were obliged to proceed to the B.D. degree on pain of forfeiting their fellowships. The exercises for the degree, which, by the Statutes, took the old-fashioned shape of formal Latin disputations between Opponents and Respondents on given theses in the Divinity School, had by an arrangement introduced by Dr. Burton, with no authority from the Statutes, come to consist of two English essays on subjects chosen by the candidate and approved by the Divinity Professor. The exercises for the degree had long ceased to be looked upon as very serious matters, and certainly were never regarded as tests of the soundness of the candidate's faith. They were usually on well-worn commonplaces, of which the Regius Professor kept a stock, and about which no one troubled himself but the person who wanted the degree. It was not a creditable system, but it was of a piece with the prevalent absence of any serious examination for the superior degrees. It would have been quite befitting his position, if Dr. Hampden had called the attention of the authorities to the evil of sham exercises for degrees in his own important Faculty. It would have been quite right to make a vigorous effort on public grounds to turn these sham trials into realities; to use them, like the examination for the B.A. degree, as tests of knowledge and competent ability. Such a move on his part would have been in harmony with the legislation which had recently added two theological Professors to the Faculty, and had sketched out, however imperfectly, the outlines of a revived theological school.

3. The numbers were 334 to 219.

This is what, with good reason, Dr. Hampden might have attempted on general grounds, and had he been successful (though this in the suspicious state of University feeling was not very likely) he would have gained in a regular and lawful way that power of embarrassing his opponents which he was resolved to use in defiance of all existing custom. But such was not the course which he chose. Mr. Macmullen of Corpus, who, in pursuance of the College Statutes, had to proceed to the B.D. degree, .applied, as the custom was, for theses to the Professor. Mr. Macmullen was known to hold the opinions of the movement school; of course he was called a Tractarian; he had put his name to some of the many papers which expressed the sentiments of his friends on current events. Dr. Hampden sent him two propositions, which the candidate was to support, framed so as to commit him to assertions which Mr. Macmullen, whose high Anglican opinions were well known, could not consistently make. It was a novel and unexampled act on the part of the Professor, to turn what had been a mere formal exercise into a sharp and sweeping test of doctrine, which would place all future Divinity degrees in the University at his mercy; and the case was made more serious, when the very form of exercise which the Professor used as an instrument of such formidable power was itself without question unstatutable and illegal, and had been simply connived at by the authorities. To introduce by his own authority a new feature into a system which he had no business to use at all, and to do this for the first time with the manifest purpose of annoying an obnoxious individual, was, on Dr. Hampden's part, to do more to discredit his chair and himself, than the censure of the University could do; and it was as unwise as it was unworthy. The strength of his own case before the public was that he could be made to appear as the victim of a personal and partisan attack; yet on the first opportunity he acts in the spirit of an inquisitor, and that not in fair conflict with some one worthy of his hostility, but to wreak an injury, in a matter of private interest, or an individual, in no way known to him or opposed to him, except as holding certain unpopular opinions.

Mr. Macmullen was not the person to take such treatment quietly. The right was substantially on his side, and the Professor, and the University authorities who more or less played into the hands of the Professor, in defence of his illegal and ultimately untenable claims, appeared before the University, the one as a persecutor, the others as rulers who were afraid to do justice on behalf of an ill-used man because he was a Tractarian. The right course was perfectly clear. It was to put an end to these unauthorised exercises, and to recall both candidates and Professor to the statutable system which imposed disputations conducted under the moderatorship of the Professor, but which gave him no veto, at the time, on the theological sufficiency of the disputations, leaving him to state his objections, if he was not satisfied, when the candidate's degree was asked for in the House of Congregation. This course, after some hesitation, was followed, but only partially; and without allowing or disallowing the Professor's claim to a veto, the Vice-Chancellor on his own responsibility stopped the degree. A vexatious dispute lingered on for two or three years, with actions in the Vice-Chancellor's Court, and distinguished lawyers to plead for each side, and appeals to the University Court of Delegates, who reversed the decision of the Vice-Chancellor's assessor. Somehow or other, Mr. Macmullen at last got his degree, but at the cost of a great deal of ill-blood in Oxford, for which Dr. Hampden, by his unwarranted interference, and the University authorities, by their questionable devices to save the credit and claims of one of their own body, must be held mainly responsible.

Before the matter was ended, they were made to feel, in rather a startling way, how greatly they had lost the confidence of the University. One of the attempts to find a way out of the tangle of the dispute was the introduction, in February 1844, of a Statute which should give to the Professor the power which was now contested, and practically place all the Divinity degrees under the control of a Board in conjunction with the Vice-Chancellor.[4] The proposed legislation raised such indignation in the University, that the Hebdomadal Board took back their scheme for further revision, and introduced it again in a modified shape, which still however gave new powers to the Professor and the Vice-Chancellor. But the University would have none of it. No one could say that the defeat of the altered Statute by 341

4. *Christian Remembrancer*, vol. ix. p. 175.

to 21 was the work merely of a party.[5] It was the most decisive vote given in the course of these conflicts. And it was observed that on the same day Mr. Macmullen's degree was vetoed by the Vice-Chancellor at the instance of Dr. Hampden at 10 o'clock in Congregation, and the Hebdomadal Board, which had supported him, received the vote of want of confidence at noon in Convocation.

Nothing could show more decisively that the authorities in the Hebdomadal Board were out of touch with the feeling of the University, or, at all events, of that part of it which was resident. The residents were not, as a body, identified with the Tractarians; it would be more true to say that the residents, as a body, looked on this marked school with misgiving and apprehension; but they saw what manner of men these Tractarians were; they lived with them in college and common-room; their behaviour was before their brethren as a whole, with its strength and its weakness, its moral elevation and its hazardous excitement, its sincerity of purpose and its one-sidedness of judgment and sympathy, its unfairness to what was English, its over-value for what was foreign. Types of those who looked at things more or less independently were Mr. Hussey of Christ Church, Mr. C. P. Eden of Oriel, Mr. Sewell of Exeter, Mr. Francis Faber of Magdalen, Dr. Greenhill of Trinity, Mr. Wall of Balliol, Mr. Hobhouse of Merton, with some of the more consistent Liberals, like Mr. Stanley of University, and latterly Mr. Tait. Men of this kind, men of high character and weight in Oxford, found much to dislike and regret in the Tractarians. But they could also see that the leaders of the Hebdomadal Board laboured under a fatal incapacity to recognise what these unpopular Tractarians were doing for the cause of true and deep religion; they could see that the judgment of the Heads of Houses, living as they did apart, in a kind of superior state, was narrow, ill-informed, and harsh, and that the warfare which they waged was petty, irritating, and profitless; while they also saw with great clearness that under cover of suppressing "Puseyism," the policy of the Board was, in fact, tending to increase and strengthen the power of an irresponsible and incompetent oligarchy, not only over a troublesome party

5. *Ibid.* pp. 177–179.

but over the whole body of residents. To the great honour of Oxford it must be said, that throughout these trying times, on to the very end, there was in the body of Masters a spirit of fairness, a recognition of the force both of argument and character, a dislike of high-handedness and shabbiness, which was in strong and painful contrast to the short-sighted violence in which the Hebdomadal Board was unhappily induced to put their trust, and which proved at last the main course of the overthrow of their power. When changes began to threaten Oxford, there was no one to say a word for them.

But, for the moment, in spite of this defeat in Convocation, they had no misgivings as to the wisdom of their course or the force of their authority. There was, no doubt, much urging from outside, both on political and theological grounds, to make them use their power to stay the plague of Tractarianism; and they were led by three able and resolute men, unfortunately unable to understand the moral or the intellectual character of the movement, and having the highest dislike and disdain for it in both aspects—Dr. Hawkins, Provost of Oriel, the last remaining disciple of Whately's school, a man of rigid conscientiousness, and very genuine though undemonstrative piety, of great kindliness in private life, of keen and alert intellect, but not of breadth and knowledge proportionate to his intellectual power; Dr. Symons, Warden of Wadham, a courageous witness for Evangelical divinity in the days when Evangelicals were not in fashion in Oxford, a man of ponderous and pedantic learning and considerable practical acuteness; and Dr. Cardwell, Principal of St. Alban's Hall, more a man of the world than his colleagues, with considerable knowledge of portions of English Church history. Under the inspiration of these chiefs, the authorities had adopted, as far as they could, the policy of combat; and the Vice-Chancellor of the time, Dr. Wynter of St. John's, a kind-hearted man, but quite unfit to moderate among the strong wills and fierce tempers round him, was induced to single out for the severest blow yet struck the most distinguished person in the ranks of the movement, Dr. Pusey himself.

Dr. Pusey was a person with whom it was not wise to meddle, unless his assailants could make out a case without a flaw. He was without question the most venerated person in Oxford. Without

an equal, in Oxford at least, in the depth and range of his learning, he stood out yet more impressively among his fellows in the
lofty moral elevation and simplicity of his life, the blamelessness
of his youth, and the profound devotion of his manhood, to which
the family sorrows of his later years, and the habits which grew
out of them, added a kind of pathetic and solemn interest. Stern
and severe in his teaching at one time—at least as he was understood—beyond even the severity of Puritanism, he was yet overflowing with affection, tender and sympathetic to all who came
near him, and, in the midst of continual controversy, he endeavoured, with deep conscientiousness, to avoid the bitterness of
controversy. He was the last man to attack; much more the last
man to be unfair to. The men who ruled in Oxford contrived, in
attacking him, to make almost every mistake which it was possible
to make.

On the 24th of May 1843 Dr. Pusey, intending to balance and
complement the severer, and, to many, the disquieting aspects of
doctrine in his work on Baptism, preached on the Holy Eucharist
as a comfort to the penitent. He spoke of it as a disciple of Andrewes and Bramhall would speak of it; it was a high Anglican
sermon, full, after the example of the Homilies, Jeremy Taylor,
and devotional writers like George Herbert and Bishop Ken, of
the fervid language of the Fathers; and that was all. Beyond this
it did not go; its phraseology was strictly within Anglican limits.
In the course of the week that followed, the University was
surprised by the announcement that Dr. Faussett, the Margaret
Professor of Divinity, had *"delated"* the sermon to the Vice-
Chancellor as teaching heresy; and even more surprised at the
news that the Vice-Chancellor had commenced proceedings. The
Statutes provided that when a sermon was complained of, or
delated to the Vice-Chancellor, the Vice-Chancellor should demand a copy of the sermon, and summoning to him as his
assessors Six Doctors of Divinity, should examine the language
complained of, and, if necessary, condemn and punish the
preacher. The Statute is thus drawn up in general terms, and
prescribes nothing as to the mode in which the examination into
the alleged offence is to be carried on; that is, it leaves it to the
Vice-Chancellor's discretion. What happened was this. The sermon was asked for, but the name of the accuser was not given;

the Statute did not enjoin it. The sermon was sent, with a request from Dr. Pusey that he might have a hearing. The Six Doctors were appointed, five of them being Dr. Hawkins, Dr. Symons, Dr. Jenkyns, Dr. Ogilvie, Dr. Jelf; the Statute said the Regius Professor was, if possible, to be one of the number; as he was under the ban of a special Statute, he was spared the task, and his place was taken by the next Divinity Professor, Dr. Faussett, the person who had preferred the charge, and who was thus, from having been accuser, promoted to be a judge. To Dr. Pusey's request for a hearing, no answer was returned; the Statute, no doubt, said nothing of a hearing. But after the deliberations of the judges were concluded, and after the decision to condemn the sermon had been reached, one of them, Dr. Pusey's old friend, Dr. Jelf, was privately charged with certain communications from the Vice-Chancellor, on which the seal of absolute secrecy was imposed, and which, in fact, we believe, have never been divulged from that day to this. Whatever passed between the Vice-Chancellor, Dr. Jelf, and Dr. Pusey, it had no effect in arresting the sentence; and it came out, in informal ways, and through Dr. Pusey himself, that on the 2d of June Dr. Pusey had been accused and condemned for having taught doctrine contrary to that of the Church of England, and that by the authority of the Vice-Chancellor he was suspended from preaching within the University for two years. But no formal notification of the transaction was ever made to the University.

The summary suppression of erroneous and dangerous teaching had long been a recognised part of the University discipline; and with the ideas then accepted of the religious character of the University, it was natural that some such power as that given in the Statutes should be provided. The power, even after all the changes in Oxford, exists still, and has been recently appealed to. Dr. Pusey, as a member of the University, had no more right than any other preacher to complain of his doctrine being thus solemnly called in question. But it is strange that it should not have occurred to the authorities that, under the conditions of modern times, and against a man like Dr. Pusey, such power should be warily used. For it was not only arbitrary power, such as was exerted in the condemnation of No. 90, but it was arbitrary power acting under the semblance of a judicial inquiry, with accusers, examination, trial, judges, and a heavy penalty. The act of a court of justice which sets at defiance the rules of justice is a very different thing from a straightforward act of arbitrary power, because it pretends to be what it is not. The information against Dr. Pusey, if accepted, involved a trial—that was the fixed condition and point of departure from which there was no escaping—and if a trial be held, then, if it be not a fair trial, the proceeding becomes, according to English notions, a flagrant and cowardly wrong. All this, all the intrinsic injustice, all the scandal and discredit in the eyes of honest men, was forgotten in the obstinate and blind confidence in the letter of a vague Statute. The accused was not allowed to defend or explain himself; he was refused the knowledge of the definite charges against him; he was refused, in spite of his earnest entreaties, a hearing, even an appearance in the presence of his judges. The Statute, it was said, enjoined none of these things. The name of his accuser was not told him; he was left to learn it by report. To the end of the business all was wrought in secrecy; no one knows to this day how the examination of the sermon was conducted, or what were the opinions of the judges. The Statute, it was said, neither enjoined nor implied publicity. To this day no one knows what were the definite passages, what was the express or necessarily involved heresy or contradiction of the formularies, on which the condemnation was based; nor—except on the supposition of gross ignorance of English divinity on the part of the judges—is it easy for a reader to put his finger on the probably incriminated passages. To make the proceedings still more unlike ordinary public justice, informal and private communications were carried on between the judge and the accused, in which the accused was bound to absolute silence, and forbidden to consult his nearest friends.

And of the judges what can be said but that they were, with one exception, the foremost and sternest opponents of all that was identified with Dr. Pusey's name; and that one of them was the colleague who had volunteered to accuse him? Dr. Faussett's share in the matter is intelligible; hating the movement in all its parts, he struck with the vehemence of a mediaeval zealot. But that men like Dr. Hawkins and Dr. Ogilvie, one of them reputed to be a theologian, the other one of the shrewdest and most cautious of men, and in ordinary matters one of the most conscientious and fairest, should not have seen what justice, or at least the show of justice, demanded, and what the refusal of that demand would look like, and that they should have persuaded the Vice-Chancellor to accept the entire responsibility of haughtily refusing it, is, even to those who remember the excitement of those days, a subject of wonder. The pleas was actually put forth that such opportunities of defence of his language and teaching as Dr. Pusey asked for would have led to the "inconvenience" of an interminable debate, and confronting of texts and authorities.[6] The fact, with Dr. Pusey as the accused person, is likely enough; but in a criminal charge with a heavy penalty, it would have been better for the reputation of the judges to have submitted to the inconvenience.

It was a great injustice and a great blunder—a blunder, because the gratuitous defiance of accepted rules of fairness neutralised whatever there might seem to be of boldness and strength in the blow. They were afraid to meet Dr. Pusey face to face. They were afraid to publish the reasons of their condemnation. The effect on the University, both on resident and non-resident members, was not to be misunderstood. The Protestantism of the Vice-Chancellor and the Six Doctors was, of course, extolled by partisans in the press with reckless ignorance and reckless contempt at once for common justice and their own consistency. One person of some distinction at Oxford ventured to make himself the mouthpiece of those who were bold enough to defend the proceeding—the recently-elected Professor of Poetry, Mr. Garbett. But deep offence was given among the wiser and more reasonable men who had a regard for the character of the University. A request to know the grounds of the sentence from men who were certainly of no party was curtly refused by the Vice-Chancellor, with a suggestion that it did not concern them. A more important memorial was sent from London, showing how persons at a distance were shocked by the unaccountable indifference to the appearance of justice in the proceeding. It was signed among others by Mr. Gladstone and Mr. Justice Coleridge. The Vice-Chancellor lost his temper. He sent back the memorial to

6. Cf. *British Critic*, No. xlvii. pp. 221–223.

London "by the hands of his bedel," as if that in some way stamped his official disapprobation more than if it had been returned through the post. And he proceeded, in language wonderful even for that moment, as "Resident Governor" of the University, to reprimand statesmen and lawyers of eminence and high character, not merely for presuming to interfere with his own duties, but for forgetting the oaths on the strength of which they had received their degrees, and for coming very near to that high, almost highest, academical crime, the crime of being *perturbatores pacis*—breaking the peace of the University.

Such foolishness, affecting dignity, only made more to talk of. If the men who ruled the University had wished to disgust and alienate the Masters of Arts, and especially the younger ones who were coming forward into power and influence, they could not have done better. The chronic jealousy and distrust of the time were deepened. And all this was aggravated by what went on in private. A system of espionage, whisperings, backbitings, and miserable tittle-tattle, sometimes of the most slanderous or the most ridiculous kind, was set going all over Oxford. Never in Oxford, before or since, were busybodies more truculent or more unscrupulous. Difficulties arose between Heads of Colleges and their tutors. Candidates for fellowships were closely examined as to their opinions and their associates. Men applying for testimonials were cross-questioned on No. 90, as to the infallibility of general councils, purgatory, the worship of images, the *Ora pro nobis,* and the intercession of the saints: the real critical questions upon which men's minds were working being absolutely uncomprehended and ignored. It was a miserable state of misunderstanding and distrust, and none of the University leaders had the temper and the manliness to endeavour with justice and knowledge to get to the bottom of it. It was enough to suppose that a Popish Conspiracy was being carried on.

XVII

W. G. Ward

If only the Oxford authorities could have had patience—if only
they could have known more largely and more truly the deep
changes that were at work everywhere, and how things were beginning to look in the eyes of the generation that was coming,
perhaps many things might have been different. Yes, it was true
that there was a strong current setting towards Rome. It was acting on some of the most vigorous of the younger men. It was acting powerfully on the foremost mind in Oxford. Whither, if not
arrested, it was carrying them was clear, but as yet it was by no
means clear at what rate; and time, and thought, and being left
alone and dealt with justly, have a great effect on men's minds.
Extravagance, disproportion, mischievous, dangerous exaggeration, in much that was said and taught—all this might have settled down, as so many things are in the habit of settling down,
into reasonable and practical shapes, after a first burst of crude-
ness and strain—as, in fact it *did* settle down at last. For Anglicanism itself was not Roman; friends and foes said it was
not, to reproach as well as to defend it. It was not Roman
in Dr. Pusey, though he was not afraid to acknowledge what
was good in Rome. It was not Roman in Mr. Keble and his
friends, in Dr. Moberly of Winchester, and the Barters. It was
not Roman in Mr. Isaac Williams, Mr. Copeland, and Mr.
Woodgate, each of them a centre of influence in Oxford and
the country. It was not Roman in the devoted Charles Marriott, or in Isaac Williams's able and learned pupil, Mr. Arthur

Haddan. It was not Roman in Mr. James Mozley, after Mr. Newman, the most forcible and impressive of the Oxford writers. A distinctively English party grew up, both in Oxford and away from it, strong in eminent names, in proportion as Roman sympathies showed themselves. These men were, in any fair judgment, as free from Romanising as any of their accusers; but they made their appeal for patience and fair judgment in vain. If only the rulers could have had patience:—but patience is a difficult virtue in the presence of what seem pressing dangers. Their policy was wrong, stupid, unjust, pernicious. It was a deplorable mistake, and all will wish now that the discredit of it did not rest on the history of Oxford. And yet it was the mistake of upright and conscientious men.

Doubtless there was danger; the danger was that a number of men would certainly not acquiesce much longer in Anglicanism, while the Heads continued absolutely blind to what was really in these men's thoughts. For the Heads could not conceive the attraction which the Roman Church had for a religious man; they talked in the old-fashioned way about the absurdity of the Roman system. They could not understand how reasonable men could turn Roman Catholics. They accounted for it by supposing a silly hankering after the pomp or the frippery of Roman Catholic worship, and at best a craving after the romantic and sentimental. Their thoughts dwelt continually on image worship and the adoration of saints. But what really was astir was something much deeper—something much more akin to the new and strong forces which were beginning to act in very different directions from this in English society—forces which were not only leading minds to Rome, but making men Utilitarians, Rationalists, Positivists, and, though the word had not yet been coined, Agnostics. The men who doubted about the English Church saw in Rome a strong, logical, consistent theory of religion, not of yesterday nor to-day—not only comprehensive and profound, but actually in full work, and fruitful in great results; and this, in contrast to the alleged and undeniable anomalies and shortcomings of Protestantism and Anglicanism. And next, there was the immense amount which they saw in Rome of self-denial and self-devotion; the surrender of home and family in the clergy; the great organised ministry of women in works of mercy; the resolute abandonment of the world and its attractions in the religious life. If in England there flourished the homely and modest types of goodness, it was in Rome that, at that day at least, men must look for the heroic. They were not indisposed to the idea that a true Church which had lost all this might yet regain it, and they were willing to wait and see what the English Church would do to recover what it had lost; but there was obviously a long way to make up, and they came to think that there was no chance of its overtaking its true position. Of course they knew all that was so loudly urged about the abuses and mischiefs growing out of the professed severity of Rome. They knew that in spite of it foreign society was lax; that the discipline of the confessional was often exercised with a light rein. But if the good side of it was real, they easily accounted for the bad: the bad did not destroy, it was a tacit witness to the good. And they knew the Latin Church mainly from France, where it was more in earnest, and exhibited more moral life and intellectual activity, than, as far as Englishmen knew, in Italy or Spain. There was a strong rebound from insular ignorance and unfairness, when English travellers came on the poorly-paid but often intelligent and hard-working French clergy; on the great works of mercy in the towns; on the originality and eloquence of De Maistre, La Mennais, Lacordaire, Montalembert.

These ideas took possession of a remarkable mind, the index and organ of a remarkable character. Mr. W. G. Ward had learned the interest of earnest religion from Dr. Arnold, in part through his close friend Arthur Stanley. But if there was ever any tendency in him to combine with the peculiar elements of the Rugby School, it was interrupted in its *nascent* state, as chemists speak, by the intervention of a still more potent affinity, the personality of Mr. Newman. Mr. Ward had developed in the Oxford Union, and in a wide social circle of the most rising men of the time—including Tait, Cardwell, Lowe, Roundell Palmer—a very unusual dialectical skill and power of argumentative statement: qualities which seemed to point to the House of Commons. But Mr. Newman's ideas gave him material, not only for argument but for thought. The lectures and sermons at St. Mary's subdued and led him captive. The impression produced on him was expressed in the formula that primitive Christianity might have been corrupted into Popery, but that Protestantism never could.[1] For a moment he hung in the wind. He might have been one of the earliest of Broad Churchmen. He might have been a Utilitarian and Necessitarian follower of Mr. J. S. Mill. But moral influences of a higher kind prevailed. And he became, in the most thoroughgoing yet independent fashion, a disciple of Mr. Newman. He brought to his new side a fresh power of controversial writing; but his chief influence was a social one, from his bright and attractive conversation, his bold and startling candour, his frank, not to say reckless, fearlessness of consequences, his unrivalled skill in logical fence, his unfailing good-humour and love of fun, in which his personal clumsiness set off the vivacity and nimbleness of his joyous moods. "He was," says Mr. Mozley, "a great musical critic, knew all the operas, and was an admirable buffo singer."—No one could doubt that, having started, Mr. Ward would go far and probably go fast.

Mr. Ward was well known in Oxford, and his language might have warned the Heads that if there was a drift towards Rome, it came from something much more serious than a hankering after a sentimental ritual or mediaeval legends. In Mr. Ward's writings in the *British Critic*, as in his conversation—and he wrote much and at great length—three ideas were manifestly at the bottom of his attraction to Rome. One was that Rome did, and, he believed, nothing else did, keep up the continuous recognition of the supernatural element in religion, that consciousness of an ever-present power not of this world which is so prominent a feature in the New Testament, and which is spoken of there as a permanent and characteristic element in the Gospel dispensation. The Roman view of the nature and offices of the Church, of man's relations to the unseen world, of devotion, of the Eucharist and of the Sacraments in general, assumed and put forward this supernatural aspect; other systems ignored it or made it mean nothing, unless in secret to the individual and converted soul. In the next place he revolted—no weaker word can be used—from the popular exhibition in England, more or less Lutheran and Calvinistic, of the doctrine of justification. The ostentatious separation of justification from morality, with all its theological

1. Cf. T. Mozley, *Reminiscences*, 2:5.

refinements and fictions, seemed to him profoundly unscriptural, profoundly unreal and hollow, or else profoundly immoral. In conscience and moral honesty and strict obedience he saw the only safe and trustworthy guidance in regard to the choice and formation of religious opinions; it was a principle on which all his philosophy was built, that "careful and individual moral discipline is the only possible basis on which Christian faith and practice can be reared." In the third place he was greatly affected, not merely by the paramount place of sanctity in the Roman theology and the professed Roman system, but the standard of saintliness which he found there, involving complete and heroic self-sacrifice for great religious ends, complete abandonment of the world, painful and continuous self-discipline, purified and exalted religious affections, besides which English piety and goodness at its best, in such examples as George Herbert and Ken and Bishop Wilson, seemed unambitious and pale and tame, of a different order from the Roman, and less closely resembling what we read of in the first ages and in the New Testament. Whether such views were right or wrong, exaggerated or unbalanced, accurate or superficial, they were matters fit to interest grave men; but there is no reason to think that they made the slightest impression on the authorities of the University.

On the other hand, Mr. Ward, with the greatest good-humour, was unreservedly defiant and aggressive. There was something intolerably provoking in his mixture of jauntiness and seriousness, his avowal of utter unworthiness and his undoubting certainty of being in the right, his downright charges of heresy and his ungrudging readiness to make allowance for the heretics and give them credit for special virtues greater than those of the orthodox. He was not a person to hide his own views or to let others hide theirs. He lived in an atmosphere of discussion with all around him, friends or opponents, fellows and tutors in common-rooms, undergraduates after lecture or out walking. The most amusing, the most tolerant man in Oxford, he had round him perpetually some of the cleverest and brightest scholars and thinkers of the place; and where he was, there was debate, cross-questioning, pushing inferences, starting alarming problems, beating out ideas, trying the stuff and mettle of mental capacity. Not always with real knowledge, or a real sense of fact, but always rapid and impetuous, taking in the whole dialectical chess-board at a glance, he gave no quarter, and a man found himself in a perilous corner before he perceived the drift of the game; but it was clear his own thought, not—for he was much too good-natured—to embarrass another. If the old scholastic disputations had been still in use at Oxford, his triumphs would have been signal and memorable. His success, compared with that of other leaders of the movement, in influencing life and judgment, was a pre-eminently intellectual success; and it cut two ways. The stress which he laid on the moral side of questions, his own gen-erosity, his earnestness on behalf of fair play and good faith, elevated and purified intercourse. But he did not always win assent in proportion to his power of argument. Abstract reason-ing, in matters with which human action is concerned, may be too absolute to be convincing. It may not leave sufficient margin for the play and interference of actual experience. And Mr. Ward, having perfect confidence in his conclusions, rather liked to leave them in a startling form, which he innocently declared to be manifest and inevitable. And so stories of Ward's audacity and paradoxes flew all over Oxford, shocking and perplexing grave heads with fear of they knew not what. Dr. Jenkyns, the Master of Balliol, one of those curious mixtures of pompous absurdity with genuine shrewdness which used to pass across the Univer-sity stage, not clever himself but an unfailing judge of a clever man, as a jockey might be of a horse, liking Ward and proud of him for his cleverness, was aghast at his monstrous and un-intelligible language, and driven half wild with it. Mr. Tait, a fellow-tutor, though living on terms of hearty friendship with Ward, prevailed on the Master after No. 90 to dismiss Ward from the office of teaching mathematics. It seemed a petty step thus to mix up theology with mathematics, though it was not so absurd as it looked, for Ward brought in theology everywhere, and discussed it when his mathematics were done. But Ward accepted it frankly and defended it. It was natural, he said, that Tait, thinking his principles mischievous, should wish to silence him as a teacher; and their friendship remained unbroken.

Mr. Ward's theological position was really a provisional one, though, at starting at least, he would not have allowed it. He had no early or traditional attachment to the English Church, such as that which acted so strongly on the leaders of the movement: but he found himself a member of it, and Mr. Newman had interpreted it to him. He so accepted it, quite loyally and in earnest, as a point of departure. But he proceeded at once to put "our Church" (as he called it) on its trial, in comparison with its own professions, and with the ideal standard of a Church which he had thought out for himself; and this rapidly led to grave consequences. He accepted from authority which satisfied him both intellectually and morally the main scheme of Catholic theology, as the deepest and truest philosophy of religion, satisfying at once conscience and intellect. The Catholic theology gave him, among other things, the idea and the notes of the Church; with these, in part at least, the English Church agreed; but in other respects, and these very serious ones, it differed widely; it seemed inconsistent and anomalous. The English Church was separate and isolated from Christendom. It was supposed to differ widely from other Churches in doctrine. It admitted variety of opinion and teaching, even to the point of tolerating alleged heresy. With such data as these, he entered on an investigation which ultimately came to the question whether the English Church could claim to be part of the Church Catholic. He postulated from the first, what he afterwards developed in the book in which his Anglican position culminated,—the famous *Ideal*,—the existence at some time or another of a Catholic Church which not only aimed at, but fulfilled all the conditions of a perfect Church in creed, communion, discipline, and life. Of course the English and, as at starting he held, the Roman Church, fell far short of this perfection. But at starting, the moral which he drew was, not to leave the English Church, but to do his best to raise it up to what it ought to be. Whether he took in all the conditions of the problem, whether it was not far more complicated and difficult than he supposed, whether his knowledge of the facts of the case was accurate and adequate, whether he was always fair in his comparisons and judgments, and whether he did not overlook elements of the gravest importance in the inquiry; whether, in fact, save for certain strong and broad lines common to the whole historic Church, the reign of anomaly, inconsistency, difficulty did not extend much farther over the whole field of debate than he chose to admit: all this is fairly open to question. But within the limits which he laid down, and within which he confined his reasonings, he used his materials with skill and force; and even those who least agreed with him and were most sensible of the strong and hardly disguised basis which so greatly affected the value of his judgments, could not deny the frankness and the desire to be fair and candid, with which, as far as intention went, he conducted his argument. His first appearance as a writer was in the controversy, as has been said before, on the subject of No. 90. That tract had made the well-worn distinction between what was Catholic and what was distinctively Roman, and had urged—what had been urged over and over again by English divines—that the Articles, in their condemnation of what was Roman, were drawn in such a way as to leave untouched what was unquestionably Catholic. They were drawn indeed by Protestants, but by men who also earnestly professed to hold with the old Catholic doctors and disavowed any purpose to depart from their teaching, and who further had to meet the views and gain the assent of men who were much less Protestant than themselves—men who were willing to break with the Pope and condemn the abuses associated with his name, but by no means willing to break with the old theology. The Articles were the natural result of a compromise between two strong parties—the Catholics agreeing that the abuses should be condemned, so that the Catholic doctrine was not touched; the Protestants insisting that, so that the Catholic doctrine was not touched, the abuses of it should be denounced with great severity: that there should be no question about the condemnation of the abuses, and of the system which had maintained them. The Articles were undoubtedly anti-Roman; that was obvious from the historical position of the English Church, which in a very real sense was anti-Roman; but were they so anti-Roman as to exclude doctrines which English divines had over and over again maintained as Catholic and distinguished from Romanism, but which the popular opinion, at this time or that, identified therewith?[2] With flagrant ignorance—ignorance of the history of

2. In dealing with the Articles either as a test or as a text-book, this question was manifestly both an honest and a reasonable one. As a test, and therefore penal, they must be construed strictly; like judicial decisions, they only ruled as much as was necessary, and in the wide field of theology confined themselves to the points at issue at the moment. And as a text-book for instruction, it was

thought and teaching in the English Church, ignorance far more inexcusable of the state of parties and their several notorious difficulties in relation to the various formularies of the Church, it was maintained on the other side that the "Articles construed by themselves" left no doubt that they were not only anti-Roman but anti-Catholic, and that nothing but the grossest dishonesty and immorality could allow any doubt on the subject.

Neither estimate was logical enough to satisfy Mr. Ward. The charge of insincerity, he retorted with great effect on those who made it: if words meant anything, the Ordination Service, the Visitation Service, and the Baptismal Service were far greater difficulties to Evangelicals, and to Latitudinarians like Whately and Hampden, than the words of any Article could be to Catholics; and there was besides the tone of the whole Prayer Book, intelligible, congenial, on Catholic assumptions, and on no other. But as to the Articles themselves, he was indisposed to accept the defence made for them. He criticised indeed with acuteness and severity the attempt to make the loose language of many of them intolerant of primitive doctrine; but he frankly accepted the allegation that apart from this or that explanation, their general look, as regards later controversies, was visibly against, not only Roman doctrines or Roman abuses, but that whole system of principles and mode of viewing religion which he called Catholic. They were, he said, *patient* of a Catholic meaning, but *ambitious* of a Protestant meaning; whatever their logic was, their rhetoric was

---

obvious that while on some points they were precise and clear, on others they were vague and imperfect. The first five Articles left no room for doubt. When the compilers came to the controversies of their day, for all their strong language, they left all kinds of questions unanswered. For instance, they actually left unnoticed the primacy, and much more the infallibility of the Pope. They condemned the "sacrifices of Masses"—did they condemn the ancient and universal doctrine of a Eucharist sacrifice? They condemned the Romish doctrine of Purgatory, with its popular tenet of material fire—did that exclude every doctrine of purgation after death? They condemned Transubstantiation—did they condemn the Real Presence? They condemned a great popular system— did they condemn that of which it was a corruption and travesty? These questions could not be foreclosed, unless on the assumption that there was no doctrine on such points which could be called Catholic *except the Roman*. The inquiry was not new; and divines so stoutly anti-Roman as Dr. Hook and Mr. W. Palmer of Worcester had answered it substantially in the same sense as Mr. Newman in No. 90.

Protestant. It was just possible, but not more, for a Catholic to subscribe to them. But they were the creation and the legacy of a bad age, and though they had not extinguished Catholic teaching and Catholic belief in the English Church, they had been a serious hindrance to it, and a support to its opponents.

This was going beyond the position of No. 90. No. 90 had made light of the difficulties of the Articles.

> That there are real difficulties to a Catholic Christian in the ecclesiastical position of our Church at this day, no one can deny; but the statements of the Articles are not in the number. Our present scope is merely to show that, while our Prayer Book is acknowledged on all hands to be of Catholic origin, our Articles also—the offspring of an uncatholic age—are, through God's good providence, to say the least, not uncatholic, and may be subscribed by those who aim at being Catholic in heart and doctrine.

Mr. Ward not only went beyond this position, but in the teeth of these statements; and he gave a new aspect and new issues to the whole controversy. The Articles, to him, were a difficulty, which they were not to the writer of No. 90, or to Dr. Pusey, or to Mr. Keble. To him they were not only the "offspring of an uncatholic age," but in themselves uncatholic; and his answer to the charge of dishonest subscription was, not that the Articles "in their natural meaning are Catholic,"[3] but that the system of the English Church is a compromise between what is Catholic and what is Protestant, and that the Protestant parties in it are involved in even greater difficulties, in relation to subscription and use of its formularies, than the Catholic. He admitted that he *did* evade the spirit, but accepted the "statements of the Articles," maintaining that this was the intention of their original sanctioners. With characteristic boldness, inventing a phrase which has become famous, he wrote: "Our twelfth Article is as plain as words can make it on the Evangelical side; of course I think its natural meaning may be explained away, for I subscribe it myself in a non-natural sense":[4] but he showed that Evangelicals, high church Anglicans, and Latitudinarians were equally obliged to

3. W. G. Ward, *The Ideal of a Christian Church*, p. 478.
4. Ibid., p. 479.

have recourse to explanations, which to all but themselves were unsatisfactory.

But he went a step beyond this. Hitherto the distinction had been uniformly insisted upon between what was Catholic and what was Roman; between what was witnessed to by the primitive and the undivided Church, and what had been developed beyond that in the Schools, and by the definitions and decisions of Rome, and in the enormous mass of its post-Reformation theology, at once so comprehensive, and so minute in application. This distinction was the foundation of what was, characteristically, Anglican theology, from Hooker downwards. This distinction, at least for all important purposes, Mr. Ward gradually gave up. It was to a certain degree recognised in his early controversy about No. 90; but it gradually grew fainter till at last it avowedly disappeared. The Anglican writers had drawn their ideas and their inspiration from the Fathers; the Fathers lived long ago, and the teaching drawn from them, however spiritual and lofty, wanted the modern look, and seemed to recognise insufficiently modern needs. The Roman applications of the same principles were definite and practical, and Mr. Ward's mind, essentially one of his own century, and little alive to what touched more imaginative and sensitive minds, turned at once to Roman sources for the interpretation of what was Catholic. In the *British Critic*, and still more in the remarkable volume in which his Oxford controversies culminated, the substitution of *Roman* for the old conception of *Catholic* appears, and the absolute identification of Roman with Catholic. Roman authorities become more and more the measure and rule of what is Catholic. They belong to the present in a way in which the older fountains of teaching do not; in the recognised teaching of the Latin Church, they have taken their place and superseded them.

It was characteristic of Mr. Ward that his chief quarrel with the Articles was not about the Sacraments, not about their language on alleged Roman errors, but about the doctrine of grace, the relation of the soul of man to the law, the forgiveness, the holiness of God,—the doctrine, that is, in all its bearings, of justification. Mr. Newman had examined this doctrine and the various language held about it with great care, very firmly but very temperately, and had attempted to reconcile with each other all but the extreme Lutheran statements. It was, he said, among really religious men, a question of words. He had recognised the faulty state of things in the pre-Reformation Church, the faulty ideas about forgiveness, merit, grace, and works, from which the Protestant language was a reaction, natural, if often excessive; and in the English authoritative form of this language, he had found nothing but what was perfectly capable of a sound and true meaning. From the first, Mr. Ward's judgment was far more severe than this. To him, the whole structure of the Articles on Justification and the doctrines connected with it seemed based on the Lutheran theory, and for this theory, as fundamentally and hopelessly immoral, he could not find words sufficiently expressive of detestation and loathing. For the basis of his own theory of religious knowledge was a moral basis; men came to the knowledge of religious truth primarily not by the intellect, but by absolute and unfailing loyalty to conscience and moral light; and a doctrine which separated faith from morality and holiness, which made man's highest good and his acceptance with God independent of what he was as a moral agent, which relegated the realities of moral discipline and goodness to a secondary and subordinate place,—as a mere sequel to follow, almost mechanically and of course, on an act or feeling which had nothing moral in it,—which substituted a fictitious and imputed righteousness for an inherent and infused and real one, seemed to him to confound the eternal foundations of right and wrong, and to be a blasphemy against all that was true and sacred in religion.

Of the Lutheran doctrine[5] of justification, and the principle of private judgment, I have argued that, in their abstract nature and

5. It is curious, and characteristic of the unhistorical quality of Mr. Ward's mind, that his whole hostility should have been concentrated on Luther and Lutheranism—on Luther, the enthusiastic, declamatory, unsystematic denouncer of practical abuses, with his strong attachments to portions of orthodoxy, rather than on Calvin, with his cold love of power, and the iron consistency and strength of his logical anti-Catholic system, which has really lived and moulded Protestantism, while Lutheranism as a religion has passed into countless different forms. Luther was to Calvin as Carlyle to J. S. Mill or Herbert Spencer; he defied system. But Luther had burst into outrageous paradoxes, which fastened on Mr. Ward's imagination.—Yet outrageous language is not always the most dangerous. Nobody would really find a provocation to sin, or an excuse for it, in Luther's *Pecca fortiter* any more than in Escobar's ridiculous casuistry. There may be much more mischief in the delicate unrealities of a fashionable preacher, or in many a smooth sentimental treatise on the religious affections.

necessary tendency, they sink below atheism itself. . . . A religious person who shall be sufficiently clear-headed to understand the meaning of words, is warranted in rejecting Lutheranism on the very same grounds which would induce him to reject atheism, viz. as being the contradiction of truths which he feels on most certain grounds to be first principles.[6]

There is nothing which he looks back on with so much satisfaction in his writings as on this, that he has "ventured to characterise that hateful and fearful type of Antichrist in terms not wholly inadequate to its prodigious demerits."[7]

Mr. Ward had started with a very definite idea of the Church and of its notes and tests. It was obvious that the Anglican Church —and so, it was thought, the Roman—failed to satisfy these notes in their completeness; but it seemed, at least at first, to satisfy some of them, and to do this so remarkably, and in such strong contrast to other religious bodies, that in England at all events it seemed the true representative and branch of the Church Catholic; and the duty of adhering to it and serving it was fully recognised, even by those who most felt its apparent departure from the more Catholic principles and temper preserved in many points by the Roman Church. From this point of view Mr. Ward avowedly began. But the position gradually gave way before his relentless and dissolving logic. The whole course of his writing in the *British Critic* may be said to have consisted in a prolonged and disparaging comparison of the English Church, in theory, in doctrine, in moral and devotional temper, in discipline of character, in education, in its public and authoritative tone in regard to social, political, and moral questions, and in the type and standard of its clergy, with those of the Catholic Church, which to him was represented by the mediaeval and later Roman Church. And in the general result, and in all important matters, the comparison became more and more fatally disadvantageous to the English Church. In the perplexing condition of Christendom, it had just enough good and promise to justify those who had been brought up in it remaining where they were, as long as they saw any prospect of improving it, and till they were driven out. That was a duty—uncomfortable and thankless as it was, and open to any amount of misconstruction and misrepresentation—which

6. *Ideal,* pp. 587, 305.
7. Ibid. p. 305.

they owed to their brethren, and to the Lord of the Church. But it involved plain speaking and its consequences; and Mr. Ward never shrank from either.

Most people, looking back, would probably agree, whatever their general judgment on these matters, and whatever they may think of Mr. Ward's case, that he was, at the time at least, the most unpersuasive of writers. Considering his great acuteness, and the frequent originality of his remarks—considering, further, his moral earnestness, and the place which the moral aspects of things occupy in his thoughts, this is remarkable; but so it is. In the first place, in dealing with these eventual questions, which came home with such awful force to thousands of awakened minds and consciences, full of hope and full of fear, there was an entire and ostentatious want of sympathy with all that was characteristically English in matters of religion. This arose partly from his deep dislike to habits, very marked in Englishmen, but not peculiar to them, of self-satisfaction and national self-glorification; but it drove him into a welcoming of opposite foreign ways, of which he really knew little, except superficially. Next, his boundless confidence in the accuracy of his logical processes led him to habits of extreme and absolute statement, which to those who did not agree with him, and also to some who did, bore on their face the character of over-statement, exaggeration, extravagance, not redeemed by an occasional and somewhat ostentatious candour, ofter at the expense of his own side and in favour of opponents to whom he could afford to be frank. And further, while to the English Church he was merciless in the searching severity of his judgment, he seemed to be blind to the whole condition of things to which she, as well as her rival, had for the last three centuries been subjected, and in which she had played a part at least as important for Christian faith as that sustained by any portion of Christendom; blind to all her special and characteristic excellences, where these did not fit the pattern of the continental types (obviously, in countless instances, matters of national and local character and habits); blind to the enormous difficulties in which the political game of her Roman opponents had placed her; blind to the fact that, judged with the same adverse bias and prepossessions, the same unsparing rigour, the same refusal to give real weight to what was good, on the ground that it was mixed with something lower, the Roman Church would show just as much deflection from the ideal as the English. Indeed, he would have done a great service—people would have been far more disposed to attend to his really interesting, and, to English readers, novel, proofs of the moral and devotional character of the Roman popular discipline, if he had not been so unfair on the English; if he had not ignored the plain fact that just such a picture as he gave of the English Church, as failing in required notes, might be found of the Roman before the Reformation, say in the writings of Gerson, and in our own days in those of Rosmini. Mr. Ward, if any one, appealed to fair judgment; and to this fair judgment he presented allegations on the face of them violent and monstrous. The English Church, according to him, was in the anomalous position of being "gifted with the power of dispensing sacramental grace,"[8] and yet, at the same time, *"wholly destitute* of external notes, and *wholly indefensible*, as to her position, by external, historical, ecclesiastical arguments": and he for his part declares, correcting Mr. Newman, who speaks of "outward notes as partly gone and partly going," that he is *"wholly unable* to discern the outward notes of which Mr. Newman speaks, during any part of the last three hundred years." He might as well have said at once that she did not exist, if the outward aspects of a Church—orders, creeds, sacraments, and, in some degree at any rate, preaching and witnessing for righteousness—are not some of the "outward notes" of a Church. "Should the pure light of the Gospel be ever restored to *this benighted land*,"[9] he writes at the beginning, as the last extract was written at the end, of his controversial career at Oxford. Is not such writing as if he wished to emulate in a reverse sense the folly and falsehood of those who spoke of English Protestants having a monopoly of the Gospel? He was unpersuasive, he irritated and repelled, in spite of his wish to be fair and candid, in spite of having so much to teach, in spite of such vigour of statement and argument, because on the face of all his writings he was so extravagantly one-sided, so incapable of an equitable view, so much a slave to the unreality of extremes.

8. *Ideal*, p. 286.
9. *British Critic*, October 1841, p. 340.

XVIII

The Ideal
of a
Christian Church

No. 90, with the explanations of it given by Mr. Newman and the other leaders of the movement, might have raised an important and not very easy question, but one in no way different from the general character of the matters in debate in the theological controversy of the time. But No. 90, with the comments on it of Mr. Ward, was quite another matter, and finally broke up the party of the movement. It was one thing to show how much there is in common between England and Rome, and quite another to argue that there is no difference. Mr. Ward's refusal to allow a reasonable and a Catholic interpretation to the doctrine of the Articles on Justification, though such an understanding of it had not only been maintained by Bishop Bull and the later orthodox divines, but was impressed on all the popular books of devotion, such as the *Whole Duty of Man* and Bishop Wilson's *Sacra Privata*; and along with this, the extreme claim to hold compatible with the Articles the "whole cycle of Roman doctrine," introduced entirely new conditions into the whole question. *Non haec in foedera* was the natural reflection of numbers of those who most sympathised with the Tractarian school. The English Church might have many shortcomings and want many improvements; but after all she had something to say for herself in her quarrel with Rome; and the witness of experience for fifteen hundred years must be not merely qualified and corrected, but absolutely wiped out, if the allegation were to be accepted that Rome was blameless in all that quarrel, and had no part in bringing about

the confusions of Christendom. And this contention was more
and more enforced in Mr. Ward's articles in the *British Critic*—
enforced, more effectively than by direct statement, by continual
and passing assumption and implication. They were papers of
considerable power and acuteness, and of great earnestness in
their constant appeal to the moral criteria of truth; though Mr.
Ward was not then at his best as a writer, and they were in composition heavy, diffuse, monotonous, and wearisome. But the attitude of deep depreciation, steady, systematic, unrelieved, in regard to that which ought, if acknowledged at all, to deserve the
highest reverence among all things on earth, in regard to an institution which, with whatever faults, he himself in words still
recognised as the Church of God, was an indefensible and an
unwholesome paradox. The analogy is a commonly accepted one
between the Church and the family. How could any household
go on in which there was at work an *animus* of unceasing and
relentless, though possibly too just criticism, on its characteristic
and perhaps serious faults; and of comparisons, also possibly most
just, with the better ways of other families? It might be the honest
desire of reform and improvement; but charity, patience, equi-
tableness, are virtues of men in society, as well as strict justice and
the desire of improvement. In the case of the family, such action
could only lead to daily misery and the wasting and dying out of
home affections. In the case of a Church, it must come to the sun-
dering of ties which ought no longer to bind. Mr. Ward all along
insisted that there was no necessity for looking forward to such
an event. He wished to raise, purify, reform the Church in which
Providence had placed him; utterly dissatisfied as he was with it,
intellectually and morally, convinced more and more that it was
wrong, dismally, fearfully wrong, it was his duty, he thought, to
abide in it without looking to consequences; but it was also his
duty to shake the faith of any one he could in its present claims
and working, and to hold up an incomparably purer model of
truth and holiness. That his purpose was what he considered real
reform, there is no reason to doubt, though he chose to shut his
eyes to what must come of it. The position was an unnatural one,
but he had great faith in his own well-fenced logical creations,
and defied the objections of a homelier common sense. He was not
content to wait in silence the slow and sad changes of old convic-

tions, the painful decay and disappearance of long-cherished ties. His mind was too active, restless, unreserved. To the last he persisted in forcing on the world, professedly to influence it, really to defy it, the most violent assertions which he could formulate of the most paradoxical claims on friends and opponents which had ever been made.

Mr. Ward's influence was felt also in another way; though here it is not easy to measure the degree of its force. He was in the habit of appealing to Mr. Newman to pronounce on the soundness of his principles and inferences, with the view of getting Mr. Newman's sanction for them against more timid or more dissatisfied friends; and he would come down with great glee on objectors to some new and startling position, with the reply, "Newman says so." Every one knows from the *Apologia* what was Mr. Newman's state of mind after 1841—a state of perplexity, distress, anxiety; he was moving undoubtedly in one direction, but moving slowly, painfully, reluctantly, intermittently, with views sometimes clear, sometimes clouded, of that terribly complicated problem, the answer to which was full of such consequences to himself and others. No one ever felt more keenly that it was no mere affair of dexterous or brilliant logic; if logic could have settled it, the question would never have arisen. But in this fevered state, with mind, soul, heart all torn and distracted by the tremendous responsibilities pressing on him, wishing above everything to be quiet, to be silent, at least not to speak except at his own times and when he saw the occasion, he had, besides bearing his own difficulties, to return off-hand and at the moment some response to questions which he had not framed, which he did not care for, on which he felt no call to pronounce, which he was not perhaps yet ready to face, and to answer which he must commit himself irrevocably and publicity to more than he was prepared for. Every one is familiar with the proverbial distribution of parts in the asking and the answering of questions; but when the asker is no fool, but one of the sharpest-witted of mankind, asking with little consideration for the condition of the wishes of the answerer, with great power to force the answer he wants, and with no great tenderness in the use he makes of it, the situation becomes a trying one. Mr. Ward was continually forcing on Mr. Newman so-called irresistible inferences: "If you say so and so, surely you must also say something more?" Avowedly ignorant of facts and depending for them on others, he was only concerned with logical consistency. And accordingly Mr. Newman, with whom producible logical consistency was indeed a great thing, but with whom it was very far from being everything, had continually to accept conclusions which he would rather have kept in abeyance, to make admissions which were used without their qualifications, to push on and sanction extreme ideas which he himself shrank from because they were extreme. But it was all over with his command of time, his liberty to make up his mind slowly on the great decision. He had to go at Mr. Ward's pace, and not his own. He had to take Mr. Ward's questions, not when he wanted to have them and at his own time, but at Mr. Ward's. No one can tell how much this state of things affected the working of Mr. Newman's mind in that pause of hesitation before the final step; how far it accelerated the view which he ultimately took of his position. No one can tell, for many other influences were mixed up with this one. But there is no doubt that Mr. Newman felt the annoyance and the unfairness of this perpetual questioning for the benefit of Mr. Ward's theories, and there can be little doubt that, in effect, it drove him onwards and cut short his time of waiting. Engineers tell us that, in the case of a ship rolling in a sea-way, when the periodic times of the ship's roll coincide with those of the undulations of the waves, a condition of things arises highly dangerous to the ship's stability. So the agitations of Mr. Newman's mind were reinforced by the impulses of Mr. Ward's.[1]

But the great question between England and Rome was not the only matter which engaged Mr. Ward's active mind. In the course of his articles in the *British Critic* he endeavoured to develop in large outlines a philosophy of religious belief. Restless on all matters without a theory, he felt the need of a theory of the true method of reaching, verifying, and judging of religious truth; it seemed to him necessary especially to a popular religion, such as Christianity claimed to be; and it was not the least of the points on which he congratulated himself that he had worked

1. A pencilled note indicates that this illustration was suggested by experiments in navigational engineering carried on at one time by Mr. W. Froude. Cf. T. Mozley, *Reminiscences*, 2:17.

out a view which extended greatly the province and office of conscience, and of fidelity to it, and greatly narrowed the province and office of the mere intellect in the case of the great mass of mankind. The Oxford writers had all along laid stress on the paramount necessity of the single eye and disciplined heart in accepting or judging religion; moral subjects could be only appreciated by moral experience; purity, reverence, humility were as essential in such questions as zeal, industry, truthfulness, honesty; religious truth is a gift as well as a conquest; and they dwelt on the great maxims of the New Testament: "To him that hath shall be given"; "If any man will do the will of the Father, he shall know of the doctrine." But though Mr. Newman especially had thrown out deep and illuminating thoughts on this difficult question, it had not been treated systematically; and this treatment Mr. Ward attempted to give to it. It was a striking and powerful effort, full of keen insight into human experience and acute observations on its real laws and conditions; but on the face of it, it was laboured and strained; it chose its own ground, and passed unnoticed neighbouring regions under different conditions; it left undealt with the infinite variety of circumstances, history, capacities, natural temperament, and those unexplored depths of will and character, affecting choice and judgment, the realities of which have been brought home to us by our later ethical literature. Up to a certain point his task was easy. It is easy to say that a bad life, a rebellious temper, a selfish spirit are hopeless disqualifications for judging spiritual things; that we must take something for granted in learning any truths whatever; that men must act as moral creatures to attain insight into moral truths, to realise and grasp them as things, and not abstractions and words. But then came the questions—What is that moral training, which, in the case of the good heart, will be practically infallible in leading into truth? And what is that type of character, of saintliness, which gives authority which we cannot do wrong in following; where, if question and controversy arise, is the common measure binding on both sides; and can even the saints, with their immense variations and apparent mixtures and failings, furnish that type? And next, where, in the investigations which may be endlessly diversified, does intellect properly come in and give its help? For come in somewhere, of course it must; and the conspicuous dominance of the intellectual element in Mr. Ward's treatment of the subject is palpable on the face of it. His attempt is to make out a theory of the reasonableness of unproducible, because unanalysed, reasons; reasons which, though the individual cannot state them, may be as real and as legitimately active as the obscure rays of the spectrum. But though the discussion in Mr. Ward's hands was suggestive of much, though he might expose the superciliousness of Whately or the shallowness of Mr. Goode, and show himself no unequal antagonist to Mr. J. S. Mill, it left great difficulties unanswered, and it had too much the appearance of being directed to a particular end, that of guarding the Catholic view of a popular religion from formidable objections.

The moral side of religion had been from the first a prominent subject in the teaching of the movement. Its protests had been earnest and constant against intellectual self-sufficiency, and the notion that mere shrewdness and cleverness were competent judges of Christian truth, or that soundness of judgment in religious matters was compatible with arrogance or an imperfect moral standard; and it revolted against the conventional and inconsistent severity of Puritanism, which was shocked at dancing but indulged freely in good dinners, and was ostentatious in using the phrases of spiritual life and in marking a separation from the world, while it surrounded itself with all the luxuries of modern inventiveness. But this moral teaching was confined to the statement of principles, and it was carried out in actual life with the utmost dislike of display and with a shrinking from strong professions. The motto of Froude's *Remains*, which embodied his characteristic temper, was an expression of the feeling of the school:

> Se sub serenis vultibus
> Austera virtus occulit:
> Timet videri, ne suum,
> Dum prodit, amittat decus.[2]

The heroic strictness and self-denial of the early Church were the objects of admiration, as what ought to be the standard of Christians; but people did not yet like to talk much about attempts to copy them. Such a book as the *Church of the Fathers* brought out

2. Hymn in Paris Breviary, *Commune Sanctarum Mulierum.*

with great force and great sympathy the ascetic temper and the value put on celibacy in the early days, and it made a deep impression; but nothing was yet formulated as characteristic and accepted doctrine.

It was not unnatural that this should change. The principles exemplified in the high Christian lives of antiquity became concrete in definite rules and doctrines, and these rules and doctrines were most readily found in the forms in which the Roman schools and teachers had embodied them. The distinction between the secular life and the life of "religion," with all its consequences, became an accepted one. Celibacy came to be regarded as an obvious part of the self-sacrifice of a clergyman's life, and the belief and the profession of it formed a test, understood if not avowed, by which the more advanced or resolute members of the party were distinguished from the rest. This came home to men on the threshold of life with a keener and closer touch than questions about doctrine. It was the subject of many a bitter, agonising struggle which no one knew anything of; it was with many the act of a supreme self-oblation. The idea of the single life may be a utilitarian one as well as a religious one. It may be chosen with no thought of renunciation or self-denial, for the greater convenience and freedom of the student or the philosopher, the soldier or the man of affairs. It may also be chosen without any special feeling of a sacrifice by the clergyman, as most helpful for his work. But the idea of celibacy, in those whom it affected at Oxford, was in the highest degree a religious and romantic one. The hold which it had on the leader of the movement made itself felt, though little was directly said. To shrink from it was a mark of want of strength or intelligence, of an unmanly preference for English home life, of insensibility to the generous devotion and purity of the saints. It cannot be doubted that at this period of the movement the power of this idea over imagination and conscience was one of the strongest forces in the direction of Rome.

Of all these ideas Mr. Ward's articles in the *British Critic* were the vigorous and unintermittent exposition. He spoke out, and without hesitation. There was a perpetual contrast implied, when it was not forcibly insisted on, between all that had usually been esteemed highest in the moral temper of the English Church, always closely connected with home life and much variety of character, and the loftier and bolder but narrower standard of Roman piety. And Mr. Ward was seconded in the *British Critic* by other writers, all fervid in the same cause, some able and eloquent. The most distinguished of his allies was Mr. Oakeley, Fellow of Balliol and minister of Margaret Chapel in London. Mr. Oakeley was, perhaps, the first to realise the capacities of the Anglican ritual for impressive devotional use, and his services, in spite of the disadvantage of the time, and also of his chapel, are still remembered by some as having realised for them, in away never since surpassed, the secrets and the consolations of the worship of the Church. Mr. Oakeley, without much learning, was master of a facile and elegant pen. He was a man who followed a trusted leader with chivalrous boldness, and was not afraid of strengthening his statements. Without Mr. Ward's force and originality, his articles were more attractive reading. His article on "Jewel" was more than anything else a landmark in the progress of Roman ideas.[3]

From the time of Mr. Ward's connexion with the *British Critic*, its anti-Anglican articles had given rise to complaints which did not become less loud as time went on. He was a troublesome contributor to his editor, Mr. T. Mozley, and he made the hair of many of his readers stand on end with his denunciations of things English and eulogies of things Roman.

> My first troubles [writes Mr. Mozley] were with Oakeley and Ward. I will not say that I hesitated much as to the truth of what they wrote, for in that matter I was inclined to go very far, at least in the way of toleration. Yet it appeared to me quite impossible either that any great number of English Churchmen would ever go so far, or that the persons possessing authority in the Church would fail to protest, not to say more. . . . As to Ward I did but touch a filament or two in one of his monstrous cobwebs, and off he ran instantly to Newman to complain of my gratuitous impertinence. Many years after I was forcibly reminded of him by a pretty group of a little Cupid flying to his mother to show a wasp-sting he had just received. Newman was then in this difficulty. He did not disagree with what Ward had written; but, on the other hand, he had given neither me nor Ward to understand that he was likely to step in between us. In

3. *Reminiscences,* 2:243, 244. Cf. *British Critic,* July 1841.

fact, he wished to be entirely clear of the editorship. This, how-ever, was a thing that Ward could not or would not understand.[4]

The discontent of readers of the *British Critic* was great. It was expressed in various ways, and was represented by a pamphlet of Mr. W. Palmer's of Worcester, in which he contrasted, with words of severe condemnation, the later writers in the Review with the teaching of the earlier *Tracts for the Times*, and de-nounced the "Romanising" tendency shown in its articles. In the autumn of 1843 the Review came to an end. A field of work was thus cut off from Mr. Ward. Full of the interest of the ideas which possessed him, always equipped and cheerfully ready for the argumentative encounter, and keenly relishing the *certaminis gaudia*, he at once seized the occasion of Mr. Palmer's pamphlet to state what he considered his position, and to set himself right in the eyes of all fair and intelligent readers. He intended a long pamphlet. It gradually grew under his hands—he was not yet gifted with the power of compression and arrangement—into a volume of 600 pages: the famous *Ideal of a Christian Church, considered in Comparison with Existing Practice*, published in the summer of 1844.

The *Ideal* is a ponderous and unattractive volume, ill arranged and rambling, which its style and other circumstances have caused to be almost forgotten. But there are interesting discussions in it which may still repay perusal for their own sakes. The object of the book was twofold. Starting with an "ideal" of what the Chris-tian Church may be expected to be in its various relations to men, it assumes that the Roman Church, and only the Roman Church, satisfies the conditions of what a Church ought to be, and it argues in detail that the English Church, in spite of its professions, ut-terly and absolutely fails to fulfil them. It is a *plaidoirie* against everything English, on the ground that it cannot be Catholic be-cause it is not Roman. It was not consistent, for while the writer alleged that "our Church totally neglected her duties both as guardian of and witness to morality, and to witness and teacher of orthodoxy," yet he saw no difficulty in attributing the revival of Catholic truth to "the inherent vitality and powers of our own Church."[5] But this was not the sting and provocation of the book.

4. *Reminiscences*, 2:225.
5. *Ideal*, p. 566.

That lay in the developed claim, put forward by implication in Mr. Ward's previous writings, and now repeated in the broadest and most unqualified form, to hold his position in the English Church, avowing and teaching all Roman doctrine.

> We find [he exclaims], oh, most joyful, most wonderful, most unexpected sight! we find the whole cycle of Roman doctrine gradually possessing numbers of English Churchmen. . . . Three years have passed since I said plainly that in subscribing the Articles I renounce no Roman doctrine; yet I retain my fellowship which I hold on the tenure of subscription, and have received no ecclesiastical censure in any shape.[6]

There was much to learn from the book; must that might bring home to the most loyal Churchman a sense of shortcomings, a burning desire for improvement; much that might give every one a great deal to think about, on some of the deepest problems of the intellectual and religious life. But it could not be expected that such a challenge, in such sentences as these, should remain unnoticed.

The book came out in the Long Vacation, and it was not till the University met in October that signs of storm began to appear. But before it broke an incident occurred which inflamed men's tempers. Dr. Wynter's reign as Vice-Chancellor had come to a close, and the next person, according to the usual custom of succession, was Dr. Symons, Warden of Wadham. Dr. Symons had never concealed his strong hostility to the movement, and he had been one of Dr. Pusey's judges. The prospect of a partisan Vice-Chancellor, certainly very determined, and supposed not to be over-scrupulous, was alarming. The consent of Convocation to the Chancellor's nomination of his substitute had always been given in words, though no instance of its having been refused was known, at least in recent times. But a great jealousy about the rights of Convocation had been growing up under the late autocratic policy of the Heads, and there was a disposition to assert, and even to stretch these rights, a disposition not confined to the party of the movement. It was proposed to challenge Dr. Symons's nomination. Great doubts were felt and expressed about the wisdom of the proposal; but at length opposition was resolved upon. The step was a warning to the Heads, who had been provoking

6. Ibid., pp. 565–67.

enough; but there was not enough to warrant such a violent departure from usage, and it was the act of exasperation rather than of wisdom. The blame for it must be shared between the few who fiercely urged it, and the many who disapproved and acquiesced. On the day of nomination, the scrutiny was allowed, *salva auctoritate Cancellarii*; but Dr. Symons's opponents were completely defeated by 883 to 183. It counted, not unreasonably, as a "Puseyite defeat."

The attempt and its result made it certain that in the attack that was sure to come on Mr. Ward's book, he would meet with no mercy. As soon as term began the Board of Heads of Houses took up the matter; they were earnestly exhorted to it by a letter of Archbishop Whately's, which was read at the Board. But they wanted no pressing, nor is it astonishing that they could not understand the claim to hold the "whole cycle" of Roman doctrine in the English Church. Mr. Ward's view was that he was loyally doing the best he could for "our Church," not only in showing up its heresies and faults, but in urging that the only remedy was wholesale submission to Rome. To the University authorities this was taking advantage of his position in the Church to assail and if possible destroy it. And to numbers of much more sober and moderate Churchmen, sympathisers with the general spirit of the movement, it was evident that Mr. Ward had long passed the point when tolerance could be fairly asked, consistently with any respect for the English Church, for such sweeping and paradoxical contradictions, by her own servants, of her claims and title. Mr. Ward's manner also, which, while it was serious enough in his writings, was easy and even jocular in social intercourse, left the impression, in reality a most unfair impression, that he was playing and amusing himself with these momentous questions.

A Committee of the Board examined the book; a number of startling propositions were with ease picked out, some preliminary skirmishing as to matters of form took place, and in December 1844 the Board announced that they proposed to submit to Convocation without delay three measures:—(1) to condemn Mr. Ward's book; (2) to degrade Mr. Ward by depriving him of all his University degrees; and (3) whereas the existing Statutes gave the Vice-Chancellor power of calling on any member of the University at any time to prove his orthodoxy by subscribing the

Articles, to add to this a declaration, to be henceforth made by the subscriber, that he took them in the sense in which "they were both first published and were now imposed by the University," with the penalty of expulsion against any one, lay or clerical, who thrice refused subscription with this declaration.

As usual, the Board entirely mistook the temper of the University, and by their violence and want of judgment turned the best chance they ever had, of carrying the University with them, into what their blunders really made an ignominious defeat. If they had contented themselves with the condemnation, in almost any terms, of Mr. Ward's book, and even of its author, the condemnation would have been overwhelming. A certain number of men would have still stood by Mr. Ward, either from friendship or sympathy, or from independence of judgment, or from dislike of the policy of the Board; but they would have been greatly outnumbered. The degradation—the Board did not venture on the logical consequence, expulsion—was a poor and even ridiculous measure of punishment; to reduce Mr. Ward to an undergraduate *in statu pupillari*, and a commoner's short gown, was a thing to amuse rather than terrify. The personal punishment seemed unworthy when they dared not go farther, while to many the condemnation of the book seemed penalty enough; and the condemnation of the book by these voters was weakened by their refusal to carry it into personal disgrace and disadvantage. Still, if these two measures had stood by themselves, they could not have been resisted, and the triumph of the Board would have been a signal one. But they could not rest. They must needs attempt to put upon subscription, just when its difficulties were beginning to be felt, not by one party, but by all, an interpretation which set the University and Church in a flame. The cry, almost the shriek, arose that it was a new test, and a test which took for granted what certainly needed proof, that the sense in which the Articles were first understood and published was exactly the same as that in which the University now received and imposed them. It was in vain that explanations, assurances, protests, were proffered; no new test, it was said, was thought of—the Board would never think of such a thing; it was only something to ensure good faith and honesty. But it was utterly useless to contend against the storm. A test it was, and a new test no one would have. It was clear that, if the third proposal was pushed, it would endanger the votes about Mr. Ward. After some fruitless attempts at justification the Board had, in the course of a month, to recognise that it had made a great mistake. The condemnation of Mr. Ward was to come on, on the 13th of February; and on the 23d of January the Vice-Chancellor, in giving notice of it, announced that the third proposal was withdrawn.

It might have been thought that this was lesson enough to leave well alone. The Heads were sure of votes against Mr. Ward, more or less numerous; they were sure of a victory which would be a severe blow, not only to Mr. Ward and his special followers, but to the Tractarian party with which he had been so closely connected. But those bitter and intemperate spirits which had so long led them wrong were not to be taught prudence even by their last experience. The mischief-makers were at work, flitting about the official lodgings at Wadham and Oriel. Could not something be done, even at this late hour, to make up for the loss of the test? Could not something be done to disgrace a greater name than Mr. Ward's? Could not the opportunity which was coming of rousing the feeling of the University against the disciple be turned to account to drag forth his supposed master from his retirement and impunity, and brand the author of No. 90 with the public stigma —no longer this time of a Hebdomadal censure, but of a University condemnation? The temptation was irresistible to a number of disappointed partisans—kindly, generous, good-natured men in private life, but implacable in their fierce fanaticism. In their impetuous vehemence they would not even stop to think what would be said of the conditions and circumstances under which they pressed their point. On the 23d of January the Vice-Chancellor had withdrawn the test. On the 25th of January—those curious in coincidences may observe that it was the date of No. 90 in 1841—a circular was issued inviting signatures for a requisition to the Board, asking them to propose, in the approaching Convocation of the 13th of February, a formal censure of the principles of No. 90. The invitation to sign was issued in the names of Dr. Faussett and Dr. Ellerton of Magdalen. It received between four and five hundred signatures, as far as was known; but it was withheld by the Vice-Chancellor from the inspection of those who officially had a right to have it before them. On the 4th of

February its prayer came before the Hebdomadal Board. The objection of haste—that not ten days intervened between this new and momentous proposal and the day of voting—was brushed aside. The members of the Board were mad enough not to see, not merely the odiousness of the course, but the aggravated odiousness of hurry. The proposal was voted by the majority, *sans phrase.* And they ventured, amid all the excitement and irritation of the moment, to offer for the sanction of the University a decree framed in the words of their own censure.

The interval before the Convocation was short, but it was long enough for decisive opinions on the proposal of the Board to be formed and expressed. Leading men in London, Mr. Gladstone among them, were clear that it was an occasion for the exercise of the joint veto with which the Proctors were invested. The veto was intended, if for anything, to save the University from inconsiderate and hasty measures; and seldom, except in revolutionary times, had so momentous and so unexpected a measure been urged on with such unseemly haste. The feeling of the younger Liberals, Mr. Stanley, Mr. Donkin, Mr. Jowett, Dr. Greenhill, was in the same direction. On the 10th of February the Proctors announced to the Board their intention to veto the third proposal. But of course the thing went forward. The Proctors were friends of Mr. Newman, and the Heads believed that this would counterbalance any effect from their act of authority. It is possible that the announcement may have been regarded as a mere menace, too audacious to be fulfilled. On the 13th of February, amid slush and snow, Convocation met in the Theatre. Mr. Ward asked leave to defend himself in English, and occupied one of the rostra, usually devoted to the recital of prize poems and essays. He spoke with vigour and ability, dividing his speech, and resting in the interval between the two portions in the rostrum.[7] There was no other address, and the voting began. The first vote, the condemnation of the book, was carried by 777 to 386. The second, by a more evenly balanced division, 569 to 511. When the Vice-Chancellor put the third, the Proctors rose, and the senior Proctor, Mr. Guil-

7. It is part of the history of the time, that during those anxious days, Mr. Ward was engaged to be married. The engagement came to the knowledge of his friends, to their great astonishment and amusement, very soon after the events in the Theatre.

lemard of Trinity, stopped it in the words, *Nobis procuratoribus non placet.* Such a step, of course, only suspended the vote, and the year of office of these Proctors was nearly run. But they had expressed the feeling of those whom they represented. It was shown not only in a largely-signed address of thanks. All attempts to revive the decree at the expiration of their year of office failed. The wiser heads in the Hebdomadal Board recognised at last that they had better hold their hand. Mistakes men may commit, and defeats they may undergo, and yet lose nothing that concerns their character for acting as men of a high standard ought to act. But in this case, mistakes and defeat were the least of what the Board brought on themselves. This was the last act of a long and deliberately pursued course of conduct; and if it was the last, it was because it was the upshot and climax, and neither the University nor any one else would endure that it should go on any longer. The proposed attack on Mr. Newman betrayed how helpless they were, and to what paltry acts of worrying it was, in their judgment, right and judicious to condescend. It gave a measure of their statesmanship, wisdom, and good feeling in defending the interests of the Church; and it made a very deep and lasting impression on all who were interested in the honour and welfare of Oxford. Men must have blinded themselves to the plainest effects of their own actions who could have laid themselves open to such a description of their conduct as is contained in the following extract from a paper of the time—a passage of which the indignant and pathetic undertone reflected the indignation and the sympathy of hundreds of men of widely differing opinions.

> The vote is an answer to a cry—that cry is one of dishonesty, and this dishonesty the proposed resolution, as plainly as it dares to say anything, insinuates. On this part of the question, those who have ever been honoured by Mr. Newman's friendship must feel it dangerous to allow themselves thus to speak. And yet they must speak; for no one else can appreciate it as truly as they do. When they see the person whom they have been accustomed to revere as few men are revered, whose labours, whose greatness, whose tenderness, whose singleness and holiness of purpose, they have been permitted to know intimately—not allowed even the poor privilege of satisfying, by silence and retirement—by the relinquishment of preferment, position, and influence—the

persevering hostility of persons whom they cannot help comparing with him—not permitted even to submit in peace to those irregular censures, to which he seems to have been even morbidly alive, but dragged forth to suffer an oblique and tardy condemnation; called again to account for matters now long ago accounted for; on which a judgment has been pronounced, which, whatever others may think of it, he at least has accepted as conclusive—when they contrast his merits, his submission, his treatment, which they see and know, with the merits, the bearing, the fortunes of those who are doggedly pursuing him, it does become very difficult to speak without sullying what it is a kind of pleasure to feel is *his* cause by using hard words, or betraying it by not using them. It is too difficult to speak, as ought to be spoken, of this ungenerous and gratuitous afterthought—too difficult to keep clear of what, at least, will be *thought* exaggeration; too difficult to do justice to what they feel to be undoubtedly true; and I will not attempt to say more than enough to mark an opinion which ought to be plainly avowed, as to the nature of this procedure.[8]

8. From a *Short Appeal to Members of Convocation on the Proposed Censure on No. 90.* By Frederic Rogers, Fellow of Oriel. (Dated Saturday, 8th of February 1845.)

XIX

The Catastrophe

The events of February were a great shock. The routine of Oxford had been broken as it had never been broken by the fiercest strifes before. Condemnations had been before passed on opinions, and even on persons. But to see an eminent man, of blameless life, a fellow of one of the first among the Colleges, solemnly deprived of his degree and all that the degree carried with it, and that on a charge in which bad faith and treachery were combined with alleged heresy, was a novel experience, where the kindnesses of daily companionship and social intercourse still asserted themselves as paramount to official ideas of position. And when, besides this, people realised what more had been attempted, and by how narrow a chance a still heavier blow had been averted from one towards whom so many hearts warmed, how narrowly a yoke had been escaped which would have seemed to subject all religious thought in the University to the caprice or the blind zeal of a partisan official, the sense of relief was mixed with the still present memory of a desperate peril. And then came the question as to what was to come next. That the old policy of the Board would be revived and pursued when the end of the Proctors' year delivered it from their inconvenient presence, was soon understood to be out of the question. The very violence of the measures attempted had its reaction, which stopped anything further. The opponents of Tractarianism, Orthodox and Liberal, were for the moment gorged with their success. What men waited to see was the effect on the party of the movement; how it would influence the advanced portion of it; how it would influence the little company who had looked on in silence from their retirement at Littlemore. The more serious aspect of recent events was succeeded for the moment by a certain comic contrast, created by Mr. Ward's engagement to be married, which was announced within a week of his degradation, and which gave the common-rooms something to smile at after the strain and excitement of the scene in the Theatre. But that passed, and the graver outlook of the situation occupied men's thoughts.

There was a widespread feeling of insecurity. Friends did not know of friends, how their minds were working, how they might go. Anxious letters passed, the writers not daring to say too much, or reveal too much alarm. And yet there was still some hope that at least with the great leader matters were not desperate. To his own friends he gave warning; he had already done so in a way to leave little to expect but at last to lose him; he spoke of resigning his fellowship in October, though he wished to defer this till the following June; but nothing final had been said publicly. Even at the last it was only anticipated by some that he would retire into lay communion. But that silence was awful and ominous. He showed no signs of being affected by what had passed in Oxford. He privately thanked the Proctors for saving him from what would have distressed him; but he made no comments on the measures themselves. Still it could not but be a climax of everything as far as Oxford was concerned. And he was a man who saw signs in such events.

It was inevitable that the events of the end of 1844 and the beginning of 1845 should bring with them a great crisis in the development of religious opinion, in the relations of its different forms to one another, and further, in the thoughts of many minds as to their personal position, their duty, and their prospects. There had been such a crisis in 1841 at the publication of No. 90. After the discussions which followed that tract, Anglican theology could never be quite the same that it had been before. It was made to feel the sense of some grave wants, which, however they might be supplied in the future, could no longer be unnoticed or uncared for. And individuals, amid the strife of tongues, had felt, some strongly and practically, but a much larger number dimly and reluctantly, the possibility, unwelcome to most, but not without interest to others, of having to face the strange and at one time inconceivable task of revising the very foundations of their religion. And such a revision had since that time been going on more or less actively in many minds; in some cases with very decisive results. But after the explosion caused by Mr. Ward's book, a crisis of a much more grave and wide-reaching sort had arrived. To ordinary lookers-on it naturally seemed that a shattering and decisive blow had been struck at the Tractarian party and their cause; struck, indeed, formally and officially, only at its extravagances, but struck, none the less, virtually, at the premises which led to the extravagances, and at the party, which, while disapproving them, shrank, with whatever motives,—policy, generosity, or secret sympathy,—from joining in the condemnation of them. It was more than a defeat, it was a rout, in which they were driven and chased headlong from the field; a wreck in which their boasts and hopes of the last few years met the fate which wise men had always anticipated. Oxford repudiated them. Their theories, their controversial successes, their learned arguments, their appeals to the imagination, all seemed to go down, and to be swept away like chaff, before the breath of straightforward common sense and honesty. Henceforth there was a badge affixed to them and all who belonged to them, a badge of suspicion and discredit, and even shame, which bade men beware of them, an overthrow under which it seemed wonderful that they could raise their heads or expect a hearing. It is true, that to those who looked below the surface, the overthrow might have seemed almost too showy and theatrical to be quite all that it was generally thought to be. There had been too much passion, and too little looking forward to the next steps, in the proceedings of the victors. There was too much blindness to weak points of their own position, too much forgetfulness of the wise generosity of cautious warfare. The victory was easy to win; the next moment it was quite obvious that they did not know what to do with it, and were at their wits' end to understand what it meant. And the defeated party, though defeated signally and conspicuously in the sight of the Church and the country, had in it too large a proportion of the serious and able men of the University, with too clear and high a purpose, and too distinct a sense of the strength and reality of their ground, to be in as disadvantageous a condition as from a distance might be imagined. A closer view would have discovered how much sympathy there was for their objects and for their main principles in many who greatly disapproved of much in the recent course and tendency of the movement. It might have been seen how the unwise measures of the Heads had awakened convictions among many who were not naturally on their side, that it was necessary both on the ground of justice and policy to arrest all extreme measures, and to give a breathing time to the minority. Confidence in their prospects as a party might have been impaired in in the Tractarians; but confidence in their principles, confidence that they had rightly interpreted the spirit, the claims, and the duties of the English Church, confidence that devotion to its cause was the call of God, whatever might happen to their own fortunes, this confidence was unshaken by the catastrophe of February.

But that crisis had another important result, not much noticed then, but one which made itself abundantly evident in the times that followed. The decisive breach between the old parties in the Church, both Orthodox and Evangelical, and the new party of the movement, with the violent and apparently irretrievable discomfiture of the latter as the rising force in Oxford, opened the way and cleared the ground for the formation and the power of a third school of opinion, which was to be the most formidable rival of the Tractarians, and whose leaders were eventually to succeed where the Tractarians had failed, in becoming the masters and the reformers of the University. Liberalism had hitherto been represented in Oxford in forms which though respectable from intellectual vigour were unattractive, sometimes even repulsive. They were dry, cold, supercilious, critical; they wanted enthusiasm; they were out of sympathy with religion and the religious temper and aims. They played, without knowing it, on the edge of the most dangerous questions. The older Oxford Liberals were either intellectually aristocratic, dissecting the inaccuracies or showing up the paralogisms of the current orthodoxy, or they were poor in character, Liberals from the zest of sneering and mocking at what was received and established, or from the convenience of getting rid of strict and troublesome rules of life. They patronised Dissenters; they gave Whig votes; they made free, in a mild way, with the pet conventions and prejudices of Tories and High

Churchmen. There was nothing inspiring in them, however much men might respect their correct and sincere lives. But a younger set of men brought, mainly from Rugby and Arnold's teaching, a new kind of Liberalism. It was much bolder and more independent than the older forms, less inclined to put up with the traditional, more searching and inquisitive in its methods, more suspicious and daring in its criticism; but it was much larger in its views and its sympathies, and, above all, it was imaginative, it was enthusiastic, and, without much of the devotional temper, it was penetrated by a sense of the reality and seriousness of religion. It saw greater hopes in the present and the future than the Tractarians. It disliked their reverence for the past and the received as inconsistent with what seemed evidence of the providential order of great and fruitful change. It could not enter into their discipline of character, and shrank from it as antiquated, unnatural, and narrow. But these younger Liberals were interested in the Tractarian innovators, and, in a degree, sympathised with them as a party of movement who had had the courage to risk and sacrifice much for an unworldly end. And they felt that their own opportunity was come when all the parties which claimed to represent the orthodoxy of the English Church appeared to have broken for good with one another, and when their differences had thrown so much doubt and disparagement on so important and revered a symbol of orthodoxy as the Thirty-nine Articles. They looked on partly with amusement, partly with serious anxiety, at the dispute; they discriminated with impartiality between the strong and the weak points in the arguments on both sides: and they enforced with the same impartiality on both of them the reasons, arising out of the difficulties in which each party was involved, for new and large measures, for a policy of forbearance and toleration. They inflicted on the beaten side, sometimes with more ingenuity than fairness, the lesson that the "wheel had come round full circle" with them; that they were but reaping as they themselves had sown:—but now that there seemed little more to fear from the Tractarians, the victorious authorities were the power which the Liberals had to keep in check. They used their influence, such as it was (and it was not then what it was afterwards), to protect the weaker party. It was a favourite boast of Dean Stanley's in after-times, that the intervention of the Liberals had saved the Tractarians from complete disaster. It is quite true that the younger Liberals disapproved the continuance of harsh measures, and some of them exerted themselves against such measures. They did so in many ways and for various reasons; from consistency, from feelings of personal kindness, from a sense of justice, from a sense of interest—some in a frank and generous spirit, others with contemptuous indifference. But the debt of the Tractarians to their Liberal friends in 1845 was not so great as Dean Stanley, thinking of the Liberal party as what it had ultimately grown to be, supposed to be the case. The Liberals of his school were then still a little flock: a very distinguished and a very earnest set of men, but too young and too few as yet to hold the balance in such a contest. The Tractarians were saved by what they were and what they had done, and could do, themselves. But it is also true, that out of these feuds and discords, the Liberal party which was to be dominant in Oxford took its rise, soon to astonish old-fashioned Heads of Houses with new and deep forms of doubt more audacious than Tractarianism, and ultimately to overthrow not only the victorious authorities, but the ancient position of the Church, and to recast from top to bottom the institutions of the University. The 13th of February was not only the final defeat and conclusion of the first stage of the movement. It was the birthday of the modern Liberalism of Oxford.

But it was also a crisis in the history of many lives. From that movement, the decision of a number of good and able men, who had once promised to be among the most valuable servants of the English Church, became clear. If it were doubtful before, in many cases, whether they would stay with her, the doubt existed no longer. It was now only a question of time when they would break the tie and renounce their old allegiance. In the bitter, and in many cases agonising struggle which they had gone through as to their duty to God and conscience, a sign seemed now to be given them which they could not mistake. They were invited, on one side, to come; they were told, sternly and scornfully, on the other, to go. They could no longer be accused of impatience if they brought their doubts to an end, and made up their minds that their call was to submit to the claims of Rome, that their place was in its communion.

Yet there was a pause. It was no secret what was coming. But men lingered. It was not till the summer that the first drops of the storm began to fall. Then through the autumn and the next year, friends, whose names and forms were familiar in Oxford, one by one disappeared and were lost to it. Fellowships, livings, curacies, intended careers, were given up. Mr. Ward went. Mr. Capes, who had long followed Mr. Ward's line, and had spent his private means to build a church near Bridgewater, went also. Mr. Oakeley resigned Margaret Chapel and went. Mr. Ambrose St. John, Mr. Coffin, Mr. Dalgairns, Mr. Faber, Mr. T. Meyrick, Mr. Albany Christie, Mr. R. Simpson of Oriel, were received in various places and various ways, and in the next year, Mr. J. S. Northcote, Mr. J. B. Morris, Mr. G. Ryder, Mr. David Lewis. On the 3d of October 1845 Mr. Newman requested the Provost of Oriel to remove his name from the books of the College and University, but without giving any reason. The 6th of October is the date of the "Advertisement" to the work which had occupied Mr. Newman through the year—the *Essay on the Development of Christian Doctrine.* On the 8th he was, as he has told us in the *Apologia,* received by Father Dominic, the Passionist. To the "Advertisement" are subjoined the following words:

> *Postscript.*—Since the above was written the Author has joined the Catholic Church. It was his intention and wish to have carried this volume through the press before deciding finally on this step. But when he got some way in the printing, he recognised in himself a conviction of the truth of the conclusion, to which the discussion leads, so clear as to preclude further deliberation. Shortly afterwards circumstances gave him the opportunity of acting on it, and he felt that he had no warrant for refusing to act on it.

So the reality of what had been so long and often so lightly talked about by those who dared it, provoked it, or hoped for it, had come indeed; and a considerable portion of English society learned what it was to be novices in a religious system, hitherto not only alien and unknown, but dreaded, or else to have lost friends and relatives, who were suddenly transformed into severe and uncompromising opponents, speaking in unfamiliar terms, and sharply estranged in sympathies and rules of life. Some of them, especially those who had caught the spirit of their leader, began life anew, took their position as humble learners in the Roman Schools, and made the most absolute sacrifice of a whole lifetime than a man can make. To others the change came and was accepted as an emancipation, not only from the bonds of Anglicanism, but from the obligations of orders and priestly vows and devotion. In some cases, where they were married, there was no help for it. But in almost all cases there was a great surrender of what English life has to offer to those brought up in it. Of the defeated party, those who remained had much to think about, between grief at the breaking of old ties, and the loss of dear friends, and perplexities about their own position. The anxiety, the sorrow at differing and parting, seem now almost extravagant and unintelligible. There are those who sneer at the "distress" of that time. There had not been the same suffering, the same estrangement, when Churchmen turned dissenters, like Bulteel and Baptist Noel. But the movement had raised the whole scale of feeling about religious matters so high, the questions were felt to be so momentous, the stake and the issue so precious, the "Loss and Gain" so immense, that to differ on such subjects was the differing on the greatest things which men could differ about. But in a time of distress, of which few analogous situations in our days can give the measure, the leaders stood firm. Dr. Pusey, Mr. Keble, Mr. Marriott accepted, with unshaken faith in the cause of the English Church, the terrible separation. They submitted to the blow—submitted to the reproach of having been associates of those who had betrayed hopes and done so much mischief; submitted to the charge of inconsistency, insincerity, cowardice; but they did not flinch. Their unshrinking attitude was a new point of departure for those who believed in the Catholic foundation of the English Church.

Among those deeply affected by these changes, there were many who had been absolutely uninfluenced by the strong Roman current. They had recognised many good things in the Roman Church; they were fully alive to many shortcomings in the English Church; but the possibility of submission to the Roman claims had never been a question with them. A typical example of such minds was Mr. Isaac Williams, a pupil of Mr. Keble, an intimate friend of Mr. Newman, a man of simple and saintly life, with heart and soul steeped in the ancient theology of undivided

Christendom, and for that very reason untempted by the newer principles and fashions of Rome. There were numbers who thought like him; but there were others also, who were forced in afresh upon themselves, and who had to ask themselves why they stayed, when a teacher, to whom they had looked up as they had to Mr. Newman, and into whose confidence they had been admitted, thought it his duty to go. With some the ultimate, though delayed, decision was to follow him. With others, the old and fair *praejudicium* against the claims of Rome, which had always asserted itself even against the stringent logic of Mr. Ward and the deep and subtle ideas of Mr. Newman, became, when closed with, and tested face to face in the light of fact and history, the settled conviction of life. Some extracts from contemporary papers, real records of the private perplexities and troubles actually felt at the time, may illustrate what was passing in the minds of some whom knowledge and love of Mr. Newman failed to make his followers in his ultimate step. The first extract belongs to some years before, but it is part of the same train of thinking.[1]

> As to myself, I am getting into a very unsettled state as to aims and prospects. I mean that as things are going on, a man does not know where he is going to; one cannot imagine what state of things to look forward to; in what way, and under what circumstances, one's coming life—if it does come—is to be spent; what is to become of one. I cannot at all imagine myself a convert; but how am I likely, in the probable state of things, to be able to serve as an English clergyman? Shall I ever get Priest's orders? Shall I be able to continue always serving? What is one's line to be; what ought to be one's aims; or can one have any?
>
> The storm is not yet come: how it may come, and how soon it may blow over, and what it may leave behind, is doubtful; but some sort of crisis, I think, must come before things settle. With the Bishops against us, and Puritanism aggressive, we may see strange things before the end.

When the "storm" had at length come, though before its final violence, the same writer continues:

> The present hopeless check and weight to our party—what has for the time absolutely crushed us—is the total loss of con-

---

1. Compare Mozley's *Reminiscences*, 2:1–3.

fidence arising from the strong tendency, no longer to be dissembled or explained away, among many of us to Rome. I see no chance of our recovery, or getting our heads above water from this, at least in England, for years to come. And it is a check which will one day be far greater than it is now. Under the circumstances—having not the most distant thought of leaving the English Church myself, and yet having no means of escaping the very natural suspicion of Romanising without giving up my best friends and the most saint-like men in England—how am I to view my position? What am I witnessing to? What, if need be, is one to suffer for? A man has no leaning towards Rome, does not feel, as others do, the strength of her exclusive claims to allegiance, the perfection of her system, its right so to overbalance all the good found in ours as to make ours absolutely untrustworthy for a Christian to rest in, notwithstanding all circumstances of habit, position, and national character; has such doubts on the Roman theory of the Church, the Ultramontane, and such instincts not only against many of their popular religious customs and practical ways of going on, but against their principles of belief (*e.g.* divine faith = relics), as to repel him from any wish to sacrifice his own communion for theirs; yet withal, and without any great right on his part to complain, is set down as a man who may any day, and certainly will some day, go over; and he has no lawful means of removing the suspicion:— why is it *tanti* to submit to this?

However little sympathy we Englishmen have with Rome, the Western Churches under Rome are really living and holy branches of the Church Catholic; corruptions they may have, so may we; but putting these aside, they are Catholic Christians, or Catholic Christianity has failed out of the world: we are no more [Catholic] than they. But this, *public opinion* has not for centuries, and *does not now,* realise or allow. So no one can express in reality and detail a practical belief in their Catholicity, in their equality (setting one thing against another) with us as Christians, without being suspected of what such belief continually leads to—disloyalty to the English Church. Yet such belief is nevertheless well-grounded and right, and there is no great hope for the Church till it gains ground, soberly, powerfully, and apart from all low views of proselytising, or fear of danger. What therefore the disadvantage of those among us who do not really deserve the imputation of Romanising may be meant for, is to break this practical belief to the English Church. We may be silenced, but, without any wish to leave the English Church, we cannot give up the belief, that the Western Church under Rome is a true, living, venerable branch of the Christian Church. There are dangers in such a belief, but they must be provided against, they do not affect the truth of the belief.

Such searchings of heart were necessarily rendered more severe and acute by Mr. Newman's act. There was no longer any respite; his dearest friends must choose between him and the English Church. And the choice was made, by those who did not follow him, on a principle little honoured or believed in at the time on either side, Roman or Protestant; but a principle which in the long-run restored hope and energy to a cause which was supposed to be lost. It was not the revival of the old *Via Media*; it was not the assertion of the superiority of the English Church; it was not a return to the old-fashioned and ungenerous methods of controversy with Rome—one-sided in all cases, ignorant, coarse, unchristian in many. It was not the proposal of a new theory of the Church—its functions, authority, and teaching, a counter-ideal to Mr. Ward's imposing *Ideal*. It was the resolute and serious appeal from brilliant logic, and keen sarcasm, and pathetic and impressive eloquence, to reality and experience, as well as to history, as to the positive and substantial characteristics of the traditional and actually existing English Church, shown not on paper but in work, and in spite of contradictory appearances and inconsistent elements; and along with this, an attempt to put in a fair and just light the comparative excellences and defects of other parts of Christendom, excellences to be ungrudgingly admitted, but not to be allowed to bar the recognition of defects. The feeling which had often stirred, even when things looked at the worst, that Mr. Newman had dealt unequally and hardly with the English Church, returned with gathered strength. The English Church was after all as well worth living in and fighting for as any other; it was not only in England that light and dark, in teaching and in life, were largely intermingled, and the mixture had to be largely allowed for. We had our Sparta, a noble, if a rough and an incomplete one; patiently to do our best for it was better than leaving it to its fate, in obedience to signs and reasonings which the heat of strife might well make delusive. It was one hopeful token, that boasting had to be put away from us for a long time to come. In these days of stress and sorrow were laid the beginnings of a school, whose main purpose was to see things as they are; which had learned by experience to distrust unqualified admiration and unqualified disparagement; determined not to be blinded even by genius to plain certainties; not afraid to honour all that is great and beneficent in Rome, not afraid with English frankness to criticise freely at home; but not to be won over, in one case, by the good things, to condone and accept the bad things; and not deterred, in the other, from service, from love, from self-sacrifice, by the presence of much to regret and to resist.

All this new sense of independence, arising from the sense of having been left almost desolate by the disappearance of a great stay and light in men's daily life, led to various and different results. In some minds, after a certain trial, it actually led men back to that Romeward tendency from which they had at first recoiled. In others, the break-up of the movement under such a chief led them on, more or less, and some very far, into a career of speculative Liberalism like that of Mr. Blanco White, the publication of whose biography coincided with Mr. Newman's change. In many others, especially in London and the towns, it led to new and increasing efforts to popularise in various ways— through preaching, organisation, greater attention to the meaning, the solemnities, and the fitnesses of worship—the ideas of the Church movement. Dr. Pusey and Mr. Keble were still the recognised chiefs of the continued yet remodelled movement. It had its quarterly organ, the *Christian Remembrancer,* which had taken the place of the old *British Critic* in the autumn of 1844. A number of able Cambridge men had thrown their knowledge and thoroughness of work into the *Ecclesiologist.* There were newspapers—the *English Churchman,* and, starting in 1846 from small and difficult beginnings, in the face of long discouragement and at times despair, the *Guardian.* One mind of great and rare power, though only recognised for what he was much later in his life, one undaunted heart, undismayed, almost undepressed, so that those who knew not its inner fires thought him cold and stoical, had lifted itself above the wreck at Oxford. The shock which had cowed and almost crushed some of Mr. Newman's friends roused and fired Mr. James Mozley.

To take leave of Mr. Newman [he writes on the morrow of the event] is a heavy task. His step was not unforeseen; but when it is come those who knew him feel the fact as a real change within them—feel as if they were entering upon a fresh stage of their own life. May that very change turn to their profit, and discipline them by its hardness! It may do so if they will use it so. Let nobody complain; a time must come, sooner or later, in every one's life, when he has to part with advantages, connexions, supports, consolations, that he has had hitherto, and face a new state of things. Every one knows that he is not always to have all that he has now: he says to himself, "What shall I do when this or that stay, or connexion, is gone?" and the answer is, "That he will do without it." ... The time comes when this is taken away; and then the mind is left alone, and is thrown back upon itself, as the expression is. But no religious mind tolerates the notion of being really thrown upon itself; this is only to say in other words, that it is thrown back upon God. . . . Secret mental consolations, whether of innocent self-flattery or reposing confidence, are over; a more real and graver life begins—a firmer, harder disinterestedness, able to go on its course by itself. Let them see in the change a call to greater earnestness, sincerer simplicity, and more solid manliness. What were weaknesses before will be sins now.[2]

"A new stage has begun. Let no one complain":—this, the expression of individual feeling, represents pretty accurately the temper into which the Church party settled when the first shock was over. They knew that henceforward they had difficult times before them. They knew that they must work under suspicion, even under proscription. They knew that they must expect to see men among themselves perplexed, unsettled, swept away by the influences which had affected Mr. Newman, and still more by the precedent of his example. They knew that they must be prepared to lose friends and fellow-helpers, and to lose them sometimes unexpectedly and suddenly, as the wont was so often at this time. Above all, they knew that they had a new form of antagonism to reckon with, harder than any they had yet encountered. It had the peculiar sad bitterness which belongs to civil war, when men's foes are they of their own households—the bitterness arising out of interrupted intimacy and affection.

2. *Christian Remembrancer*, January 1846, pp. 167, 168.

Neither side could be held blameless; the charge from the one of betrayal and desertion was answered by the charge from the other of insincerity and faithlessness to conscience, and by natural but not always very fair attempts to proselytise; and undoubtedly, the English Church, and those who adhered to it, for some years after 1845, to hear from the lips of old friends the most cruel and merciless invectives which knowledge of her weak points, wit, argumentative power, eloquence, and the triumphant exultation at once of deliverance and superiority could frame. It was such writing and such preaching as had certainly never been seen on the Roman side before, at least in England. Whether it was adapted to its professed purpose may perhaps be doubted; but the men who went certainly lost none of their vigour as controversialists or their culture as scholars. Not to speak of Mr. Newman, such men as Mr. Oakeley, Mr. Ward, Mr. Faber, and Mr. Dalgairns more than fulfilled in the great world of London their reputation at Oxford. This was all in prospect before the eyes of those who had elected to cast in their lot with the English Church. It was not an encouraging position. The old enthusiastic sanguineness had been effectually quenched. Their Liberal critics and their Liberal friends have hardly yet ceased to remind them how sorry a figure they cut in the eyes of men of the world, and in the eyes of men of bold and effective thinking.[3] The "poor Puseyites" are spoken of in tones half of pity and half of sneer. Their part seemed played out. There seemed nothing more to make them of importance. They had not succeeded in Catholicising the English Church; they had not even shaken it by a wide secession. Henceforth they were only marked men. All that could be said for them was, that at the worst, they did not lose heart. They had not forgotten the lessons of their earlier time.

It is not my purpose to pursue farther the course of the movement. All the world knows that it was not, in fact, killed or even much arrested by the shock of 1845. But after 1845, its field was at least as much out of Oxford as in it. As long as Mr. New-

3. *E.g.* the Warden of Merton's *History of the University of Oxford,* p. 212. "The first panic was succeeded by a reaction; some devoted adherents followed him [Mr. Newman] to Rome; others relapsed into lifeless conformity; and the University soon resumed its wonted tranquility." *"Lifeless* conformity" sounds odd connected with Dr. Pusey or Mr. J. B. Mozley, and the London men who were the founders of the so-called Ritualist schools.

man remained, Oxford was necessarily its centre, necessarily, even after he had seemed to withdraw from it. When he left his place vacant, the direction of it was not removed from Oxford, but it was largely shared by men in London and the country. It ceased to be strongly and prominently Academical. No one indeed held such a position as Dr. Pusey's and Mr. Keble's; but though Dr. Pusey continued to be a great power at Oxford, he now became every day a much greater power outside of it; while Mr. Keble was now less than ever an Academic, and became more and more closely connected with men out of Oxford, his friends in London and his neighbours at Hursley and Winchester. The cause which Mr. Newman had given up in despair was found to be deeply interesting in ever new parts of the country: and it passed gradually into the hands of new leaders more widely acquainted with English society. It passed into the hands of the Wilberforces, and Archdeacon Manning; of Mr. Bennett, Mr. Dodsworth, Mr. W. Scott, Dr. Irons, Mr. E. Hawkins, and Mr. Upton Richards in London. It had the sympathy and counsels of men of weight, or men who were rising into eminence and importance—some of the Judges, Mr. Gladstone, Mr. Roundell Palmer, Mr. Frederic Rogers, Mr. Mountague Bernard, Mr. Hope Scott (as he afterwards was), Mr. Badeley, and a brilliant recruit from Cambridge, Mr. Beresford Hope. It attracted the sympathy of another boast of Cambridge, the great Bishop of New Zealand, and his friend Mr. Whytehead. Those times were the link between what we are now, so changed in many ways, and the original impulse given at Oxford; but to those times I am as much of an outsider as most of the foremost in them were outsiders to Oxford in the earlier days. Those times are almost more important than the history of the movement; for, besides vindicating it, they carried on its work to achievements and successes which, even in the most sanguine days of "Tractarianism," had not presented themselves to men's minds, much less to their hopes. But that story must be told by others.

"Show thy servants thy work, and their children thy glory."

Index

INDEX

Authors—*Continued*
  Newman—*Continued*
          125, 126, 139, 141,
          149, 184–87, 191, 213,
          215; "Catholicity of the
          English Church," 156;
          Essay on Development,
          264; *Grammar of Assent,* 175; *Letter to the
          Bishop of Oxford,* 188–
          91; *Parochial Sermons,*
          71; *Prophetic Office,
          The* (i.e., *Romanism
          and Popular Protestantism*), 142–48, 178;
          "State of Religious Parties," 137–39, 173–74,
          184–85; Tract no. 1,
          80–84, 171; Tract no.
          71, 141; Tract no. 90,
          see Tracts for the
          Times
Newsome, D., xxvii, xxix–xxx
Palmer, W., xix, 9, 69, 74, 121
Pattison, M., xxvii, xxxi
Perceval, A. P., 74, 77, 90
Phillpotts, H., 172
Pusey, E. B., 104
Sanday, W., xxviii
Shairp, J., 100–101
Smith, B. A., xiii
Smyth, C., xxv
Stanley, A. P., 9
Stephen, J., xxiv
Stephens, W. R. W., xxv
Storr, V. F., xxv, xxix
Sumner, J. B., 138, 172
Taylor, H., 31
Thucydides, 202–3
Trench, R. C., 19
Tuckwell, W., xxx
Tulloch, J., xxiv
Uniomachia, 62
Walton, 193
Ward, W. G., 236, 239
Ward, W. R., xxvi
Webb, C. C. J., xxix

Whately, R., 9, 12, 108, 128,
          141
Williams, I., 26, 44
Wordsworth, W., 11, 169

Badeley, E., 272
Badham, C., 59
Barter brothers, 227
Bennett, W. J. E., 272
Bentham, Jeremy, 20
Bernard, M., 272
Beveridge, 85
Bickersteth, E., 137
Bishops. *See* Episcopate
Bisley, 54, 55, 58
Bliss, J., 94
Blomfield, C. J., 75, 148, 171,
          215
Bowden, J., 92
Bowdler, J., 60
Bramhall, 185, 222
British Critic, 137, 156, 173–74,
          181, 185, 200, 230, 237,
          243, 245, 248–50, 269
British Magazine, 29, 69, 133
Brougham, H., 20
Bull, 185, 193, 242
Burton, E., 73, 112, 217
Bussage, 213
Butler, 43, 46, 128, 146

Calvinism, xii, 16, 17, 24, 37, 86,
          152, 157, 193, 197, 207–8,
          215, 230, 238. *See also*
          Evangelicalism and Evangelicals; Puritanism
Capes, J. M., 264
Cardwell, E., 221, 229
Carlyle, T., 238
Catholic Emancipation, xiv, xxx,
          38, 39, 142
Cecil, R., 16
Celibacy, 248
Chalmers, T., 18
Christian Remembrancer, xii, 98,
          219, 220, 269, 270
Christie, A., 264

INDEX

INDEX

Lyra Apostolica, 29, 38, 92, 134, 143

Macmullen, of Corpus, xxv, 218–20
Margaret Chapel, 249, 264
Marriott, Charles, 30, 59–67, 227, 265; helps with Pusey's *Fathers,* 63–64, 98; relations with Newman, 63–64, 66
Marsh, H., 171
Martyn, Henry, 31
Martyrs' Memorial, 152–53
Maurice, F. D., 9, 16, 19, 59, 110, 215
Melbourne, Lord, xxiv, 118–19
Methodism, xv, 10, 17, 24, 25, 28, 53, 88, 105, 113
Meyrick, T., 264
Middle classes, 16, 91
Midlands, 13, 16
Mill, J. S., xxxi, 163, 230, 238, 247
Miller, John, 16
Milman, H. H., 19
Milner brothers, 17
Moberly, G., xii, 63, 227
Montalembert, 229
Morris, J. B., 162, 264
Mozley, J. B., xii, xix, 33, 34, 40, 65, 94, 98–100, 131, 151, 196, 198, 200, 207, 217, 228, 269, 270, 271
Mozley, T., xxv, 34, 50, 65, 66-67, 71, 79, 85, 94, 230, 245, 250, 266

Newman, John Henry:
  early share in Oxford Movement, 70, 77, 125
  starts *Tracts for the Times,* 79–80
  sermons, 22, 92–93, 99–103, 107, 130, 132, 133, 135, 159, 212–13
  lectures, 132–33
  as party leader, xv, xx, xxi, 93–94, 129–32
  elucidates Hampden, 111, 118–19, 125
  Romanism and Popular Protestantism, 132–33, 142–48, 157–58, 178
  Tract no. 90, 131, 194–206, 208–9, 212
  changes mind about Rome, xxiii, 155–61, 164, 182–97, 259, 264
  relations with Church, xvi–xxiii
  relations with Froude, 27–28, 31, 37–39, 45, 47–49
  relations with Keble, 27–29, 139
  relations with Marriott, 63–64, 66
  relations with Pusey, 94–96, 139
  relations with Ward, xix, 229, 244–45, 249
  relations with Whately, 12, 27, 39, 54, 139
  relations with Williams, 50, 54–58, 94, 266
Newton, John, 17
Neotics, xxvi, 19
Norris, H. H., 50, 53, 89
Northcote, J. S., 264

Oakeley, F., 249, 264, 271
Ogilvie, C. A., 223, 224
Otter, W., 63
Oxford, xiii-iv, 113–15
Oxford movement: beginnings, 80, 85–87, 91–93, 94–95, 108, 126–28, 139; leading characteristics, xv, 91–92, 133–35, 246–48; as a party, 126–28, 135, 151; early hostility to, 86–87, 106–8; developments c. 1835–36, 137, 139; internal differences, before Tract 90, 151–55, 161–66, 173–75, 201;

INDEX

Wordsworth, C., 77, 89

Wordsworth, W., 24, 105

Wynter, P., 203, 221, 225–26, 251

Young, P., 213

Zwinglianism, 37, 86, 116, 152–53